DONNE

PUBLISHED BY

Constable and Company Ltd

LONDON

*The Macmillan Company
of Canada, Limited*

TORONTO

JOHN DONNE, AGED 44

DONNE

A SPIRIT IN CONFLICT

by

EVELYN HARDY

with five illustrations

CONSTABLE & CO LTD
LONDON

BOOK
PRODUCTION
WAR ECONOMY
STANDARD

*This book is produced in complete
conformity with the authorized
economy standards*

First Published 1942

PRINTED IN GREAT BRITAIN BY ROBERT MACLEHOSE AND CO. LTD.
THE UNIVERSITY PRESS, GLASGOW

CONTENTS

CONTENTS

ILLUSTRATIONS

ACKNOWLEDGMENT

I am indebted to the following people for the thoughtful assistance which they have given me:

To Mr. John Hayward for permission to use his chronological table as a basis for mine.

To Mr. O. F. Morshead, Windsor Castle, for lending me the micro-film of the Oliver miniature of Donne from which the photograph in this book was taken.

To Mr. A. M. Hind of the British Museum for the table of engraved portraits of Donne in my Appendix.

To Mr. H. M. Hake and Mr. C. K. Adams of the National Portrait Gallery for information concerning the extant portraits of Donne, and those of Lucy, Countess of Bedford, at Woburn Abbey, and for permission to use the negative of the photograph of Donne's Tomb.

To Mr. John Johnson and the Delegates of the University Press, Oxford, for his assistance and their permission to use the Walpole's Society's negative of the photograph of Donne's tomb, and the facsimile of Donne's handwriting:

To Messrs. Monger & Marchant, Ltd., for supplying the print of the portrait of Lucy, Countess of Bedford.

In quoting from the poems I have followed the text and punctuation of the Nonesuch edition but I have modernized the spelling, as Mr. Fausset has done in the Everyman edition, since antique spelling very often wearies the reader and fails to bring home the force of the words, still so modern. The Nonesuch edition has been my guide throughout and I owe Mr. Hayward much for his scholarly treatment.

Next to him I owe a debt of gratitude to the late Sir Edmund Gosse for his 'Life and Letters', to Mrs. Percy Simpson for her 'Study of the Prose Works', and to Sir Herbert Grierson for his exhaustive and sympathetic interpretation of the poems. For the many authors whose work has stimulated or clarified my mind, the titles of whose books or articles I give in footnotes and in my Bibliography, I have nothing but admiration and gratitude.

CHRONOLOGICAL TABLE FOR THE LIFE
OF JOHN DONNE

Born in London	Winter	1571/2
Death of John Donne, senior		1576
Matriculated Hart Hall, Oxford	October,	1584
Transferred to Trinity College, Cambridge		1587
Admitted to Lincoln's Inn	May 6th,	1592
Death of Henry Donne	Summer	1593
Foreign Travel	Nov. 1594–June 1596	
Foreign Service with the Earl of Essex, Cadiz	June,	1596
The Azores Expedition	August,	1597
Secretary to Sir Thomas Egerton		1598–1602
Married Ann More	December,	1601
Imprisoned in the Fleet	February,	1601/2
Marriage ratified	April,	1602
Residence at Pyrford		1602–1604
„ „ Mitcham		1605–1609
Employed by Thomas Morton		c.1605–1607
Hon. M.A. Oxford	April,	1610
Residence at Drury House and Foreign Travel with Sir Robert Drury	Nov. 1611–Sept. 1612	
Ordained Priest	Jan. 23rd,	1614/5
Doctor of Divinity, Cambridge	April,	1615
Reader in Divinity to the Benchers of Lincoln's Inn	Oct., 1616–Feb., 1622	
Death of Ann Donne	August,	1617
Foreign Travel with Lord Doncaster	May, 1619–Dec., 1620	
Appointed Dean of St. Paul's	November,	1621
Severe illness	Winter	1623
Appointed to 'St. Dunstan's in the West'	March,	1624
In retreat at Chelsea	Autumn	1625
Preaching of 'Death's Duell'	Feb. 12th,	1630
Died in London	March 31st,	1631

'The pattern is given by what goes on in the mind rather than by the exterior events which provoke the mental activity, play of thought and feeling.'

T. S. Eliot on Donne

'We are beginning to see man not as the smooth self-acting agent he pretends to be, but as he really is, a creature only dimly conscious of the various influences that mould his thought and action, and blindly resisting, with all the means at his command, the forces that are making for a higher and fuller consciousness.'

Ernest Jones on Hamlet

...her. Their choice lay between faith and country. Open ...giance to the Church incurred disgrace, alienation and the ...nalties of high treason; to the State and Sovereign, spiritual ...amnation. Earthly and temporal citizenship, or the glorious and eternal welfare of the Soul? Thinking subjects of her Majesty could not afford to disregard this question, vital to life itself, and spying, counter-spying, imprisonment, mock trial, torturing and the public spectacle of hanging, with all its revolting accompaniments, went on as a desperate undercurrent to the happy expansion of the realm.

In the years preceding the issue of the Bull the measures against Catholics, which had formerly been precautionary, gradually assumed the character of a systematic policy of persecution. Imprisonment for attending mass was enforced, even upon the Ambassadors from foreign countries. Mary, Queen of Scots, became a prisoner within the land. Scotland, openly allied with France, lay dissatisfied to the North; Ireland, resentful and smouldering, to the West; Spain, the arch enemy, far to the South, with the remainder of the Continent, a hotbed of conflicting and vacillating religio-political tendencies, in between. The feeling of insecurity in England reached its climax, with consequent measures of suppression and torture. The prisons were full of Catholics, so full that the State did not know how to keep them. The laws grew into inflexibility, each new edict marking an advance in the campaign against the church. Lord Bacon noted in cold, scientific manner that 'harsher methods were adopted against the Catholics':[1] until, in the year before Donne's birth, there came the 'Act against Fugitives over the Sea',[2] the unfortunate ones who, following the dictates of their conscience, had forsaken their homes in order to settle at one of the hospitable communities, like Louvain or Malines, where they might worship unafraid. The Channel ports were narrowly watched. No communication with the religious exiles was permitted and the

---

[1] *In Felicem Memoriam Elizabethae.*   [2] 13 Eliz. c. 3., and 14 Eliz. c. 6.

CHAPTER

THE YEARS OF GRO

'I had my first breeding and conversation with men of su
afflicted religion, accustomed to the despite of death and hu
imagined martyrdom.'

'Biathana

I

On a night in May, 1570, less than two years before the birth of John Donne, a hand went up in the seely dark and struck at the door of the Bishop of London's Palace, and in the morning, in the wan river-light before the dawn, passers-by read with horror the Bull of Pope Pius the Vth proclaiming the excommunication of Queen Elizabeth.

It was not the first time that an English sovereign had been cut off from grace. Elizabeth's father had brought down the papal fire upon his head, and nearly four centuries earlier England had ceased to be, to all outward appearances, a Christian land, for no bells were rung, no services held, the statues of the saints had been laid flat upon their carven faces, and the doors of the churches closed and barred. Plague and famine stealing in to distress and destroy the body had been calamities to be borne with greater fortitude than spiritual starvation.

But with the buoyancy of the Elizabethan mind, the popularity of the Queen, and the growth of the country as an international power, the matter was handled vigorously. Threats against the Sovereign and her Protestant subjects were parried by counter-threats against the Pope and his adherents. Yet not without inconceivable misery for those who remained loyal to their faith, for by his Bull the Pope had placed English Catholics in a desperate position which tore them

A

Act severed, once and for all, the slender cord tethering Catholics abroad to their mother country which they still loved.

Amongst these were John Donne's ancestors[1] and into this whirlpool of dark, controversial waters he was thrown at his birth. His mother was a Catholic and her stock of such eminence in that faith that constant persecution and exile was their lot. The influence of heredity upon him is strangely marked and an examination of the lives of his ancestors reveals both the richness of his inheritance and many individual traits which he himself shared with them. Sir Edmund Gosse goes so far as to say that 'every salient feature in his mind and temperament is foreshadowed by the general trend of his family, or by the idiosyncrasy of some member of it'.[2]

His mother was descended from a sister of Sir Thomas More, the Lord Chancellor, and the author of *Utopia*, who was beheaded for allegiance to his faith in 1536. The sister married John Rastall, a friend of More's who shows, even in retrospect, that marked originality which was one of the chief characteristics of Donne and which is generally at variance with the temper of the age into which its owner is born. He was a barrister of exceptional ability, used to pleading his cases in Westminster Hall where Kings were arraigned. He compiled a history of the laws of the realm which became a reference for future generations, and being a printer and artist as well, he was able to issue his own works and illustrate them into the bargain. Amongst other things he wrote morality plays in one of which he adopted the rare device of attempting to popularize science.[3] But apparently along with his conservative legal tastes there went a need for reformation, for he questioned the doctrine of Purgatory and attacked the practice of paying tithes, much in advance of his time. He was keenly interested in geographical exploration and got

[1] See Pedigree in Appendix I.
[2] *Life and Letters of John Donne*, vol. i, p. 3.
[3] *A New Interlude and a Merry, of The Nature of the Four Elements.*

together a number of ships bound, like Cabot's, for New-foundland, a plucky venture which came to nought owing to the jealousy of rival members of the fleet.[1] He published, too, articles of a derisive and lively nature (certain to provoke controversy), revealing ingenuity, a disputatious spirit and a talent for satire. In their pertness, their licence and their unconventionality, they plainly suggest Donne's *Paradoxes and Problems*, written towards the close of the same century, and foreshadow Donne, the satirist.

'Can any learned man prove that bag-pipes, horse-coursers, jailors, or ale-tasters, should be admitted to the clergy?'

'That a friar of over sixty years should become a bishop and marry a woman of nineteen.'

'That the residue of the sacrament should be taken away by a priest and buttered for his children.'

'That the Lenten Fast is a matter of civil policy and not of devotion.'[2]

Strangely enough, John Rastall, like Donne, turned Protestant. He died in prison.

His son William Rastall, like his father an Oxford man and a member of Lincoln's Inn, (and Donne and his brother were destined for both universities) became, like his grandfather, Sir Thomas More, Judge of the Common Pleas. His translation of his father's legal works out of Latin into English went the rounds of the country and one can read in diaries of the period how owners lent it proudly to their neighbours.[3] Like his wife's parents he was forced to flee the country for his faith, and died in banishment.

His daughter Elizabeth married John Heywood, the dramatist, grandfather of John Donne. Heywood's fortunes flared and sank, according to the fanatic winds now blowing

[1] Williamson, *Voyages of the Cabots and The Discovery of N. America*, pp. 85–93, and 246–8.

[2] Frere, p.89, *History of the English Church in the Reigns of Eliz. and James*, 1558–1625.

[3] See *Winthrop Papers*, Massachusetts Historical Society.

hot, now cold, under four successive sovereigns, so that he escaped hanging under Henry VIII, rose to favour with Mary Tudor, and, under Elizabeth, found it expedient once again to retire to Malines, where he too died in banishment. As a boy Heywood had been a royal chorister.

> 'Longe have I been a singing man
> And sundry parts oft have I songe'

he tells us, after the manner of Chaucer, and for these services received the sum of eightpence a day. He also played on the virginal. Eventually he became Master of a company of child actors who played his interludes before the Court of the Princess Mary, at whose coronation he sat under a vine in St. Paul's Churchyard, and made her a Latin oration. But if his presence on this day was an ornament, it later, on the same spot, became a public humiliation, for Heywood, old and infirm, was forced to recant and to deny his faith beneath the very Cross from which his famous grandson was to preach. It is said that Mary loved him and that when she was dying she called him to her to distract her with his ready wit, which was broad, wholesome and pleasantly rich. His Interludes form a bridge between the early Morality plays and modern comedy and in them he made use of personal types as characters instead of personified abstractions, such as Piety, Pity, Lust or Envy, a startling innovation. Like Donne he wrote Epigrams and he was also an anonymous translator of the Spanish *Celestina*, 'the first connected long story with a complete plot in modern literature,'[1] which had a tremendous popularity in its day in half a dozen countries.

John Heywood's two sons, uncles of John Donne, undiscouraged by the fate of almost all of their immediate forebears, were even more aggressive champions of their faith, and were amongst the earliest English members of the Society of Jesus. Elias, a Fellow of All Souls', became Cardinal Pole's

---

[1] Martin Hume, *Spanish Influence on English Literature*, p. 125.

secretary. His dialogues, representing Sir Thomas More's imagined conversations with the famous men of his day,[1] are, after the Italian manner, set in the open, an example which English writers followed. Elias seems to have been of a gentle, more retiring nature than his brother, and after the expulsion of the Catholic community from Antwerp when a mob attacked his house, he fled to Louvain to die, it is said, from the effects of the strain. It is not likely that Donne ever saw him.

But with Jasper Heywood it is a different story. This man of powerful but fanatic disposition shadowed Donne's youth and may have influenced him profoundly. His career was startling from the first. A Page of Honour to the Princess Elizabeth he was, like Donne, intellectually precocious and 'in disputations at home and in the public schools he bare away the bell'.[2] At Merton College, he was made 'Christmas Prince' or 'Lord of Misrule' and behaved himself with such boisterousness that he received no less than three warnings from the warden and senior fellows. Subsequently he boldly resigned his fellowship of the disapproving college only to step into one at All Souls' which his brother Elias had vacated. Cardinal Pole called him a 'Polite Scholar, able disputant and steady Catholic'. After joining the Society of Jesus he taught in the English colleges in Rome and Bavaria until, with the Pope's agreement, he was sent home on the Jesuit Mission as Vice Prefect, or Superior, in succession to Parsons, the talented intriguer who had had to flee the country. Very likely, Heywood, after seventeen years abroad, was ill-informed as to the true temper of the new generation, or his zeal and position went to his head, for he behaved with eccentricity and indiscretion. He 'vaunted and bragged as if he were legate of the Apostolic See, called, without authority, an English Council' and overstepped his duties in other ways, until he was recalled to the continent. But nature, which

[1] *Il Moro d'Helisio heivodo Inglese.*
[2] Anthony à Wood, *Athenae Oxonienses.*

sometimes reacts with equal violence upon violent natures, blew him ashore again, whereupon he was arrested and clapped into prison. Banished from England, he too died in exile.

Is it any wonder that Donne, reflecting, in the full powers of manhood, upon his ancestry should write those measured words given at the head of this chapter, or two years later:

'No family, which is not of far larger extent and greater branches, hath endured and suffered more in their persons and fortunes for obeying the teachers of Roman doctrine.'[1]

The melancholy saga was rounded with the death of his only brother Henry.

Thus if Donne is indebted to his ancestors for those intellectual traits which make him such a vital, fascinating character,—his wit, originality and dramatic ability, his taste for music, for Italian and Spanish trends of thought, his interest in law, geographical discovery, science and philosophy, his persistent need to express himself in writing and to shape his thoughts in a new manner,—he inherits also their failings— an adherence both rigid and intense to scholarly matters, too great a pride in intellectual attainment, an apparent intolerance for those less quick or gifted, extreme sensitivity, and a downward cast of the mind, predisposing it to melancholy introspection.

2

John Donne was born in London in the winter of 1571/2, at some time after Christmas.[2] The place of his birth,

[1] *Pseudo-Martyr*—Preface.

[2] For a long time the year of his birth was given as 1573. 'Donne may have been born towards the end of 1571, or between January and June 19, 1572. . . . The evidence of the portraits and of the epitaph is not perhaps of much value, but it may be noted that a birth date between January and June 1572 can be reconciled with the statement on Marshall's engraving . . . and with that on the epitaph which says that Donne was 42 years old when he took orders in January 1614/5'.

F. P. Wilson, p. 277. *Notes on the Early Life of Donne.*

together with its fellows, was destroyed in the Great Fire of London, but it stood in Bread Street which lay to the south of St. Paul's Churchyard and ran from Cheapside down to the river. It was a street of paradoxical extremities with three churches and six inns, one of which was the famous 'Mermaid'. Here Donne's ancestor, the printer-satirist, had hung out his sign, at 'a house situated at Pollis (Paul's) Gate next to Cheapsyde', and here Donne, as if by hereditary right, was to recreate himself with other poets of the day. In Bread Street Milton's father, the scrivener, worked and here the poet, whose religious thought and interest in astronomy are so much akin to Donne's, was later to be born.

Donne's father was a Welshman and was probably a younger son of good family come to London to make his fortune, for Donne, when Dean of St. Paul's bore the arms *Azure a wolf rampant* and had for a crest, a sheaf of snakes. During the latter half of the sixteenth century many of his compatriots, encouraged by a friendly dynasty on the English throne, flowed into the capital, seeking careers suitable to their ability. They were men 'proud of their lineage, well-educated, averse to menial labour, physically and mentally alert'.[1] Such men produced skilled craftsmen, competent engineers, sound lawyers, apt courtiers and thrusting churchmen. Two Welshmen filled the Deanery of Westminster successively. The Queen's favourite guard were Welshmen as well as her foremost statesmen, and under James Ist another supplied the city with its first proper supply of water.

John Donne senior was a freeman of the City of London and a member of one of the seven great Livery Companies— the Worshipful Company of Ironmongers. 'Whence hath the Crown in all times better servitors, more liberal of their lives and fortune?',[2] asks Donne's friend Ben Jonson, writing of the Welsh, and that Donne's father was a good 'servitor'

---

[1] Contemporary writer—Humphrey Llwyd of Denbigh.
[2] *For the Honour of Wales.* 1618.

and liberal with his fortune is obvious from the facts that he was made Warden of his Company two years before his death and bequeathed his money generously. Thus, although superior in lineage on his mother's side to some of his famous contemporaries, Donne, like Marlowe who was the son of a shoemaker, Spenser of a clothier, Shakespeare of a woollen-merchant and Herrick of a goldsmith, was sired by a man of sound practical nature. The interrelation of commerce and literature constantly recurs in the lives of Elizabethans and the trees which bore such lovely blooms had their roots firmly nourished.

Unfortunately for the happiness of his family the older Donne died in 1576 in the prime of life. His will, together with that of his more famous son, is preserved for us in Somerset House. One receives from it the impression of a just and charitable man, since five succeeding clauses are devoted to the distribution of sums to 'the poor, needy and impotent', not necessarily in his own parish. Two of these clauses concern 'The prisons in London and the suburbs thereof,' and 'the great hospitals,' both of which he lists with scrupulous care.

'To Newgate, Ludgate, the Fleet, the two Compters in the Poultry and Woodstreet, and the Bedlam: and to the relief of the poor prisoners in the King's Bench, the Marshalry, the White Lion and the Compter in Southwark, twenty shillings apiece. . . .[1]
'and unto the poor people harboured in the hospitals of Christ Church, St. Bartholomew's, Bidwell and St. Thomas in Southwark . . . to every of the same hospitals five pounds.'

He knew the misery of the dark, unwholesome places: his wife's people had languished in them, possibly his own, but the fact that his sons would one day experience their wretchedness was mercifully hidden from him.

John Donne, senior, left six children, four daughters and two sons, as well as one not yet born—'the child with whom

[1] About ten pounds in modern currency.

my wife now goeth'—the thoughtful merchant called it. The poet was the third child and he was five years old at the time of his father's death. His brother Henry was four and Anne, the only other child to grow to maturity, somewhat older than either.

Less than six months after the Master-Ironmonger's death, their mother, Elizabeth Donne, married a second time. Her second husband, Dr. Symmings, was a distinguished London physican, a Fellow of New College, Oxford, who had added continental degrees to his native, graduating from the University at Bologna. He practised in both London and Oxford, and was twice elected President of the Royal College of Physicians. He died in 1588 and thus he and Elizabeth Donne had thirteen years together, years of the utmost importance to a sensitive and precocious child like Donne.

What was the effect upon him of his mother's second marriage? The custom of the day caused widows to remarry quickly if they did not wish the State to take over their property. But a child cares nothing for laws of the realm,— property acts, courts of wardship, or Orphanage Courts, beneath whose jurisdiction the children of freemen, under age at the time of their father's decease, automatically came. He is concerned, like the young nestling that he is, with what he will put in his belly, with the amount of love he may absorb from his parents, and above all, with adjusting himself to a changing environment which, in Donne's case, altered with terrifying swiftness.

Now it is a curious fact, and in keeping with his cautious nature, so vexing to the biographer, that Donne never once mentions his stepfather, from whose conversation, work or library he almost certainly drew his interest in medicine, anatomy, chemistry and biology. In one of the 'Songs and Sonnets' he remarks that 'racked carcases make ill anatomies'; he wonders what phlegm is made of, how the heart pumps blood from one ventricle to the other, how a stone gets in to the bladder, the child in the womb, and what chemical constituents cause blood to be red and grass green. What part did this important man, the physician-stepfather, play in Donne's life? Was he a staunch Catholic and if so did he encourage the lad in his faith? Did he foster the boy with understanding and sympathy or merely tolerate his presence? Alas, Donne's attitude to him cannot be known because of his own reticence.

But his attitude to women who, throughout his life, either comforted or tormented him, is of greater importance and may find its roots in this early transferring of his mother's affections. For if Donne had adored his father doubtless he resented the intrusion of a newcomer, looking upon him as plain usurper: but if he adored his mother her action would bewilder him and hatred for his stepfather would be added to jealousy. The victim of this psychological misfortune, realizing his hatred for his parent, begins to feel guilty and so comes to hate himself. This inner imagined guilt, unconscious and primitive, may cause the child, even the adult, to react with enhanced respect towards the hated parent, but the lurking sense of guilt will lower the powers of resistance, break down inner defences, and in time cause both physical and mental illness. As he grows to manhood, and misfortunes, inevitable in human existence, occur to him, the sufferer will look upon them as intended and so increase their importance. The conflict in Donne's mind with regard to women and his lifelong habit of uselessly repenting for actual, or imagined, sexual experience in widening vortices of remorse, very likely sprang from this early, painful, emotional upheaval centring round his mother's marriage.[1]

Apparently Dr. Symmings left the tutelage of the young

[1] For the information on Mrs. Donne's remarriage, the particulars of her second husband's career, the date of Donne's birth and other valuable additions to our knowledge of his early years see 'Notes on the Early Life of Donne', F. P. Wilson, pp. 272–9, *Review of English Studies*, vol. iii, July 1927.

Donnes entirely to his wife's conscience, for in the solitary
letter which we have from Donne to his mother when she
was an old woman, he especially states this. 'All those children
for whose education you were so carefully and chargeably
diligent', he writes, and if he had not given us this grudging
crumb of information we would have surmised as much
from the tenor of his mind which shows unmistakeable
traces of the school of thought in which it was first formed.
For Donne's early tutors, chosen by his mother, were Catholic, probably Jesuit, and the influence of his training amongst
men of this persuasion persisted throughout his life. 'The
Jesuits were at this time the most learned and able champions
of the counter-reformation. They paid particular attention to
education, and their methods showed their intimate knowledge of the psychology of children's minds.'[1]

His debt to the Jesuits was profound. He owed to them the
thoroughness of his grounding, the breadth of his interests,
and his controversial ability. Much that has been remarked
upon in Donne as being exceptional, such as his interest in
science, astronomy and geography, was the product of their
training, for the Jesuits were noted for the attention they
gave in their curricula to mathematics and the natural
sciences. Father Clavius, the Jesuit 'Euclid', speaks of the
need for good grounding in mathematics for a 'knowledge of
the movements of heavenly bodies, of their distances, of the
oppositions and conjunctions of the comets, of the tides, the
winds, the rainbow and other physical phenomena.'[2] In the
seminaries attention was given to the geography of the countries in which they stood as well as to that of the newly-dis-
covered and expanding continents. 'The Jesuits had, during
the sixteenth and seventeenth centuries, better advantages
for obtaining geographical information than any other body
of men. The missionaries scattered all over the world sent

[1] Evelyn Simpson, *A Study of the Prose Works of John Donne*, p. 16.
[2] *Monumenta Paedagogica*, pp. 471–478.

regular accounts of their journeys and observations to their brethren in Europe.[1] They recorded these in notebooks and maps, of whose accuracy in the days of early cartography they were justly proud. Although Donne did not, as far as is known, attend any of the great continental seminaries, the breadth of knowledge observable in the Jesuit 'Plan of Study', begun in his boyhood, was to be found in earlier plans and was significant of all Jesuit teaching, private as well as communal.

The Jesuits were alleged, by their critics, to have an almost supernatural hold over their charges. It was said that they used black magic to entice and bind the young to them or secret charms to hasten their mental progress: 'They anoint their pupils with secret salves of the devil, by which diabolical practices they so attract and attach the children to them that they can only with difficulty be separated from these wizards, and always long to go back to them'.[2] Other less bigoted critics realized the value of their training. 'The Jesuits know how to treat boys according to their nature, and to keep alive a zeal for studies . . . They know how to accommodate themselves to the natural gifts of every pupil and are the finest and most dexterous of teachers.'[3]

The truth lay between these allegations. The Jesuits were remarkable people, in advance of their day in the scope of their learning and in the penetration with which they studied the minds of the young. Their plans of study were the first attempt at a uniform curriculum of international scope, modified according to the needs of the locality and individual. They may perhaps be called the first organized group of psychologists upon whose consciences and mercy the young were thrown. The instructors were commanded to obtain the esteem and affection of their pupils, by the depth of their

---

[1] *Jesuit Education*, Schwickerath, p. 126.

[2] *Ibid.*, pp. 147 and 148.

[3] Protestant criticisms quoted by Schwickerath, pp. 146–7.

own learning, the integrity of their character and the firmness and moderation of their behaviour, but also through the agency of *fear*. It was pointed out that this fear must be the 'reverent' fear of a child, not the servile fear of a slave, and they styled it 'wholesome fear'.

This question of the employment of fear as a corrective in education involves the whole theory of discipline, punishment and moral values, and the interpretation of Christian law. Like all good systems, that adopted by the Jesuits was open to mishandling by individuals, or groups, in authority, and that it *was* mishandled, that an odious plant grew out of the good seed, cannot be denied. Dissatisfaction in the English College at Rome, controlled by the Jesuits, flared into open revolt and, all over the world, the Jesuits grew to be first mistrusted and then abhorred. Their justness became tempered with injustice, their mildness with inhuman severity: the vine became proud, luxuriant and twisted in growth, bearing bitter and poisonous fruit.

In addition to his tutor's influence there was that of his mother.

'Having . . . provided him with a fit tutor, she commended him to his care; yet she continued there with him, and still kept him in a moderate awe of herself, and so much under her own eye as to see and converse with him daily; *but she managed this power over him without any such rigid sourness as might make her company a torment to her child*, but with such a sweetness and compliance with the recreations and pleasures of youth, as did incline him willingly to spend much of his time in the company of his dear and careful mother; which was to her great content . . .'[1]

This is Isaac Walton's description of Donne's friend and patroness, the gracious Magdalen Herbert, handling her eldest son, Lord Herbert of Cherbury. Seeing all things, as he did, with a holy eye, Walton might have given a like picture of Elizabeth Donne's treatment of her elder son John,

[1] Sir Isaac Walton, *Life of George Herbert*.

but he does not do so and we are left to conjecture about their relationship. We know from the Sermons that she forbade that he be handed over to servants for punishment, but the passage—'And as in the tenderness of our childhood we suffer, yet are whipt if we cry'[1]—rings too true to be pleasantly imaginative, and the enigma of the character of Elizabeth Donne never yet disclosed, has to be taken into account. She was a woman unhesitatingly loyal to the Catholic faith, unflinching in courage and determination. Protestantism was hateful to her and she bent every effort to being up her children in a religion both proscribed and secret. She visited her brother in prison, fled to the continent because of her scruples, and, wealthy at the death of her husband, lived to be old and penniless, no doubt because of benefactions to the distressed religious. Such tenacity of purpose, such loyalty to principle does not make for easy living and it is more than likely that Elizabeth Donne matched the softer side of her nature with an almost fierce fanaticism. Unless she was of saint-like simplicity, the strain of nurturing her children in a faith openly condemned may have made her apprehensive, even bitter and aggressive. Her fiery egoism, proud of its stubborn resistance to authority other than that of the Pope and God, may have amounted to passionate intractability, and such a disposition, were it hers, would not incline to a broad, open sunlit mind, or to an even tenor of thought.

Thus the two powerful influences of childhood, heredity and environment, conspired against Donne's happiness. His early masters inculcated into the young and pliant mind a fear, a conflict, which he never outgrew and which turned him against them with a vitriolic hatred upon the death of his brother. A nature suppressed and twisted from its natural heritage, when it comes to adult growth, will throw off the

[1] From Donne's Second Prebend Sermon, LXVI, Jan. 29, 1625/6, 'one of the most magnificent pieces of religious writing in English literature.' Gosse, vol. ii, p. 239.

hated yoke, first with hesitancy, next with bravado, and then with increasing conviction and exhilaration. The rational, healthy side of Donne resented the morbidity, the maceration, the immolation of useful life typified by martyrdom and its glorification, but the imagery of martyrdom (visualized in the frescoes of Circignani, depicting the torture chamber, the scaffold and various forms of violent death[1]), long haunted his unconscious mind and troubled its serenity.

The mind was early set with an emphasis on suffering, negation, annihilation: the speculative doctrines of the Neo-Platonists and the repressive tenets of the Schoolmen merely took root in a soil which had already been prepared for them. The chiaroscuro of the canvas of life became of more import than the light itself, which could not fall softly for him. Either the sharp, blinding, brilliant light towards which ambition drove him, or the profound and melancholy blackness of non-attainment—desire and achievement, balance and completion, spiritual illumination or unredeemed darkness. Donne's writings are full of this preoccupation with light and dark, signifying more than an Aristotelian interest: 'There are birds which, when their eyes are cieled, still soar up and up, till they have spent their strength. Saul had such a blindness so that he fell with it.'[2] No doubt he identified himself, as he wrote, with the soaring lark pitifully blinded, in the same way that Shelley did when he invoked his wind of 'skiey speed'. The sense of height, of striving, of crippled effort are peculiarly personal and the note of suffering and torture strikes a discordant second to that of dizzy aspiration.

[1] Those of the English College at Rome have been preserved in a series of engravings by Cavalleri. There is another group on the walls of San Stefano Rotundo in Rome. See Meyer, p. 109, *England and The Catholic Church under Elizabeth.*

[2] Sermon XLVI. St. Paul's. The Sunday after the Conversion of St. Paul, Jan. 30, 1624/5.

3

Mrs. Donne's connections with the Worshipful Company ceased almost immediately after her husband's death but very likely her son, who came under the care of the Court of Orphans and whose age was, at 21, witnessed by heads of the Ironmongers' Company,[1] kept in touch with the place of his father's business. The mediaeval quadrangular pile of the old hall lay not far from Bread Street, and Donne, as a boy, may have wandered through the gatehouse into the Great Hall, whose roofs were securely covered with lead, whose floors were strewn with rushes, and whose walls were warmly wainscoated. The buildings included Chapels with vestments of cloth of gold: a Court Chamber hung with 'grene sey' and furnished with down cushions, likewise covered: an Armoury stocked with weapons, a Buttery with platters of pewter and chests of precious silver and 'napery of damaske, diaper-wrought, woven with the flower-de-luce and crown'.[2] The arms of the Company, *two scaly lizards erect, gorged with plain collars*, hung over the gates and the courtyard was garnished with vines, roses and rosemary.

Indeed, the rustic appearance of the London of Donne's boyhood was notorious. Travellers from the Continent— Spanish, Dutch, French and German—remarked first upon the clouds of pale swans which welcomed them—

'so tame that you can almost touch them (yet it is forbidden to injure them upon pain of corporal punishment, for royalty has them plucked every year in order to have their down for Court use)'[3]—

and then upon the gardens ... There were the roses of Temple Gardens, the strawberries and saffron-gold crocuses

[1] *Notes on the Early Life of Donne*, Wilson.

[2] *History of the 12 Great Livery Companies of the City of London*, William Herbert, 1836.

[3] The Duke of Wirtemberg, 1592. W. B. Rye, *England as seen by Foreigners*, p. 6.

of Ely Place and the beds which Gerarde, the herbalist, lovingly tended round Lord Burleigh's house in the Strand. Opposite, the gardens of Essex and Somerset Houses, stretching down to the unfettered water, threw out their scent and colour to rival the plots of the city companies and the greenery of the royal parks.

London's chief highway and artery was the Thames. Along the river, the stairs went down from the palaces,—dark, narrow-light fortresses, or congeries of buildings, of a later date and of conflicting styles of architecture, eyeing each other across the water. The Tower, oppressive in its significance, dwarfed every other fortified building, 'A Prison of Estate for the most daungerous offenders, a Citadel to defend or command the Citie, an Armoury for warlike provisions'.[1]

> 'The cloud-capped towers, the gorgeous palaces,
> The solemn temples,'

were not the mere poetic imagery of Shakespeare's brain, for the great monastic buildings taken over by the Crown, the Nobles or charity, at the dissolution of the monasteries, as well as the more recent palaces of the favourites which rose with a rush of domestic architectural activity, these, together with the Royal and Ecclesiastical palaces, the Cathedral, the Abbey and the countless city churches, as yet unmolested by the scouring Fire, all bore witness to Prospero's vision.

From the five great palaces of the Queen giving onto the river, processions and water pageants came forth with the gilded state barges of the Sovereign, the Archbishops, the Mayor and City Companies, with banners, music and garlands of flowers, with men in scarlet and azure, carrying torches an ell long, with musicians and trumpeters and the singing 'boys from Westminster'. One of the entries in the

---

[1] Stowe, *Survey of London,* p. 55.

accounts of the Ironmongers' Company brings back such a procession to our minds with homely force:

> Breakfast and fire in the apparelling room at 'The Bell'. . 14/8
> For the children's drink at the same. . . . . .8d.[1]

Among the sights of Tudor London were the Wall, punctured by its seven gates, running in a rough semicircle from the Thames by the Tower to the Thames by Fleet Ditch: London Bridge, of nursery rhyme, with its towers and portcullises, its shops, dwellings and watermills and the grisly row of blanched heads grinning at the open sky: the Royal Exchange, newly opened by the Queen: Westminster Hall, in which the chief law courts sat: the exquisite chapel of Henry VII, 'stone . . . robbed of its weight and density . . . the airy security of cobwebs'[2]: the Holbein arch at the head of lost King Street, of which Donne speaks in his Fourth Satyre: old Charing Cross, lovingly placed by the mourning Edward: Temple Bar, and the countless, galleried mediaeval inns, precursors of the primitive circular theatres, the 'wooden o's' of Shakespeare, just coming into being.

All these Donne knew for he was a Londoner born, proud of his native city from which, when he had entered the Church, no country living could tempt him. Even the place of his birth, close to old St. Paul's, whose gothic aisles and long nave—the longest in England—were later to ring with his fiery eloquence and under whose stones his body was to be laid, was significant. This was the church in which Wycliffe had been tried for heresy and Tyndale's New Testament burned, yet it was the common news-room of the day, the resort of wits and gallants about town, where masterless men set up their bills for service, where lawyers stood at their pillars like merchants on 'change, waiting for clients, where bread, fish, and ale were sold as in any common tavern or shop, and

---

[1] Herbert, *History of the 12 Great Livery Companies of the City of London.*

[2] Washington Irving.

through which mules and horses were often led'.[1] In the crypt coopers loudly plied their trade and the cathedral vaults were used as storeplaces for booksellers' stocks.

Indeed, the Churchyard, jealously guarded by a high wall and resembling the close of a country cathedral, was the nursery of bookselling. The deanery, which Donne was to occupy, lay to the south, and the Bishop of London's Palace, upon whose doors the Papal Bull had been fixed, to the north, yet in and about, the smaller homes of the former petty canons and the shops of the recent vendors of rosaries, candles and censers, had turned book and printing shops. Here were sold programmes for the plays and foreign as well as English books, which indulgent shopkeepers ventured to lend out to trustworthy individuals. Perhaps Donne, like the young Shakespeare, sampled at will the hand-blocked pages and, since he had an interest in books amounting to avidity, availed himself of the privilege of borrowing.

Possibly too, he watched with keen intensity the choir-boy actors of St. Paul's in the music room of the little church of St. Gregory, nestling under the wing of the Cathedral, or, when outdoor performances were given, in the yard enclosed by the high walls of the Convocation House. And, like all boys, fascinated by the miraculous voyages of the times, he must have gone to Deptford to see the ship which had encircled the globe—the *Golden Hind*, upon whose decks the Queen had knighted Drake, and which now tide, wind, weather and the rapacity of sight-seers was slowly demolishing.

When Donne, a boy of sensitive nature, preternaturally advanced in learning, was eleven years old, his uncle, Jasper Heywood, was thrown into prison, either the Clink, lying across the river in Southwark, or the Tower, to which Heywood was removed when he was found to be obdurate in his

---

[1] See Wheatley, 'London and the Life of the Town,' *Shakespeare's England*, vol. ii, p. 166.

faith. Here his sister visited him (nursing him in illness[1]) and perhaps took with her her precocious son, whose mind and writings show every sign of having been bruised by contact with these unfortunate places. The prison scene, reinforced by a more tragic visit upon a later occasion, the arrogant spirit of the prisoner and his contempt for life as well as for death, made an ineffaceable impression upon the mind of Donne, sensitive as a photographic plate.

From the Clink Jasper had been fetched away to be examined by the Privy Council, to be bribed by the offer of a Bishopric if he would recant and use his talents to forward the Established Church, to be publicly arraigned, and to see his miserable companions taken out and executed.

This was the height of the heroic period of the English mission when the martyrs, those incomprehensible ones, 'kissed the instruments of torture, blessed their hangmen and embraced the ladders as they mounted to the gallows'.[2] Jasper Heywood might thank the particular protecting angel which watched over him that he was not called upon to join their numbers. A few months later, together with twenty other priests and a solitary layman he was put on board a ship, moored off the Tower stairs, and was taken across the Channel. Safe conduct was granted the recusants from Boulogne to Abbeville and here, fortunate in having escaped with their lives, they were abandoned with the knowledge that if ever they returned to their native shores the scathing death of traitors to the realm awaited them.

Jasper Heywood had the failings as well as the virtues of the Jesuits. He aimed at supremacy and monopoly, and in his handling of those with whom he was associated there was a certain chilly lack of consideration. At the same time his ability, his courage, his open espousal of the lost cause of English Catholicism as a national religion, his impatience to

---

[1] Morris, *The Troubles of our Catholic Forbears*, ii, p. 14.
[2] Meyer, p. 110.

forward it, all bespeak the positive side of his character which we are forced to admire. He died in 1598 at the Court of Naples, and unless Donne went abroad without permission from the Government—an act of the highest indiscretion in a family already marked for its religious stubbornness—it is doubtful if he ever saw him again. But the powerful personality of the eccentric Jasper, who probably advised Donne's mother on his early education, must have subtly impressed the lad.

4

In October of 1584, the year in which Raleigh, with whom Donne was later associated, equipped two ships and sent them on a voyage of discovery to America, John and Henry Donne, aged twelve and eleven respectively, went up to Oxford and were admitted to Hart Hall. The extreme youthfulness of the candidates was not exceptional: Robert Devereux, Earl of Essex, the path of whose life was to cross Donne's for several years, took his M.A. at Cambridge at the age of sixteen, and he was only one of many such graduates. The University education of the day was often spun out for seven years and entailed progression from one University to another.

The Master of Hart Hall (a hostel later merged with Hertford and then with Magdalen College) was old Philip Rondell, who had 'weathered out several changes of religion, though in his heart he was a Papist and durst not show it'.[1] Despite the objections of some of his Catholic colleagues he had managed to hold his position and thus the Hall was, at the time of Donne's entrance, a resort for the sons of Catholics who hoped for a favourable reaction in religion, but who dared not excite it. Some of these boys crossed over to Douai, the first English seminary, and some were destined to die for

[1] Anthony à Wood, *Athenae Oxonienses*.

their religion. This refuge for adherents of the older faith lacked a chapel and consequently those services, which, although hateful to some, were by others regarded merely with grudging tolerance. It was a popular Hall and according to a census taken earlier in the troublous times of the visitation, had stood eighth in the whole list of colleges. It was particularly favoured by Welsh students, receiving in Donne's day, together with Christ Church, more students from the Principality than Jesus, notably Welsh in foundation and sympathy.[1] For a time, New College men lived at Hart, amongst whom was Henry Wotton, a lad more than three years Donne's senior but destined to become a lifelong friend. Richard Baker, the future chronicler who describes Donne, and Henry Fitzsimon, the Irish Jesuit, were also contemporary students, but it is an extraordinary fact that not one of the five remained to take a degree. They sped away on foreign travel, or to Cambridge, or up to London, in all probability to escape too careful scrutiny into their religious beliefs, and to avoid taking the Oath of Allegiance, particularly abhorrent to Catholics and 'not to be refused by those that expect titular honour of their studies,'[2] that is, their degree.

The year before Donne went up to Oxford the University had a distinguished foreign visitor, Giordano Bruno, the philosopher, who has left us his derogatory impressions of English students strangely addicted to toasting in ale-houses, duelling and general horseplay. 'They graduated in the noble science of defence and took their ease alike in lecture room or tavern'.[3] But for the dons Bruno had even less use. He caricatured them as men in long robes whose hands were covered with jewels, whose throats were plastered with chains of gold, but whose manners were 'as devoid of courtesy as

---

[1] *History of The University of Oxford in the 16th and 17th Centuries*, Charles & Edward Mallet, and *Oxford University College Histories, Hertford*, S. G. Hamilton.

[2] I. Walton, p. 4, *Life of Dr. John Donne*.

[3] *Life of Bruno*, Frith, p. 121.

cowherds'.[1] The dons were, of course, Court nominees and were forced to be much in attendance upon the Queen: the students were mere ungrown boys, let loose from home restrictions, and Bruno did not speak a word of English, so perhaps he may be forgiven his misinterpretation. But if fiery-hearted Bruno was displeased with English culture he had much more contempt for the University's intellectual development, for the parrots and sophists who could only praise Aristotle and his doctrines. The hide-bound tutors 'who pursued words and neglected matter'[2] roused his ire the most.

Let us look at what boys of those days studied. We may still do so in the diary of two lads who went up to Oxford from Cornwall, just ten years before Donne's matriculation. They speak of their petty purchases (paper, tallow, a cap and garters, a penny for a haircut and twopence for cobbling)— and then of their studies—how they made 'definitions of *homo* by the five ways' and 'exercises to Master Vice Principal', since the Head had gone up to 'the Parliament'.[3] The books which they bought and about which they wrote home to their father were Aristotle's *Ethics*, Calton on Logic, Melanchthon and Calvin. When they were not listening to lectures on 'natural philosophy' they were hard at work translating Fox's *Martyrs* into Latin, Cicero, Sallust and Cebes out of it.

Formidable, dry and barren the University statutes sound. The praelector in Theology is to lecture on 'sound literature' alone: the one in Dialectic expound the 'Elenchi' of Aristotle or the 'Topica' of Cicero: the one in Rhetoric, Quintilian and Hermogenes, or (a daring innovation), the rhetorical works of Cicero. Civil Law is to be studied in the Pandects, the Code and the Ecclesiastical Laws of the Realm. The textbooks of the lecturers in Medicine are confined to

---

[1] *Life of Bruno*, Frith, p. 121.   [2] Sir Philip Sydney's words.

[3] The Diary of William Carnsew, i & ii, *The Spectator*, January 17th & 24th, 1941. A. L. Rowse.

Galen and Hippocrates, Mathematics to Tunstall and Carden, Geometry to Euclid, Astronomy and Cosmography to Ptolemy, in addition to Pliny, Strabo and Pomponius Mela. The professor of Greek is to lecture on Homer, Isocrates, Demosthenes and Euripides, and to instruct in grammar and style: the Hebrew professor, on the scriptures and grammar. Lastly, the lecturer in Philosophy, with which the physical science of the ancients was included, must expound the Problems, Ethics and Politics of Aristotle, together with Plato or Pliny.[1] From this summary one sees that Aristotle, dead more than three hundred years before the birth of Christ, was still the guiding light of English learning. Two thousand years had passed, yet when Donne went up to Oxford no one had tested whether the laws of falling bodies were other than those laid down by the Greek philosopher.

From Plotinus and the Neo-Platonists of the second century before Christ, through Christianity and the Church Fathers, like Augustine and Tertullian, through the Aristotelian revivalists and Scholastics of the Middle Ages, like the Angelic Doctor, Thomas Aquinas, the laws came down immutable and sacred. The Church which had begun by being the enemy of Aristotle and had found him too strong, had so allied herself with him that it became, literally, a matter of life and death to disprove him. The Aristotelian dictatorship set bounds to the intellect even more effective than those of dogma, and the follower of Socrates remained the supreme authority in both the natural and metaphysical world.

Bruno, for his pantheistic philosophy, full of an ardent enthusiasm for beauty and nature, for his questioning of the Aristotelian doctrines and his opposition to the Church, was tortured and burnt at the stake a year before Donne's marriage. A dweller in a star, he felt himself to be cloistered in the very precincts of heaven. The sky itself seemed meagre, narrow and ill-proportioned to the true greatness of man.

[1] *Education*, Sir John Sandys, *Shakespeare's England*, vol. i.

Had Donne been liberated by such an attitude to life in adolescence he would have escaped that hardening of the intellectual muscles which prevented him from giving birth to the germ of dawning scientific thought within him. A philosophy like Bruno's which 'opens the senses, satisfies the mind, enlarges the understanding and leads man to the only true beatitude',[1] would have been Donne's salvation and the lost key to the 'cabinet' of his nature.

5

While Donne was at Oxford he was doubtless in touch with various Spanish scholars, among whom was Antonio Corrano, a Spanish Protestant, recently nominated Divinity Reader, who was constantly called upon to free himself publicly from charges of heresy. The Reformation had gone far to destroy the intellectual intercourse of Oxford with the continent, but from the time of Henry VIII's marriage to Katherine of Aragon a tenderness for certain trends of Spanish thought had flowed in the University. Donne's taste for the mystical transcendentalists, whose austerity of mortification and rapture of vision have never been excelled, may have begun at Oxford or may have been fostered, earlier, by his Jesuit tutors and uncles. Always an individualist, interested in foreign thought and learning, he was early attracted to the fierce and fantastic, as yet unexpressed in his own writing. And, as Gosse points out, the great Spanish mystics, St. Theresa, Granada and John of the Cross, whose deaths the Jesuits especiallly mourned, all died during his boyhood 'while he was still in close family contact with Rome'.[2]

After three years at Oxford Donne went up to Cambridge. At Oxford he had found an atmosphere which differed but little from that in which he had been enveloped at home,

[1] Bruno's words. Frith, pp. 42–46.   [2] Gosse, vol. i, pp. 17–18.

steeped in Catholicism and the traditions of the schoolmen. Now, suddenly 'translated', as Walton formally puts it, he found himself breathing a sharp, rarefied, invigorating air. For Cambridge, unlike her more conservative sister Oxford, had lately shown encouraging inclinations towards independent religious thought and scientific study.

Under the determined and fearless guidance of Archbishop Whitgift, late Master of Trinity, the college which Donne is alleged to have entered, Anglicanism had grown and flourished, until Cambridge came to be regarded as its fountainhead and the nurturing source of Anglican clergy. Here too, Puritan sympathies were aggressively luxuriant and the emphasis, as Donne was quick to appreciate, shifted from Catholic versus Protestant, to Anglican versus the newer dissenter. If Donne's 'fires of inward dissatisfaction' had been 'silently fostered'[1] at Oxford, at Cambridge, in the temporary respite from religious combats occurring during his residence, he might watch with astonishment and dawning delight the struggle for existence of divers factions, and, when partisanship had cooled in him, sit down to plot with temperate mind the beginnings of his 'middle way', of which he remained a life advocate.

'With the Anglican party securely entrenched at Cambridge against the Catholics, it is not likely that any Catholic could have escaped detection if cause for suspicion had been aroused. . . . Either Donne conducted himself so sensibly as to be above reproach, or he no longer felt so heavily constrained by the bonds of his family Church as to find Anglicanism entirely uncongenial. It is not improbable that there was already developing within him that dissatisfaction with his Roman background which, in the course of years, was to impose upon him the necessity of "surveying all Divinity" before accepting the position of the Church of England. . . .

'Here, he found himself not necessarily involved, but, nevertheless, a fascinated spectator of a great religious epic. Authority, which had nourished him so far, was not only tacitly questioned

[1] C. H. Coffin, p. 35, *John Donne and The New Philosophy.*

but openly challenged. Though the challengers were not of
the Catholic faith, Donne could share their dislike for arbitrarily
enforced authority'.[1]

Hand in hand with this questioning of Papal, or Anglican
authority went the gradual dethronement of Aristotle, whose
influence Francis Bacon had lately deplored in robust manner—(for he had gone down from Cambridge 'carrying with
him a profound contempt for the course of study pursued
there, a fixed conviction that the system of academic education in England was radically vicious, a just scorn for the
trifles on which the followers of Aristotle had wasted their
powers, and no great reverence for Aristotle himself.'[2])—and
the advancement of scientific knowledge. The University
registers for the latter half of the century show an increasing
number of names of mathematical scholars, the first translators of Euclid and Copernicus into English, the first authors
of English arithmetical and geometrical works, the first brave
draughtsmen of the heavens under the new and terrifying
astronomical system. These were 'honourable and distinguished men whose minds were kindled by the Renaissance to enrich her tradition in behalf of the advancement of
human learning. Nor is it mere coincidence that they were
nurtured by a University whose atmosphere had been the
breath of the chief reformers of the Church and the most
enthusiastic champions of a logic that looked away from
Aristotle'.[3]

Thus mysticism was countered by honest scepticism, and
antiquity by a spirit of exciting modernity. Thus the balance
was redressed and Donne, who is himself the exponent of
violent antitheses, experienced, while still pliant and adapt-

[1] Coffin, p. 35.   [2] Macaulay's *Essay on Bacon*.

[3] John Dee, Leonard Digges, Robert Recorde, and, 'closer to Donne's
own time, Edward Wright, Fellow of Caius . . . mathematical tutor to Prince
Henry, and Henry Briggs . . . Fellow of St. John's and . . . first Savilian
Professor of Geometry at Oxford'. *Ibid.*, p. 38-9.

able, the opposing currents of thought and learning flowing less than one hundred miles from each other.

6

During these tumultuous years England had been reaching the climax of a period of urgent growth. There had been the Spanish invasion of Ireland, the advent in England of the Jesuits, the execution of gentle Campion, the rise and fall of plot and counter-plot against the throne. Mary had been beheaded, the black and scarlet of her robes startling the eyes of avid spectators as still they slash the pages of dull history. Douai, the great English seminary, had removed to Rheims, owing to growing anti-Catholic feeling in the Low Countries. The English students in the College at Rome had begun to rise against the interference of the Jesuits, and the English college at Valladolid, fostered by the King of Spain, had been founded.

The threads of international intrigue for succession to the English throne, for resuscitation of the Catholic religion, for fostering the important woollen trade, entangled in their warp and woof the crowned heads of European sovereigns. The Mission priest, landing in remote saltwater inlets, hiding by day and stealing on by night, influenced the life of the noble or peasant who sheltered him, while Elizabeth flirted with her French suitor, and the heir to the Spanish throne fomented trouble in the Netherlands. The balance of power shifted warily from Spain to France, and back to Spain, and then more assuredly over to England, until the great and newly appointed ambassador to the Court of St. James, Don Bernardino de Mendoza, came bearing instructions almost 'piteously apologetic'.[1] Sir Philip Sidney, beloved of the nation died. Drake went on his plundering expedition, and the merchants of London and Bristol, the two great ports

[1] *State Papers Spanish*, vol. ii, Martin Hume's Preface.

of England, began to raise troops for Ireland, which the Spaniards might use as a base.

Many likened England, in this heroic period just before the coming of the Armada, to Athens in the age of Pericles, but we, in retrospect, see a resemblance to our own troubled times. There was the fear of undiscerned treachery: 'Without all doubt there is some great mischief meant towards us, and I pray God that when all is done that there is not found some false traitors within our realm'.[1] All foreigners had to be registered and to give their occupations. There was a fear of risings in London: 'No man shall walk in the streets after ten o'clock at night under pain of death'[2]—and the fear of assassination of the Sovereign—'No pistol is to be carried in any part of the country, nor no musket shot within two miles of the Queen'.[3] And while these latter fears have no modern counterpart the question of an invasion of England by foreign forces then, as now, occupied each one's mind. Some, like Raleigh, advocated immediate action. An open rupture, a policy of rank aggression seemed healthier than seeming friendship with a subtle enemy. 'I pray God that I may rather see England invade than be invaded'.[4]

The terrible religious massacres on the Continent exceeded anything known in England and the suppression of individual liberty and conscience existed then as now it exists. Modern writers speak of Europe as 'The Dark Continent', a name equally applicable in those days when England, small and defiant, sheltered the persecuted, fleeing across the narrow seas. For Dutch and German protestants, Flemings, and French Huguenots, all were encouraged by Elizabeth, until London became so full of foreign craftsmen plying their trades in security that 'complaints against the strangers' were

[1] Thomas Dutton, An English Protestant in Antwerp, *State Papers Spanish*, 1558–1567, pp. 671 and 684.

[2] Strype's *Annals*, August 1578.　　[3] *Ibid*.

[4] Thomas Wilson, English Envoy at the Court of the Spanish Governor of the Netherlands, in his report to Walsingham.

made, riots occurred, and the English apprentices rose in righteous fury.

The cleansing fire of the Armada, which swept over England while Donne was at Cambridge, the tremendous surge of national pride and the solace of sweet victory refreshed and reinvigorated her, but it was long before a sense of national security and consequent religious toleration brought peace to the minds of all men, no matter what creed they believed or upheld.

7

In 1591 John and Henry Donne entered Thavies Inn, a preparatory school for the Law, and on the 6th of May following, John, as the elder, in advance of Henry, was admitted to Lincoln's Inn. The Inns of Court were then regarded as the third university of England, in which 'the laws of the realme only are read and learned by such as give their minds unto the knowledge of the same.'[1]

What was Donne's appearance by now? In answer we have the most exciting of all his portraits, for it stirs the mind in many directions. It is a contemporary engraving by William Marshall, after a miniature thought to be by the earliest English miniaturist, Hilliard,[2] of whom Donne speaks in 'The Storm'—

> ... 'a hand, or eye
> By Hilliard drawn, is worth an history,
> By a worse painter made;'

Taking into account the facts that the portrait is seen first through the eyes of the limner and then through those of the engraver—in other words that it is a portrait done in two mediums and likely to have been distorted in the processes—it is still arresting and the only authentic early likeness.

[1] Holinshed's Chronicles, vol. 1, *England*, by Harrison, p. 249, 1586, London 1807.

[2] Mr. Laurence Binyon's opinion, p. 134, vol. ii. Sir Herbert Grierson, *Poems of John Donne with Introduction and Commentary*, 2 vol. 1912.

It shows the large appraising eyes, a nose coarse, yet with sensitive nostrils, finely modelled temples, narrowing at the top. It gives the high cheekbones, the indentation of the jaw suggesting a double plane across the cheek, the chin pointed, firm and prominent, and the mouth sensual but not loose, capable of gravity as well as humour. The eyebrows, more like a woman's than a man's, have about them a trace of impatience and questioning. The gallant wears earrings, and the hair, worn long, curls slightly after the newer fashion of the day. ('For see, how the hair is suffered sometimes to grow long like women's locks' . . . 'And how some lusty courtiers and gentlemen of courage do wear either rings of gold, stones or pearls in their ears, whereby they imagine the workman-ship of God to be emended.'[1]) The loose collar, worn instead of the tremendous ruff popular in the beginning of Eliza-beth's reign, lies over the doublet which buttons straight down the front and has neat sleeves, similarly cuffed, and padded-out at the shoulders. The hand, execrably drawn, yet suggestive of shapeliness and purpose, grasps a rapier below the pommel.

Above the oval of the portrait in one corner is the Latin inscription, 'In the Year of our Lord, 1591. Aged 18,' and in the other a Spanish tag, which reads, 'Sooner dead than changed',[2] together with a small crest, the *wolf rampant* of the Donnes.

In writing of the portrait critics have spoken of Donne as being the typical Shakespearian gallant, 'audacious and witty',[3] or of the face having 'a haunted look, as of a soul fearful of the form that housed it'.[4] Neither of these descrip-tions is a fitting interpretation, the one understates and the other exaggerates. It is a face which strikes one with its arrogance and intensity: arresting and uneasy, it betokens future conflict: it is a face in which the intelligence and the

---

[1] Harrison, pp. 229 and 289.   [2] See page 263.
[3] Grierson, vol. ii, p. 270.   [4] Fausset, *John Donne, A Study in Discord.*

This was for youth, Strength, Mirth, and wit that Time
Most count their golden Age; but t'was not thine.
Thine was thy later yeares, so much refind
From youths Drosso, Mirth, & wit; as thy pure mind
Thought (like the Angels) nothing but the Praise
Of thy Creator, in those last, best Dayes.
    Witnes this Booke, (thy Embleme) which begins
    With Love; but endes, with Sighes, & Teares for sins.
Will: Marshall. sculprit.   IZ: WA:

JOHN DONNE, AGED 18

senses will forever be at war, the one demanding supremacy
over the other. At the same time it suggests competence and
great assurance: it presages a leader, but in what sphere?
Anything may be in store for such a man, yet one shrewdly
suspects that the impatient forcefulness of life driving
him forward will be trammelled by the critical tendencies
of the mind. Impulse and passion may be the undoing of
reason and reflective vision. Which in the long run will hold
sway?

The appraising look in the eyes is found in other contemporary portraits. Compare it with the Grafton Portrait of
Shakespeare, and that of John Bull, the brilliant organist of
the day, both painted within a space of four years.[1] Was it a
convention, a trick of the nameless Elizabethan artists, or is it
significant of the wariness and caution prevalent when
brother suspected brother and when, despite the solid commercial ground beneath their feet, the whole world seemed to
men to be in flux?

'The Evil lies in the universal distrust', wrote the Spanish
ambassador in his despatches. 'A father dares not trust his
own son.'[2] The most tragic legacy of the period are the letters
from Protestant fathers pleading with their Catholic sons, or
sons begging forgiveness from their fathers. For instance, an
only son has disgraced his father, loyal to the State, by openly
acknowledging his allegiance to Rome. He has paid penalty
by being whipped through the town and branded with hot
irons. For the last time, the father asks, will the son accept
his judgment, or shall he be to him a stranger? And the son
replies that he is beyond the reach of doubt and can obey
no earthly power.

Another pledges his father's name without authority in order
to procure £100 with which to flee the country. So great is his

[1] In the Rylands Library, Manchester, and The Ashmolean Museum,
Oxford, 1591, 1588 and 1599. Dates of three portraits respectively.

[2] Spanish Calendars, 1558–67, p. 389.

distress of mind that, although he is a young man of integrity, he is forced into dishonesty by the exigencies of the situation and his mental torment. This torture, into which Catholics, or Catholic converts, were thrown throughout the first twenty years of Donne's life, surrounded him, and that he did not escape from it unscathed is evident from his letters, his writings and the subsequent events of his life.

Here is a letter from the young man mentioned above. Like Donne, Markham had been a student of the law. Like Donne, he had a promising career opening before him—Markham was Secretary to the Lord Treasurer as Donne was to be to the Lord Keeper—and, like Donne, he adopted the same painful method of sifting and resifting the evidence in favour of both faiths before coming to a decision.

'Robert Markham to his father, upon his departure beyond the Seas, for conscience's sake.

Gravesend. The 27th of August, 1592.

Most dear Father and Mother:
My mind is overburdened with grief and not able to endure one word tending towards departure. . . . For tears I cannot see to write and for inward grief cannot endure to read again. . . . Upon my knees I humbly crave pardon and forgiveness.

Being perplexed in mind I endeavoured to settle my conscience as well as I could. I betook myself to the study of divinity, wherein for the space of some two years I have bestowed some time, together with the conference of divers learned on both sides. Upon reading and conference, my conscience grew at length undoubtedly settled that the Romish religion was the most true, catholic church, whereof unless I should become a member, I could not be saved. Hereupon, endeavouring to be reconciled I find that that reconciliation is high treason by act of Parliament. Which odious name of traitor I do so much detest as I rather choose to leave my country than to hazard the staining of our house and name with high treason, which as yet was never attainted.'

He then explains how he 'took up' the £100 falsely and continues:

'I assure you, by the duty I owe unto you, that I will never serve in France or in Flanders against her Majesty: neither whatsoever beggary betide me, will I ever serve the King of Spain, nor any of his agents, so long as he remaineth enemy to England: neither be guilty to any conspiracy against her Majesty's person, but reveal it if ever any such matter chance to come to my hearing. I am, and will be, as good a subject to her Majesty for allegiance as any is in England. But such is my present state at this time that every hour presenteth a hell unto me. On the days, I go like a man distract of senses for fear of death at this instant. In the night, I cannot sleep, nor take any rest: when I pray I am discomforted, for I pray without hope to be heard because I am not of that church which I believe to be His.

Forgive me, and forget me, who desire to be forgotten. For since it is not God's will to suffer me by my study at law to do you some service I will so behave myself as to do you no harm. Be good to this poor man my servant, in helping him to a master, better than myself. . . .'[1]

This letter was written three months after Donne was admitted to Lincoln's Inn and just a year before the death of his brother Henry.

8

Descriptions of the impression which Donne made upon his friends agree in speaking of his charm. 'Very neat, not dissolute,' is Richard Baker's description of him,[2] and there is Hackett's more illuminating comment—'Neither was it possible that a vulgar soul should dwell in such promising features.'[3] 'He was of stature moderately tall, of a straight and equally proportioned body, to which all his words and actions gave an unexpressible addition of comeliness,'[4] writes Walton, and he speaks of his 'winning behaviour, which when it would entice, had a strange kind of elegant irresistible art'.[5]

---

[1] Strype's *Annals of the Reformation*, vol. 7, p. 157.

[2] Baker, *Chronicle of the Kings of England*, 1730, p. 424.

[3] Hackett's *Life of the Lord Keeper Williams*, 1693, p 74.

[4] Walton, p. 59.   [5] *Ibid.*, p. 10.

Amongst later authors, Jessop's summary is the best: 'A vein
of peculiar tenderness runs through the expressions in which
friends speak of him as if he had exercised over their affections for him an unusual and indefinable witchery. The
charm of his person and manners was irresistible. He must
have had much love to give, or he could never have had so
much bestowed upon him.'[1]

Chief among Donne's friends at this period were the sons
of a wealthy Mayor of York, Christopher and Samuel Brooke.
Like portions of Donne's own soul, for one was a poet and
lawyer, the other a scholar and divine, they intertwined their
lives with his until all three became knit in a relationship
forced to stand the test of rash action as well as time.

Christopher had been Donne's friend at Trinity and was
now his chamber-fellow at Lincoln's Inn. His friends were
mainly poets and he himself was a writer. From his will we
glean another fact, that he was probably one of the group
who hovered around Shakespeare, for he left to Donne 'the
portrait of Elizabeth, Countess of Southampton'. Her husband, the young Earl, was Shakespeare's patron who was to
embark on the Cadiz and Azores voyages with Donne.

Between their studies these young men, trying their wings
in London, amused themselves at inn and theatre, or in
amatory escapades. At the public playhouses the seats in
the galleries were largely occupied by gentlemen and pro-
fessional men, 'a large number of them being students of the
Inns of Court.'[2]

'Of study and play made strange hermaphrodites'[3] is
Donne's own description of himself and his companions at
this time in his expanding life. He was always a lover of the
theatre and it was his good fortune to live in the greatest
dramatic era since the age of Pericles. In his *Sermons*, he

[1] Augustus Jessop, *John Donne, sometime Dean of St. Paul*, p. 18.

[2] *The Essential Shakespeare*, J. Dover Wilson, p. 29.

[3] *Epithalamion made at Lincoln's Inn*.

speaks of the 'obscenities and scurrilities of a Comedy, or the drums and ejaculations of a Tragedy',[1] and he championed the stage against the Puritans, those who search his works for allusions to contemporary authors, or any individual play, will be disappointed.

The club at the 'Mermaid Tavern', said to have been founded by Raleigh in 1603 and to have been frequented by Donne, must have had many earlier unrecorded counterparts, for in these years towards the close of the century poets, soldiers, artists, scholars, legal and political lights in embryo came easily together.

> '. . . words that have been
> So nimble and so full of subtle flame,
> As if that everyone from whence they came
> Had meant to put his whole wit in a jest
> And had resolved to live a fool the rest
> Of his dull life . . .'

Beaumont's lines have mirrored the magic warmth of those meetings for us so perfectly that nothing will ever excel them.

Amongst men of such stature as Shakespeare, Jonson and Inigo Jones, whom he probably knew as a boy,[2] Donne, even at the age of nineteen or in the early twenties, must have cut a figure not easily ignored. His voice which was full of music, his grace in movement, his singular charm of manner and his wit, which could be sharp and satiric as well as gentle and humorous, all marked him out as exceptional. Moreover, he was known to have a fortune and to be generous, to love life passionately in any guise in which she might reveal herself—what better passport could he carry?

Now when did Donne begin to write? Certainly very early, but owing to the fact that writers did not one and all crave publicity in print, the finest verses were often simply copied

---

[1] *Sermons Eighty*, 38.

[2] Inigo Jones was the son of a Welshman and was christened in the parish of St. Bartholomew, in which Donne's stepfather lived and to which he probably removed him as a boy.

into note or commonplace books, or merely circulated from hand to hand and his were no exception. The Dutch poet Constantine Huyghens, who was Donne's ardent admirer, describes his lyrics as 'ripe medlars', when he comes upon them towards the close of Donne's life. 'Many rich fruits from the green branches of his wit have lain mellowing among the lovers of art, which now, when nearly rotten with age, they are disturbing.'[1]

Only four of his poems were published in his lifetime and two of these he regretted making public.[2] No collected edition was issued until two years after his death, and thus we, the rich inheritors, are often dependent upon the manuscript collections of the private libraries. The confusing number of extant manuscripts, of different dates and of varying texts, together with references to his poems in contemporary collections, proves how well known Donne's verses were without being printed. Bound in vellum and neatly transcribed, the manuscripts proudly bear the names of Donne's friends or their children—Henry, ninth Earl of Northumberland, or the second Earl of Bridgewater, elder brother of Milton's 'Comus' and son of his friend John Egerton.

Apart from the question of modesty or indifference in his early years, and of deprecation in his later, caution must also have influenced Donne in avoiding print so consciously. Members of the great Catholic families had learnt to be wary of their actions and not to bring themselves forward imprudently. Those who admired the Court and had ambition must keep their tongues and pens close, for with fame and success there came peril. The flowery path was treacherous and over it hung the shadows of Marlowe and Kyd who had meddled with State matters and died young.

In reading Donne's letters to his friends, his Sermons, or

[1] Grierson, vol. ii, p. lxxvii.

[2] *The Anatomy of the World* with *A Funeral Elegy*, and *Of The Progress of the Soul* in 1611 and 1612; *The Elegy upon the Untimely Death of the Incomparable Prince Henry*, (King James's son), in 1613; and the lines prefixed to *Coryat's Crudities* in 1611.

the whole volume of his verse, one fails to find a single direct reference, (such as a man might drop in conversation or use to emphasize a point by way of simile), to any biographical fact of his early years. In the case of the *Satyres* this is comprehensible, since, in 1599, the Bishops prohibited their printing and those already printed by other braver authors were burnt in public places. But in other forms, less notorious, this omission, unnatural and almost self-conscious, amounts to constriction and implies a trained habit of mind.

9

Upon this period of study and gaiety fell an act of violence which diverted part of Donne's stream of thought into the deepest channel of his life—that of meditation upon the justness of various religious creeds and his own ability to believe and uphold one. This was the imprisonment and death of Donne's younger brother, Henry, whose life at home, at Oxford and in London, had outwardly run parallel with John's, but which inwardly was as far divorced from his as 'darkness, light's elder brother'. For Henry remained unquestioningly true to the faith of his ancestors. He was, like his brother, highly compassionate, and his tenderness was tinctured with courage and rash thoughtlessness for himself in the danger of others, for in May of 1593, he sheltered a young seminary priest called William Harington.

More than ten years earlier complaints had been made to the Government about the Inns of Court harbouring 'a sort of persons detected to be in the same houses, of disordered demeanour, and ecclesiastical',[1] and the benchers and ancients had been summoned, for the second time in Elizabeth's reign, to inquire into the fomenting of such 'disorders'. Then began the period of severest persecution for the

[1] Strype's *Annals*, iii, p. 44, 1581.

Catholics, with fines beyond the means of most, sequestration of property and landed goods. In 1582 came the 'Proclamation denouncing Jesuits and Seminary Priests as Traitors', and those sheltering them as accomplices. In 1583 Burleigh publicly justified torture. In 1584 William of Orange was murdered and the fear of assassination for Elizabeth increased the measures of repression. In 1585 appeared the Act insisting that all priests must leave the country within forty days; that all those remaining were to be condemned as traitors and that all those sheltering them were now, not merely accomplices, but traitors themselves, until finally, in the year of Henry Donne's imprisonment, came the last of the Elizabethan Acts against Catholics, that 'Against Popish Recusants'.

The Catholics were now hunted beings with laws and restrictions hedging them in like the plague-stricken. They were shut out from public office, banned by public opinion, cut off from communication with their friends and relations. The knowledge that they were constantly under suspicion, not only in groups at home and abroad, but as individual citizens, often intensely loyal to the Crown, was a sorrow and irritation which brought them near madness. Listen to Richard Holtby, whom Donne must have known as a tutor at Hart Hall, writing to his Superior, Father Garnett:

'If we converse openly, if we buy or sell, if we traffic in our necessary affairs, or take care of our own commodities, if we laugh, recreate ourselves, or carry any indifferent countenance, then are we either too wealthy, or else too well to live: such prosperous fortune is not tolerable in men of our profession. . . . If we live in secret and delight ourselves to be solitary, if we cut off all access of our neighbours, or refuse to keep company with such as love us not, then do we busy our heads, in their conceit, to devise against them secret conspiracies: and our leisure is with them sufficient argument that we occupy ourselves about no other matters, save only to stir and contrive seditious factions.'[1]

[1] Dodd-Tierney, *Church History*, iii, p. 78.

The prison into which Henry Donne, now nearly of age, was thrown was the very one in which his uncle Jasper had first suffered imprisonment. Women and children were his companions and, since religion was a crime, the worst type of criminal might be placed with people of gentle breeding and hope for more lenient treatment than the offender for his faith. 'There is no room for thieves in the prisons . . . there are so many Catholics,'[1] was the cry, and for every four or five Catholics who suffered death by persecution, one died in prison.[2] At some time in the summer, Henry was removed from the Clink to Newgate and there, taking either the plague or gaol fever, he sickened and died.[3]

If Donne loved his brother the blow was a heavy one, and if he did not, then his conscience smote him. The martyr's crown, which he as the elder, if he were like the single-minded mission priests, coveted had been taken from him. Now, if ever, he might reproach himself for not sharing the danger, or for not more openly leading a religious life, unwise and dangerous though this might be. The clues to his disturbed mental state are the numerous references to 'the little room', 'the dark chamber,' the 'prison,' throughout early poems and late Sermons. Six years after Henry's death he writes:

'Withering like prisoners, which lie but for fees,'[4]

(referring to the custom of bribing the gaolers for every comfort, sometimes freedom itself), and thirty-three years later in *Death's Duell*, the last powerful, macabre oration which he was ever to deliver, he uses the self-same simile.

Again, in *The Obsequies to Lord Harington*, written before

[1] *Concertatio Eccles. Catholic.* Ed. 1583. See Meyer, p. 166.

[2] Meyer, p. 184.

[3] The Stonyhurst MSS. *Anglia*, i, 77, suggest that Henry's removal from one prison to another infected one was purposeful and connected with designs upon his patrimony, but of this there is no proof. See footnote p. 275, F. P. Wilson, *Notes on the Early Life of Donne*.

[4] *The Storm.*

his Ordination, when merciful visitations to the prisons became part of his round of life:

> 'Time's dead low-water; . . .
> . . . when the condemned man,
> (Who, when he opes his eyes, must shut them then
> Again by death) although sad watch he keep,
> Doth practise dying by a little sleep.' . . .

Such a passage rings too true for casual knowledge and the sight of those in whom 'the pulse of life beat tremulous and faint'[1] must have oppressed him long in memory.

In reading the biting *Satyres*, especially the Fourth upon 'The Court' and the Third upon 'Religion', one has no need to be reminded of Donne's brother's death, for one sees how he is still at heart a sympathizer with the Catholic minority, hating pursuivants and informers with a corrosive hatred.

The alienation from his mother which would have begun at a very early age if, as I have suggested, he resented his stepfather's intrusion, or later, when she discovered his heretical and libertine trends of thought, would now be increased. There is evidence in the only surviving letter which Donne wrote to his mother that he regarded himself as lost to her, and the lines from an Elegy[2] upon the loss of his mistress's bracelet (which Ben Jonson knew by heart), written about this time,[3] suggest that Elizabeth Donne had looked upon Henry as her favourite son:

> '*Yet with such anguish, as her only son*
> *The mother in the hungry grave doth lay,*
> Unto the fire these Martyrs I betray.
> Good Souls, (for you give life to everything)
> Good Angels, (for good messages you bring)
> Destin'd you might have been to such an one,
> As would have lov'd and worship'd you alone:
> One that would suffer hunger, nakedness,
> Yea death, ere he would make your number less.'

---

[1] *Sartor Resartus*, Carlyle. See Grierson, ii, p. 207.
[2] Elegy XI. *The Bracelet*, (Italics mine).
[3] See Grierson, vol. ii, p. 61 *et seq*.

Exceptional egoists have been known to speak of 'only sons' dying while yet another child lives and, although it is dangerous to conjecture from such material as the verse above, the poignancy of the first two lines, the Catholic cast of thought, the reflection of martyrdom, and the inverted manner of handling scathingly that which was near to his heart, all indicate that the poem is of this period in Donne's emotional life and that it may hinge on the tragedy of his brother's death, and his warped relation to his mother. It is even plausible that Donne's overthrow of the religion of his ancestors was due, not to pressure put on him from civil power, nor to the speculative and rational tendencies of his mind, but to a revulsion from everything connected with his mother and an unhappy infancy.

At some time, while he was a student at the Inns of Court, Donne began his sifting of religious tenets, his 'cribrating and recribrating', as he terms it. Although outwardly 'an atheist and rebel'[1] and frankly a pagan in search of sensual pleasures and physical experience, such study would not be incompatible with a kind of 'dormant religiosity', as Gosse calls it, and his brother's death, would be the sure incentive to work of this questioning, laborious kind, provided the mind was early in conflict over creeds, persecutions and martyrdom.

The letter from Robert Markham to his father, quoted earlier, shows that such study might easily go hand in hand with that of the law, even if the student were engaged on worldly adventures as well. Donne, we know, had the fortunate habit of requiring little sleep. 'In the most unsettled days of his youth his bed was not able to detain him past the hour of four in the morning: and it was no common business that drew him out of his chamber till past ten; all of which time was employed in study, though he took great liberty after it. And if this seems strange, it may gain a belief by the visible fruits of his labours, some of which remain as testimonies of

[1] *Love's Deity.*

what is here written, for he left the resultance of 1,400 authors, most of them abridged and analysed with his own hand. . . .'[1]

Some of these 'resultances' date from later periods, from study while unemployed at Mitcham or while he worked with Bishop Morton. They cover a wide range of human learning, which he attacked with what he called 'an hydroptique, immoderate desire'. He devoted especial attention to the work of Cardinal Bellarmine, a prime defender of the Roman cause. When he had finished his annotations he showed them to Thomas Morton, then Dean of Gloucester, and when he died he willed them as studies, still valuable in his eyes, to a dear friend. His wearisome work, early begun, stood him in good stead eventually.

The black grief which fell on the home of Donne's mother was not exceptional, for the year 1593 was a terrible one for the whole country. Dearth and famine emptied the land and the plague, often rampant and seldom controlled, burst out afresh with violence. Some 15,000 persons succumbed in London alone: there were pleas to the Lord Chancellor for the restraint of plays for fear of increased infection,[2] not only in London but in the University towns as well. Marlowe, the brilliant theatrical reformer, died and Shakespeare had to seek favour from indulgent patrons. Torrential rains, thunder and lightning and a blazing star added to the terror of the people:

'Our years are turned upside down: our summers are no summers, our harvests are no harvests: our seed-times are no seed-times . . . and the nights are like the days. . . . The Lord hath bowed the Heavens with tokens and earnests of His wrath . . . so terrible that the child unborn shall speak of it.'[3]

[1] Walton, p. 44.
[2] Strype, vol. 7, p. 228.
[3] Strype, vol. 7, p. 292. Bishop of York's words.

In April of the following year, Donne received his patrimony, sadly augmented by his brother's death, from the
Chamber of London, and his signatures exist to prove his
presence in the city. In November he was appointed 'Steward
of Christmas' at Lincoln's Inn and if he filled this post, as he
had filled that of 'Master of the Revels' previously, it would
demand his presence in London until January, 1595. But
what do we find? That his name is missing from the vacation
list of the Inn for Christmas and he is fined for not performing
his merry duties. We may safely assume that Donne was
abroad.[1] The disturbing events of the previous, miserable,
plague-ridden year, his brother's death, an excess of study
and an unsatisfactory love affair, threw him into a state of
restless mental confusion which urged him to break away.
The young man had money to spend, his interests were wide,
his energy and curiosity keen, why should he not visit France,
Italy and Spain, countries with whose languages he was
already familiar,—even the Holy Land?[2]

The latter journey was never accomplished but it strikes
one as significant that Donne, who has been labelled a
wordly character who only accepted the Church as a last
resource when all other avenues of promotion failed him,
should have contemplated this pilgrimage. What was in his
mind? Penance, supplication, identification with the Holy
place? Whatever the inclination, it emphasizes the presence
of a latent spirituality which some, cutting his life across
with a sharp knife as though the late and early man were
two distinct entities, are apt to deny in the years before his
marriage.

But at the moment he is still the lover, the poet, the ad-

[1] *Times Literary Supplement*, April 10, 1930, Article by J. E. Butt, and
2 articles, Oct. 16 & 23, 1930, I. A. Shapiro. See 'The Date of Donne's
Travels,' John Sparrow in *A Garland for Donne*, edited by Theodore
Spencer, Harvard University Press, 1931. [2] Walton, p. 4.

venturer, 'walking in expectation' in the galleries of life. In the
Elegy, On His Mistress, (which we might call the *Rosalind*,
since it answers the girl's suggestion that she accompany him
upon his travels disguised as a page-in-waiting—a fantastic
ambition actually accomplished by the mistress of an acquaintance of Donne's[1] eleven years later)—he pleads with
her:

> 'When I am gone, dream me some happiness,
> Nor let thy looks our long-hid love confess.'

There have been many definitions of poets, furnished by
poets themselves. There is Wordsworth's—'A poet is a man
speaking to men . . . a man who rejoices more than other men
in the spirit of life that is in him'—(and how true this is of
the young Donne!): Or Browning's—'A poet is only a person
more alive than other men': or Rupert Brooke's less succinct:
'It consists in looking at people and things as themselves—
neither as useful, nor moral, nor ugly, nor anything else; but
just as being. At least that's a philosophical description of it.
What happens is that I suddenly feel the extraordinary value
and importance of everything I meet, and almost everything
I see.'

This heightening of perception and appreciation, and the
realization of the value of life, is vividly evident in Jack Donne.
But it throws in its wake revulsions quick and unaccountable
and the note of sudden anguish, sometimes forced into a last
line, is almost unbearable in poignancy. Such intensity held
him hard at work when he had made up his mind to stick to
it, drove him to bouts of wild distraction, and kept him up
half the night, until like Chaucer's young Squire he slept no
more than the nightingale.

Ben Jonson's description of an unknown writer[2] applies

---

[1] Elizabeth Southwell and Sir Robert Dudley, illegitimate son of the Earl
of Leicester. 'At this period the most fantastic poetry was never more
fantastic than life itself.' Grierson, ii, p. 88.

[2] In the posthumous *Discoveries*.

with strange and forceful pertinence to Donne whom he loved and admired. Is it he whom Ben describes?

'The mind is like a bow, the stronger by being unbent. But the temper in spirits is all, when to command a man's wit, when to favour it. I have known a man vehement on both sides; that knew no man either to intermit his studies or call upon them again. When he hath set himself to writing, he would join night to day; press upon himself without release, not minding it till he fainted; and when he left off, resolve himself into all sports and looseness again: that it was almost a despair to draw him to his book: but once got to it, he grew stronger and more earnest by the case. His whole powers were renewed: he would work out of himself what he desired, but with such excess as his study could not be ruled; he knew not how to dispose his own abilities or husband them, he was of that immoderate power against himself.'[1]

The last phrase is particularly true of Donne.

Just now his restlessness was acute.

> 'Who e'er rigg'd fair ship to lie in harbours,
> And not to seek new lands, or not to deal withal?'[2]

He set out upon his travels, leaving behind him a reputation for nonchalance and libertine thought, beneath which it would be difficult for all but the closest observers to spy anything but levity, and bidding his mistress 'Rob me, but bind me not, and let me go'.[3]

Within eighteen months he was home again, but only to embark on further adventures.

---

[1] Dover Wilson, *The Essential Shakespeare*, p. 77, quotes the passage; in his estimation a portrait of Shakespeare.

[2] *Confined Love.*

[3] *The Indifferent.*

CHAPTER II

THE YEARS OF ACTION

> 'Twice or thrice had I loved thee,
> Before I knew thy face or name;
> So in a voice, so in a shapeless flame,
> Angels affect us oft, and worship'd be;'
> 'Air and Angels.'

I

In June, 1596, there lay secretly gathered together in Plymouth harbour an extraordinary number of ships and men —'300 green-headed youths, covered with feathers, gold and silver lace, and at least 10,000 soldiers, as tall, handsome men as can ever be seen: in the navy, at least 150 ships, besides hoys and flyboats,' augmented by twenty-four ships of war from the Dutch States. One of these 'soldiers' was John Donne and the expedition for which these forces were gathered together was the daring descent on the city of Cadiz.

The distinction of having fought the Spaniard was coveted by all the young gallants, unbreeched in Armada days, and so numerous were the applicants for service that many had to be turned away. Lord Howard of Effingham was again chosen Lord High Admiral, Sir Walter Raleigh, the promoter, organizer and adviser of the expedition, Rear-Admiral, and the Queen's favourite, Robert, Earl of Essex, under whom Donne took service, Lord General of the Land Forces. Among Donne's comrades-in-arms were the young Earl of Southampton, to whom Shakespeare had already dedicated 'Venus and Adonis' and 'Lucrece', and Thomas, son of Sir Thomas Egerton (later Lord Ellesmere) who had only just been made Lord High Chancellor and Keeper of the Great Seal.

It would be interesting to learn the relation of officer to

subordinate on these historic voyages, when amateur rubbed shoulder with seasoned warrior and poet jostled illiterate sailor. What were their contacts? For Raleigh, who was then turned an experienced forty-six to Essex's thirty, and who played the Capulet to his Montagu, had an eye for poets. Inspired with visions of El Dorado, of mountains of gold and crystal, he was the very man to set light to the imaginative fire in Donne's mind, whose verse and prose is interlaced with references to the West and East Indies, Virginia and the Canaries, to fair ships, new-rigged, seeking new lands, to 'myne and spice', the fruits of Raleigh's and the other discoverers' voyages. But Raleigh and Essex were bitter competitors and it is unlikely that Donne, as a subordinate, came into close contact with his superior officer's rival.

For something like eight centuries Cadiz, 'la Joyosa', as the Andalusians still call her, had been the great mart of the west. Her citizens had, at one time, ranked second only to those of Rome and now, with the discovery of America a century earlier, and the opening of new trade routes to the Indies and Orient, she had become the wealthiest port in western Europe and headquarters of the Spanish treasure-fleet. The destruction of this fleet and, if possible, of the city as well, was the object of the Elizabethan forces. Both were accomplished. During the naval encounter the Spaniards were forced to fire some of their ships, amongst them the great Royal galleons, the *St. Thomas* and the *St. Philip*, by whose sides Sir Walter Raleigh had laid out a warp in order, as he humorously put it, 'to shake hands with her.' Finding that there was no escape from their desperate pursuers the Spaniards:

'all let slip and ran aground, tumbling into the sea heaps of soldiers, so thick, as if coals had been poured out of a sack . . . some drowned and some sticking in the mud. . . . The spectacle was very lamentable . . . for many drowned themselves, many half burnt leapt into the water, very many hanging by the ropes ends

by the ship's side under the water, even to their lips: many swim-
ming with grievous wounds, strucken under water, and put out of
their pain. And withall so huge a fire and such tearing of the
Ordnance in the "Great Philip" and the rest, when the fire came to
them, as if any man had a desire to see Hell itself, it was there
most lively figured.'[1]

That is Raleigh's version. Now listen to Donne, a fascinated spectator of this holocaust:

> 'Out of a fired ship, which, by no way
> But drowning, could be rescued from the flame,
> Some men leap'd forth, and, ever as they came
> Near the foes' ships, did by their shot decay;
> So all were lost, which in the ship were found,
> They in the sea being burnt, they in the burnt ship drown'd.'[2]

This is one of his *Epigrams* which seems like a line-drawing
dashed off in the heat of the battle.

The mind registers and holds that which appeals to it in
the light of its own experience, and the predicament of the
doomed men might well seem to Donne a portrayal in the
flesh of his own mental conflict which had already begun,—
a terrible hovering between the ruinous sensual fires of youth
by which he attempted to burn away his torment, and the
more appalling spiritual death of doubt and endless horror.
Fire and water remained for him always symbols of destruction rather than constructive elements. He wrote four other
epigrams on this voyage, which, with later ones, earned for
him the exaggerated eulogy that 'if he would, he might easily
be the best epigrammatist we have found in English, of which
I have not yet seen any come near the ancients'.[3]

The razing, despoiling and defacing of Cadiz being
'happily finished' as Raleigh puts it, and only the churches
left standing as reminders of English piety, the fleet was
embarked and then set sail. But, fattened with plunder and

---

[1] Raleigh's Report written immediately after the action. Hadow's *Selec-
tions*, p. 174.

[2] *A Burnt Ship.*   [3] Drummond of Hawthornden.

made heady with success, the leaders could not resist one last foray. They needed food and fresh water, but discovering none where they landed, they penetrated inland to the town of Ferrol, which the inhabitants had obligingly abandoned, carrying away their goods and chattels.

'But there was in the Nunnery some stuff, and in the palace of the Bishop of Ossorius a library of books, valued at 1,000 marks. There was also in the town some fruit and wine and a few hens. . . .'[1]

The library (and doubtless the latter objects) was plundered and carried aboard.

There is something incongruous to modern readers in the stealing of the Portuguese Bishop's books. True, two of the leaders of the expedition were poets, Essex writing in charming adolescent, nostalgic verses of the robin redbreast and brambleberry, and Raleigh more competently of love, ambition and his own soul, but there was more in the act than mere literary covetousness. Ossorius, whose books became the nucleus of the Bodleian, had long been one of Elizabeth's most virulent antagonists. Under the auspices of the Catholic continental exiles he had repeatedly attacked her in a series of letters on religious questions and as a result, for twenty years, a fierce literary controversy had raged between the English seminarists abroad and Protestant scribes at home. Donne was to take part in a similar polemic. No doubt, as a lyricist and satirist already remarked, he was allowed to dip into the stolen combs, the 'nectar suckets' of honeyed learning, as the fleet sailed triumphantly north.

2

In the following year Donne again took service with Essex, in the naval expedition which set out with the intention of punishing a new Armada and ended by attempting merely to

[1] Stowe's *Annals*.

intercept the Spanish plate-ships off the Azores. He frankly admits his reasons for volunteering. His end was threefold: a 'hope of gain', (presumably prize money, at any rate the bettering of what he calls 'a rotten state'): 'the thirst of honour or fair death':

> 'Or to disuse me from the queasy pain
> Of being belov'd, and loving—'[1]

What a world of emotional experience lies in the adjective 'queasy'! Love for the exacting, restless, enquiring Donne had become fulsome and unsettling. The diet was too rich or too unwholesome for his fastidious palate. He needed the stimulants of action and masculine companionship, of danger and adventure, as antidotes.

> 'I can love first, and (if I win) love still;
> And cannot be remov'd, unless she will.
> It is her fault if I unsure remain,
> She only can untie, and bind again.
> The honesties of love with ease I do,
> But am no porter for a tedious woo. . . .'[2]

he declared, but there is something excessive in the protestation.

The gallants for the Azores, or Island, Voyage assembled in garments even more resplendent than those worn on the late expedition. Indeed they became the laughing-stock of England and were publicly ridiculed on London stages.[3] High plumes, embroidered jackets and gold jerkins were the order of the day but many of their wearers, like birds with plumage too fine for unseasonable work and weather, soon deserted.

> 'They secretly retired themselves home, forgetting either to bid their friends farewell or to take leave of their General.'[4]

---

[1] *The Calm.*   [2] *Verse Letter to the Countess of Huntingdon.*
[3] See Ben Jonson's *Silent Woman*, vol. i, lv.
[4] Sir Arthur Georges, *A larger Relation of the said Island Voyage.*

For a sudden storm had overtaken the fleet with 'infinite lightning, and thunder, and great wind, with the night exceeding dark save when the flashes of lightning came'[1] and the ships put back into Plymouth harbour, but Donne, unseasoned warrior as he was, stuck it out with the best of them. On the 12th of July they set out again, but on the 20th were driven back by storms so violent that:

'the beams, knees and stanching of Sir Walter's ship were shaken wellnigh asunder, and on Saturday night they thought to yield themselves up to God, having no way to work that offered any hope, the men wasted with labour and watching, and the ship so open, her bulkhead rent, and her brick cook-room shaken to powder. Many of the gentlemen are returned weak and dangerously sick. . . . The ships are now repairing, but much of the victual is spoiled, and water lost by leaking of the casks; moreover the beer carried aboard the victual ships is found to be unsavoury by the great abuse of the victuallers and London brewers, as well for their careless brewing as for the unseasonable stinking casks.'[2]

That Donne did not escape the horrible sea-sickness which so weakened some of the voyagers, including the Physician to the Fleet, that they nearly died, is evident from his writings. While the ships, battered and crippled, lay at anchor for repair he, like Raleigh, took to his pen, despatching letters to his friends. Fortunately we can still read three of these, two in verse and one in prose. One was to the Countess of Huntingdon, a lady who had lately lost her husband, and whose son and future daughter-in-law were to play a more than providential part in Donne's career, one to Christopher Brooke, to whom Donne was to owe more than any man alive; and one to an unknown friend. Here is the last:

(To?)—   August 1597

The first act of that play which I said I would go over the water to see is done and yet the people hiss. How it will end I know not *ast ego vicissim* (Cicero). It is true that Jonas was in a whale's belly three days but he came not voluntary as I did nor was troubled

---

[1] Devereux, vol. i, p. 421.   [2] *Purchas His Pilgrimes*, Part II, book 10.

with the stink of 150 land soldiers as we; and I was there twenty
days of so very very bad weather that even some of the mariners
have been drawn to think it were not altogether amiss to pray, and
myself heard one of them say God help us. For all our pains we
have seen the land of promise Spain; whether we shall enter or no
I guess not; I think there is a blot in their tables but perchance not
on our dice to hit it. We are now again at Plymouth quasi Plymouth; for we do nothing but eat and scarce that: I think when we
came in the burghers took us for the Spanish fleet for they have
either hid or conveyed all their money. Never was extreme beggary so extremely brave except when a company of mummers had
lost their box. I do not think that seventy-seven Kellys could
distill 10£ out of all the town. He that hath supped and hath two
or three shillings is a king! for none hath a crown, faith; lands,
jerkins, knighthoods, are reprobate pawns and but for the much
gay clothes (which yet are much melted) I should think we were
in Utopia: all are so utterly coinless. In one bad bare word the
want is so general that the Lord General[1] wants, and until this day
we wanted the Lord General. You will pardon me if I write
nothing earnest. Salute all whom thou lovest in my name and love
me as I would deserve.

Written from Plymouth.[2]

From this letter we get the impression of a young man with a
slightly sardonic sense of humour who looks out at the world
with amused audacity. His humour takes the form of pun-
ning, common to the day. His interests range from the Spanish business at hand, to the theatre, to alchemy (for Kelly was
a noted searcher for the Philosopher's Stone)—a subject
which always held Donne's Paracelsan mind[3]—and to classical
and biblical authors. His thirst after knowledge, which was
truly Renaissance in character, was to be both the blessing
and bane of his life. He 'relieved himself' on books, as he puts
it, and upon the making of books, until his eyesight nearly

[1] The Earl of Essex.

[2] *John Donne, Complete Poetry and Selected Prose,* John Hayward,
p. 439. I have modernized the spelling, and substituted a comma between
'crown' and 'faith'.

[3] See Donne's *Loves Alchemy, Loves Growth,* and letter to Sir Henry
Goodyer. Gosse, vol. ii, p. 49.

failed him, but in so doing he clogged his mind and gained
little wisdom about life or his own complex nature. The
mention of *Utopia* harks back to the work of his collateral
ancestor, Sir Thomas More, published some fifty years before
Donne's birth.

But it is in the Verse Letters to Brooke that Donne as an
artist may be watched. *The Storm* is a poem full of imagery
almost electric in its vitality, a picture painted in the lurid
colours of lightning, sea-sickness, noise and confusion. He
speaks of the sailors 'coffined in their cabins', of the rigging
snapping 'like too high-stretched treble strings', of the
tattered sails hanging like the clothing of a man long suspended from the gallows, and finally of the roar of the ordnance breaking loose, rolling and crashing about the decks.

> 'Pumping hath tir'd our men, and what's the gain?
> Seas into seas thrown, we suck in again;
> Hearing hath deaf'd our sailors; and if they
> Knew how to hear, there's none knows what to say.'

For nearly a month the Fleet lay at anchor. Then it set
sail again, only to be pursued by further storms, becalmings
and discouragements. The enterprise, pockmarked by the
quarrels and separation of its leaders, by disunited purpose
and action, was doomed from the start to failure. It was while
becalmed off the coast of Spain with the major portion of the
Fleet that Donne wrote his second Verse Letter[1] to Christopher Brooke, packed with even more descriptive force than
the first and making a marked contrast with the other. The
ships' rigging now seems to him like the limp garments of an
old-clothes shop and the parched and fevered sailors, like
the dying Falstaff, 'babble o' green fields.'

Donne's companions on the Island Voyage included
Thomas Egerton again, his younger brother John, and their
stepbrother, Francis Wolley. Their father, the Lord Keeper,
a faithful and influential member of Lincoln's Inn, may have

---

[1] *The Calm.*

remarked Donne as a student there, or he may have taken note of him at Court in some unascertainable moment when Donne had drifted in and out seeking, as all the young world did, a sign of grace from Essex, the favourite. But the deciding influence must have been the friendship which sprang up between the four young adventurers. At any rate, by the end of October Donne was back in London and in the closing weeks of the year, or early in the new, he had reaped an abundant harvest from an adventure spelling disappointment to its leaders, for he obtained the appointment of Secretary to the Lord Keeper, Sir Thomas Egerton, one of the Queen's most trusted officers of State.[1]

The Lord Keeper, says Walton, 'taking notice of his learning, languages and other abilities, and much affecting his person and behaviour, took him to be his secretary: supposing and intending it to be an introduction to some more weighty employment in the state: for which his Lordship did often protest he thought him very fit.'[2]

Donne's foot was set on the rungs of the golden ladder of success and fortune.

3

During these close-packed years before the close of the century, when life for Donne was full, turbulent and progressive, when the heart was being continually torn in a kind of exquisite torture, and the mind, extraordinarily active, had not yet reached a period of remorseful introspection, he was turning out an astounding number of verses as well as some witty prose. When it is remembered that such writing was in addition to his studies at the Universities and Lincoln's

[1] For a denial of Chambers' theory that Donne was employed as confidential agent by Sir Robert Cecil to carry despatches to the French coast in the months after his return, see Sparrow's 'The Date of Donne's Travels' in *A Garland for Donne;* and Chambers' 'Donne, Diplomatist and Soldier', *Modern Language Review*, vol. ii, Cambridge, 1910.

[2] Walton, p. 6.

Inn, and his work for the Lord Keeper, and that it was thrown off despite military and amatory escapades, diplomatic and private travel, then the restlessness of the enquiring mind and the abundance of the bourgeoning may equally astonish. In addition to the *Songs and Sonnets* there came *Elegies*, *Satires*, the early *Verse Letters*, the *Epigrams*, a *Funeral Elegy*, an *Epithalamion* and the prose *Juvenilia* all in the space of a decade.

As yet, nothing was published, but Donne's verses went the rounds of literary and Court society and made for him the reputation of a rebel and heretic in form, 'one who deserved hanging for not keeping the accent,' one 'who, for not being understood, would perish', but who, 'for some things' was 'the first poet in the land'.[1] These criticisms from a brother poet who did not hesitate to speak his mind in blunt fashion, were valuable praise, indicative of contemporary opinion. Ben Jonson was not to be bribed into adulation and, since he ranked close to Shakespeare, had no need of binding lesser poets to him with flattery, either faint or strong.

Donne's prose *Juvenilia* are chiefly interesting as the counterpart of his verse in theme. In them he discusses gibingly such questions as the prevalence of good rather than evil, whether virtue and chastity may be found in women, whether women have souls or ought to paint, why courtiers are atheists, and why the Puritans make long sermons. *News from the Very Country* is a collection of short, sharp apophthegms—*bon mots*, tossed off like squibs to admiring listeners, and jotted down by his friends as testimony to his lively and amusing speech.[2] One or two will serve as samples:

'Jesuits are like apricocks; heretofore, here and there one succoured in a great man's house, and cost dear, now you may have them for nothing in every cottage.'

[1] Conversations with Drummond of Hawthornden, 3 and 7.
[2] See Evelyn Simpson, *Modern Language Review*, xviii, 4, October 1923, and John Sparrow, 'Donne's Table Talk,' *London Mercury*, xviii, 1928.

'Women are not so tender fruit, but that they do as well, and bear as well, upon beds, as plashed against walls.'

'Atheists in affliction, like blind beggars, are forced to ask, though they know not of whom.'

Even in these biting remarks one notes Donne's concern with religious problems, running current with his licentiousness.

But it is his verse which startles, draws and holds us, sometimes, like the man himself, repelling with crudity, sometimes enticing with silken endearments. Yet its fibre, for all the airiness of conceits and occasional limpidity, is tough and durable below. Donne had the greatest disdain for men who served up a flummery of froth with nothing to recommend it but sweetness and air. When he had become a divine he spoke with scorn of the fashionable preacher who, 'having made a pie of plums, without meat, offers it to sale in every market, and having made an oration of flowers, figures and phrases without strength, sings it over in every pulpit.' The same holds true for the *Songs and Sonnets* and in an Elegy he voices the same belief:

> 'For one night's revels, silk and gold we choose
> But in long journeys, cloth, and leather, use.'

Next to the *Songs and Sonnets*, the *Elegies* (not to be confused with the Funeral ones) will live as memorials of Donne as a lay poet, but it is in the *Satires* that he stands out, sharp and naked against the Elizabethan sky, now leaden, now streaked with the flames from a martyr's burning. The former are the history of his heart, the latter of his growing soul.

Here was a young man who could write of love in many veins, either passionately, like a deceived and bitter amorist; or simply and ethereally, like one who has known the ecstasy of reciprocation; or in reflective Petrarchan strains of admiration and restraint. Sometimes his mistress regarded him

with the inscrutable eyes of a Gioconda, or mocked him with
the elfin charm of a 'Belle Dame sans Merci', and he hated
her: sometimes she looked at him with the unstudied simplicity of an angel and, transported into bliss, he adored her:
sometimes she had for him the gravity of a classical goddess,
and he both revered and admired her. Listen to him speaking
to the merciless beauty:

> '. . . so, the taper's beamy eye
> Amorously twinkling, beckons the giddy fly,
> Yet burns his wings; and such the devil is,
> Scarce visiting them, who are entirely his.
>
> . . . .
>
> Yet let not thy deep bitterness beget
> Careless despair in me, for that will whet
> My mind to scorn; and oh, love dulled with pain
> Was ne'er so wise, nor well arm'd as disdain.
> Then with new eyes I shall survey thee, and spy
> Death in thy cheeks, and darkness in thine eye.'[1]

or:

> 'Will no other vice content you?
> Will it not serve your turn to do, as did your mothers?
> Or have you all old vices spent, and now find out others?
> Or doth a fear, that men are true, torment you?
> Oh we are not, be not you so,
> Let me, and do you, twenty know.'[2]

here, to his true love who has comforted and reassured him:

> 'I will not look upon the quick'ning sun,
> But straight her beauty to my sense shall run;
> The air shall note her soft, the fire most pure;
> Water suggest her clear, and the earth sure.
> Time shall not lose our passages; the spring
> How fresh our love was in the beginning;
> The summer how it ripened in the ear;
> And autumn, what our golden harvests were.
> The winter, I'll not think on to spite thee,
> But count it a lost season, so shall she.'[3]

[1] *Elegy VI.* [2] *The Indifferent.* [3] *Elegy XII.*

and:

> 'As lightning, or a taper's light,
> Thine eyes, and not thy noise wak'd me;
>   Yet I thought thee
> (For thou lovest truth) an angel, at first sight,
> But when I saw thou sawest my heart,
> And knew'st my thoughts, beyond an angel's art,
> When thou knew'st what I dreamt, when thou knew'st when
> Excess of joy would wake me, and cam'st then,
> I must confess, it could not choose but be
> Profane, to think thee anything but thee.'[1]

and here, to his grave-eyed goddesses:

> 'First, we lov'd well and faithfully,
> Yet knew not what we lov'd, nor why,
> Difference of sex no more we knew,
> Than our guardian angels do;
>   Coming and going, we
> Perchance might kiss, but not between those meals.'[2]

The *Songs and Sonnets* are constant food for both lover and student. One scholar has found that Donne employs forty-six different verse forms for his thought and that out of these, forty-two are his own invention;[3] another notes his mediaeval doctrines, another his habit of 'perplexing the minds of the fair sex with the speculations of philosophy, where he should engage their hearts';[4] another his interest in astronomy, or his imagery, drawn from the voyages and discoveries. The list of approaches possible is infinite and perennially attractive, but to the superficial student, the amateur in learning, the poems remain chiefly attractive, for their impetuosity of feeling, their variety of thought and emotion, their boldness and originality of diction. They are dramatic lyrics of the highest order, concerned with time, place, situation and character, like any full-act play. Sometimes the poet is hampered, like a colt being broken into harness, by his very

---

[1] *The Dream.*   [2] *The Relique.*

[3] Professor Legouis in *Donne, the Craftsman,* Paris, 1928.

[4] Dryden, *Essay on Satire.*

ardour, too hot to curb; or by the form which his taste dictates, too intricate, too trammelling for thought and ardour.
Sometimes his wit impedes him, like a sharp stone striking
the foot of both poet and reader: sometimes his knowledge,
rich and deep or simply arid; sometimes his interest, which
travels over vast fields, like the Italian bee, sipping here,
sipping there, not content with single diet; sometimes the
quickness of his mind, which cannot be bothered with ordinary words, but snatches at foreign ones, carries them forward
from old sources, and even invents them; sometimes the
thought itself, which is so complex that he has to pack a
double negative, like a two-tailed scorpion, into a single
closing line.

On the whole Donne fails to be lyrical, but not from lack of
ability. His very susceptibility to the flow of word and line
makes him suspicious of his own facility, and he shies away
from the current love of the purely beautiful with positive
distaste. Convention only bores him—the conventional
elements of poetry appear to him a falsity. The words and
phrases of ordinary conversation must take the place of forced
poetic ones and thus Donne becomes a reformer of both
English poem and tongue.

His tenderness, which he cloaks with cynicism in his spoken
words, he hides, in his verse, beneath roughness and scepticism. He even elevates ugliness to beauty's throne in the
violence of his attempt to break away, and if for a moment he
should show his gentler, more trusting nature, it is with
something of shame and self-effacement. Arrogance and impatience must take the place of subservience and idyllic
adoration. The prelude must be abrupt, almost blasphemous,
and no quiet introduction to his matter. Instead of respecting
the traditional values and attributes of love poetry, he settles
down to passion with an earnestness and an intensity which
must have both disgusted and horrified poets of the older
school. 'To read Pope and Dryden, you need only count

syllables; but to read Donne you must measure time, and discover the time of each word, by the sense of the passion.'[1]

'Before, behind, between, above, below' this lusty, or this headstrong, passion he hangs the festoons of doctrine, of metaphysical conceit, of analogy,—all the shining spider-webs and musty cobwebs of his mind and imagination, every extravagance, every ingenuity, until he gives the impression of 'wreathing iron pokers into true-love knots'. What does it matter if the result be half like prose? or the effect too start-ling for immediate appreciation? The heart beats serious beneath and, after one has known Donne's verse, the work of other poets often appears soft, deceptively melodious, even frivolous.

4

Now turn to the *Satires*, repellent in their savagery, but strong with the strength of a young tiger, straight with the sincerity of a seminarist, and strange with the originality of the inventor, or rebellious experimenter. They are remark-able poems for many reasons, but when one considers that they were written either when Donne was coming of age, or in the years immediately following, they appear really astounding.

They are amongst the earliest Satires of the period and far exceed contemporary productions—those of Hall, Guilpin, Marston and Lodge, in originality, boldness and harshness. There had been little of Satire, in the limited sense, in Eng-lish literature before the sixteenth century. A number of medi-aeval works, similar to those produced on the continent, had dealt with the problems of contemporary distress—abuse, ill-conduct, famine and the plague—and even in these early works, (since Satire concerns itself with current, not past, history), the Church, the consistory courts, the ladies of leisure and luxury, the minority friars, all had come in for censure.

[1] Coleridge.

The five Satires of Donne imitate Juvenal and have for their subjects London Society, Lawyers, Religion, the Court, and the Bribing of Judges. The Third is a valuable clue to his mental unrest and his attitude to religious matters at this period in his life when he was loosening himself from the Catholic church and authority. It is a testament of the first importance which contradicts those thoughtless critics who cut Donne's life rudely in half and declare that religion did not trouble him until the world had turned a face of stone towards his entreaties.

Two years before he wrote this Satire, Spenser published his *Mother Hubbard's Tale*, in which the Ape and the Fox, falling in with a priest, ask his advice about earning their living. His reply is a scathing criticism of the lives and attitudes of parish priests, whose ranks Donne never joined, but with whom he was to come in contact more than twenty years later. Did Donne know Spenser, then in London for a twelve-month, eating out his heart as a suitor for the favours of Elizabeth? There is nothing to show that they ever met.

Yet both knew the same city and nothing could be more stimulating than to look for a moment at Elizabethan London as Donne reveals it in the 'Satires', the harvest of an eye which roves wide and pierces deep, whose searchings are recorded with tantalizing brevity. To read them is like being present at the opening of a play. The drop-curtain is a street, a room at Court, one of the 'gardens' with menageries, an inn, a ship's deck, or a ruined Abbey. And the stage is always crowded. The Masques of Ben Jonson and Inigo Jones, written and designed a decade later and enacted by many of Donne's court friends, were not festooned with more stuff and finery, or packed with more sketched characters, than these early works of his. We have the Captain, 'bright parcel-gilt,' the 'brisk perfumed, piert Courtier', the

> '. . . velvet Justice with a long
> Great train of blue coats, twelve or fourteen strong':

the Puritan with 'formal hat', the needy broker, and the weather-spy—a kind of meteorologist-cum-astrologer. There is the North American Indian, imported as a curiosity, silently drinking his tobacco, after the custom of the day: the 'starving idiot actor', the noon or night-watchman, the street-singer-beggar, the boring old man who shows one round the Abbey tombs and prates of nothing but dead Kings, Edwards or Harrys, as you please. There is the London apprentice indignantly 'rising against the stranger'—the workmen whom Elizabeth encouraged in her policy of Protestant toleration: the boy in the street playing 'span counter' or 'blow point', games whose primitive art we might now deride, the scholar poring over Cheapside books. In the dark, unwholesome kitchen there is a girl, like Shakespeare's 'greasy Joan', scraping

> '. . . kitchen-stuff
> And barrelling the droppings, and the snuff
> Of wasting candles, which in thirty year
> (Relique-like kept) perchance buys wedding-gear:'

while outside the rumbling of wheels over the rough stones tells of some wretched man, condemned to die, being carted off to Tyburn.

His allusions to the Court and Courtiers all bespeak an extravagance and a superficiality galling to a man whose mind was hungry for deeper matter. Something of the weight and lavishness of the ornate, and often tasteless, tombs of the period hangs over these Satires and burdens them unpleasantly. He refers to those spectacles for the idle,—the ape, the elephant, or performing horse, and speaks of the young man who has shaken off the boredom of a leisure morning in 'the mews or stews', that is, in fencing, riding, playing football or tennis, in drinking and promiscuous love-making before appearing at Court again. He speaks of 'old, rich wardrops[1] out of fashion', of scarlet robes and astonishing hose fit for a king,

[1] Wardrobes.

of the 'lace, pink, panes, print, cut and pleat' of some
poor silken fool who has had to sell half his lands to squan-
der the proceeds on finery, and of the painted, simpering
court ladies with their 'loose set hair', a phrase curiously
modern. He describes the terrible court spy, who creeps about
the Palace, insinuating himself everywhere, refers to the
court jester and those amazing monumental men, the
Queen's guard of Welshmen,

'Living barrels of beef, flagons of wine:'

and with the eye of a falcon hovering so high above the
crowded plain that it appears no more than a pasture and the
Channel no more than a mill-pond, he notes the taking of
Amiens, the 'mutinous Dutch' seamen, the great Spanish
prize-ships laden with cochineal and spices, the frozen discoverers of the North, the fighters off Dunkirk, and those who:

'. . . thrice
Colder than salamanders, like divine
Children in th'oven . . .'

face 'fires of Spain and the line'. He sees the woods cut down
and the hillside bared by the ignorant new owner, false to the
land, he hears the wind roaring pitilessly through the Abbeys
loved by his fathers and despoiled by those hostile to the
faith in which he was nurtured. And in the middle of all this
grandeur, this live and fermenting scene, he introduces
Dürer's anatomical skeleton with limbs which jerk like a
marionette, or the miniature waxen gardens, recently imported from Italy, with tasteless fruits and trees of sapless
foliage. One would augur much for a mind so rapacious and
at the same time so discerning.

To return to the *Third Satire*, although written in 1593 or
'4 this was not published until after Donne's death, and like
his poem *The Will*, the 18th *Holy Sonnet*, and passages in
his prose writings, it would have been exceedingly dangerous
for him had it appeared in print in his lifetime, especially

E

when Elizabeth was still on the throne, when the Acts against
Popish recusants and Jesuits had just reached the maximum
of severity, when his only brother had been taken up for
harbouring a seminary priest, and when he himself still had
his way to make. It shows a breadth of mind and a toleration
far in excess of that of his contemporaries and much in advance of the normal development of a young man. True,
he had as a child been precocious and as an adolescent
forward, but now in young manhood he burst forth in
extraordinary vigour and fierceness, formulating views
from which, even as an old man he deviated but little,
only modifying and adapting them to his changing development.

In reading this Satire one senses first of all Donne's perplexity. The mind which is so versatile, quick and infinitely
aware, is suspicious of intolerance and dreads imprisonment
behind the bars of any one creed, as the falcon dreads the
wires of a cage. He ridicules the Catholic, the Anglican and
the Calvinist alike, for worship of tradition, of civil and
ecclesiastical tyranny, or of newfangled dogmatism. He
realizes the weakness of the man who decries all, or of his
opposite who unthinkingly accepts all. He longs for Truth
and Unity and pleads for a recognition of the fundamental
values underlying factions, sectaries and the unhappy divi-
sions of the Church. The young and ardent Donne fore-
shadows the mature prelate whose 'sinful' toleration earned
the name of 'Soul Murder'.

'Fool and wretch,' he cries impatiently,

'. . . wilt thou let thy soul be tied
To man's laws, by which she shall not be tried
At the last day? Oh, will it then boot thee
To say a Philip, or a Gregory,
A Harry, or a Martin taught thee this?
Is not this excuse for mere contraries,
Equally strong? cannot both sides say so?
That thou may'st rightly obey power, her bounds know;'

Obeisance to Spain, the Pope, an English monarch, or Luther, is of little worth in the long run, and the gentle service of the heart which Christ taught has been exchanged for idolatry of a tyrant Church and God. An individualist and a rebel in thought, he mistrusts blind adherence to authority and absolute power, and prefers the Protestant simplicity of a direct approach to God.

The poet-philosopher's preoccupation with spiritual light and his sense of the insufficiency of reason as an aid to its appreciation are manifest:

> '. . . mysteries
> Are like the Sun, dazzling, yet plain to all eyes.'

Before the close of his life Donne enlarged this in a Sermon;[1]

'In all philosophy there is not so dark a thing as light; as the sun which is *fons lucis naturalis*, the beginning of natural light, is the most evident thing to be seen, and yet the hardest to be looked upon, so is natural light to our reason and understanding. Nothing clearer, for it is clearness itself, nothing darker, it is enwrapped in so many scruples. Nothing nearer, for it is round about us, nothing more remote, for we know neither entrance nor limits of it. Nothing more easy, for a child discerns it, nothing more hard, for no man understands it. It is apprehensible by sense, and not comprehensible by reason. If we wink, we cannot chuse but see it, if we stare, we know it never the better.'

On the whole, Walton's phrase that from the age of eighteen onwards Donne had 'betrothed himself to no religion that might give him any other denomination than a Christian' may be accepted. In one of the *Songs and Sonnets* he frankly calls himself, in the sphere of love, both rebel and atheist. Is it too far-fetched to suggest that he considered himself such in religion too, in the first stages of his transition? It is certain that at an early age he broke away from the rigorous tenets of his mother's faith and began to think matters out for himself. Gosse puts it with beauty and force:

[1] *Sermons 50*, 36. See Grierson, vol. ii, p. 117.

'As soon as Donne found himself free from his mother's tutelage, his attachment to the Catholic faith began to decline; presently his indifference to its practice, combined with an intellectual scepticism as to its tenets, led him away from any Christian communion, yet all the while he nourished a kind of dormant religiosity, ready to break forth into flame as soon as the tumult of the senses and the enraged curiosity of life had been somewhat assuaged by experience. Inwardly, the seed of the spiritual life was healthy and was biding its time for expansion. . . .'[1]

Thus in this *Satire*, Jack Donne the libertine, anticipates John Donne the great divine, and his plea for uniformity, although not clearly stated, is the same as that in his *Essays in Divinity*, written just as he was joining the Church, and in the later *Sermons*. 'The great patriarchal Catholic Church, of which every one of us is a little chapel'[2] was a more mature way of putting what he had attempted to say in the rough verse of 'dromedary trot'. The poem rises to impersonal magnificence in the impassioned advocacy of the search for Truth, the most 'dangerous' passage of the whole *Satire*.

> '. . . though Truth and Falsehood be
> Near twins, yet Truth a little elder is;
> Be busy to seek her, believe me this,
> He's not of none, nor worst, that seeks the best.
> To adore, or scorn an image, or protest
> May all be bad; doubt wisely; in strange way
> To stand enquiring right, is not to stray;
> To sleep, or run wrong, is. On a huge hill,
> Cragged, and steep, Truth stands, and he that will
> Reach her, about must, and about must go.
> And what the hill's suddenness resists, win so;
> Yet strive so, that before age, death's twilight,
> Thy Soul rest, for none can work in that night.
> To will, implies delay, therefore now do
> Hard deeds, the body's pain; hard knowledge too
> The mind's endeavours reach, and mysteries
> Are like the Sun, dazzling, yet plain to all eyes.
> Keep the Truth which thou hast found. . . .'

---

[1] Gosse, vol. i, pp. 27–28.   [2] *Essays in Divinity*.

But what *is* Truth?

'The question, What is Truth, has no prospect of obtaining a speedy answer—but the question, What is the Spirit of Truth? may be discussed with much greater prospect of agreement. By the spirit of Truth, I mean that frame of mind in which men who acknowledge their own fallibility and who desire above all things to discover what is true, should adjudicate between conflicting arguments. . . . The persecutor can never be certain that he is not persecuting truth rather than error, but he may be quite certain that he is suppressing the spirit of truth. . . . Until the seventeenth century, every mental disposition which philosophy pronounces to be essential to a legitimate research was almost uniformly branded as a sin, and a large proportion of the most deadly vices were deliberately inculcated as virtues. It was a sin to doubt the opinions that had been instilled in childhood before they had been examined. It was sinful to study with equal attention and with an indifferent mind the writings on boths sides: sinful to resolve to follow the light of evidence wherever it might lead: sinful to remain poised in doubt between conflicting opinions: sinful even to recognize the moral or intellectual excellence of opponents. . . . A critical, impartial and enquiring spirit was the worst form of vice.'[1]

In the earnestness of his search, the dogged way in which he pursues his lodestar, the 'wrastling' manner, Donne is like another great English writer who lived more than two centuries before him, William Langland, the author of *Piers Plowman*. Both observed with a penetrating eye the weaknesses of contemporary society in which they mingled, but from which they kept themselves mentally detached and philosophically indifferent.

Like Dante, like Shakespeare in *Hamlet*, both Langland and Donne felt that 'the times were out of joint': both set to work to analyse them and to find what maggot was eating out the heart of goodness. The Church and religion, Court life and the courtier, Law, with its magnificent effrontery, and Society, are Donne's as well as Langland's mommets for

[1] Lecky, vol. ii, pp. 86–88, *Rise and Influence of Rationalism in Europe*.

destruction and raillery. To Langland, the Church seemed the great plunderer of the land, stocked with mere pocket-fillers and cheaters of the common people too ignorant, too helpless to withstand. For Donne concerned with a more particular problem, in an age of transition, and influenced by his own bitter experience, the scurrilous and witty reformer, the dangerous Jesuit disseminating sedition, the hired pursuivant and informer spying upon unsuspecting souls, the torturing judge, like Topcliffe, who puts gentle and innocent poets and mystics upon the rack, the lawyers and judges who mulct the patient catholics, wringing from them fine after heavy fine, and the wanton destroyer of property, going out of his way to make havoc when tracking down the fugitive priest, are the men who rouse him to harsh intolerance.

Langland's canvas is more crowded, and the poor throng through it crying out more piteously, but Donne is equally discerning. Both write with anger hot in their hearts: both, with comprehension of the current evils but with no reforming knowledge or zeal, since they cannot answer the vast riddle—how evil grows from fertile good. Neither counsels opposition by revolt: both advise action, work and tolerance. Langland took a lifetime to write, revise and reconsider *Piers Plowman* (surviving still in nearly fifty manuscripts), popular before his death, long before its printing in 1550, only twenty-three years before Donne's birth. Donne's *Satire* was short and probably written quickly. Probably too, he kept it close, fearful of its licence. We know that it was not printed for forty years, so dangerously broad was it in its avoidance of schism. Langland used the old irregular alliterative long line, cherished in tradition since the Conquest, and sprung into new and splendid life in his time on the Welsh marches: Donne, the heroic couplet, with beats not too scrupulously marked. But the frankness, the ruggedness, the moral force behind each work, the steady querying to know what Life is and what it means,—where Truth, goodness and an enlightened interpretation of Christ's teaching, apart from man-made ecclesiastical doctrine, may be found—are apparent in both. In the century intervening between Langland and Donne an anonymous author, writing with singular pathos and beauty, tells the story of the divine and compassionate nature seeking its sister, the soul of man:

'She flytt, I followed, I loved her so.'[1]

And Francis Thompson was to render it again, dramatically, in the nineteenth century. The divine mercy, 'true love, that false was never,'[1] is inescapable and Donne was only stating the reverse of this patient fidelity in his tenacious search for it. Unfortunately for him, 'about must and about must go' summed up the process. The muscles of his mind had been so mercilessly developed by his study of the Schoolmen that he never broke out into new and original thought. Into form, yes, but not into fresh thought, and his circuitous mental paths forced him to repeat his steps in the manner of one threading a Tudor maze, ever cursing his 'riddling, intricated, perplexed, labyrinthical soul'.[2]

5

Jack Donne, as he called himself, has in posterity two charges of a serious nature to rebut—that of being a cynic, and that of being an amorist of the most licentious kind.

Much has been falsely deduced from his cynicism. Critics have used it to prove that the mature man was a hypocrite and that, upon going into the church, he must have subscribed to the Thirty-Nine Articles with his tongue in his cheek. They have sworn that its presence indicates a fellow of coarse, low, worldly tastes, incapable of appreciating human goodness or of rising sincerely to spiritual heights. They have labelled it final proof of Donne's dissimulation.

[1] 'Quia Amore Langueo' in *Oxford Book of Mystical Verse*, Nicholson & Lee, Clarendon Press, 1932.
[2] Sermon XLVIII. St. Paul's, In the Evening, Jan. 25, 1628.

But what lay behind the cynicism? What was it that saved him from being, with all his introspective and self-torturing tendencies, a hermit, or a scholarly recluse? What enabled him to hold vast audiences under the shadow of St. Paul's until individuals felt their hearts pierced with true and penetrating shafts? His love and knowledge of mankind, for he was, by nature, primarily social. His capacity for lifelong friendship indicates this; his early interest in character and of the workings of the mind reinforces the impression, his pity and compassion as a mature man show it. This humanity joined with reason saved him from madness in the years at Mitcham, from stupefying dejection in the years before he entered the Church and from complete collapse upon his wife's death. For his constant resort to books and scholastic matters was not the sign of a purely pedantic mind but of the inner discord, disturbing a complex nature which sought relief in writing and endless study. In the same way a musician may play out his emotion, or the victim of morphia seek to extend and dissipate the mind's horizon in elusive and expanding dreams.

The youthful cynicism was a cloak with which to hide incipient tenderness. But it was the thief as well as the protector of Donne's young heart, robbing his natural stores of pity, while at the same time it attempted to conceal them from prying, and possibly destructive, eyes. The fierceness with which he expressed his cynicism was, in the course of time, mellowed into sternness, but not into bitterness, which might have been more easily understood and more highly prized by the zealous partisans of Jacobean anglicanism. But in his young days the fierceness was due, more than anything else, to 'the exasperation of a particularly sensitive temperament'.[1]

This extreme sensitivity both helped and hindered him in the annals of love. Of the number of Donne's adventures, or

---

[1] Simpson, p. 63.

of the seriousness of their character, no proof at all exists,[1] except his own writings, and the significant refutation in his letter to his father-in-law, soon after his marriage, of the charge 'of having deceived some gentlewoman before'.[2]

In the words of a modern poet:

'Some of the best informed critics and scholars are still inclined to take for granted a period of debauchery and to emphasize it . . . and yet I do not think that we have sufficient evidence that Donne was so *very* dissipated: we are in danger of making an attractive romance about him. . . . We can easily exaggerate the erotic element. My intention here is not to whitewash the evidence of a dissipated or immoral youth; but merely to affirm that we have no satisfactory evidence, and that it is a point of the very slightest interest anyhow. The courtly cynicism was a poetic convention of the time; Donne's sometimes scoffing attitude towards the fickleness of women may be hardly more than immature bravado; it comes to me with none of the terrible sincerity of Swift's vituperation of the human race. Nor can I take very seriously Donne's later remorse or repentance. It is pleasant in youth to think that one is a gay dog, and it is pleasant in age to think that one *was* a gay dog; because as we grow old we all like to think that we have changed, developed and improved; people shrink from acknowledging that they are exactly the same at fifty as they were at twenty-five. . . . If Donne in youth was a rake, then I suspect that he was a conventional rake; if Donne in age was devout, then I suspect that he was conventionally devout. An observation which, even if true, is not necessarily destructive.'[3]

While I cannot agree with the entire conventionality of both Donne's profligacy and piety, since his character swung on the hinges of reckless abandon and ensuing repentance, joy and ultimate despair, complementary to each other, yet this 'needed saying'.

A lad like Donne, whose mind was filled with a tangle of harrowing thoughts on the subject of feminine worth and

[1] Baker in his *Chronicles of the Kings of England*, 1732, p. 424, calls him 'a great visitor of ladies' but expressly adds that his old acquaintance 'was not dissolute'.

[2] Gosse, i, p. 106.

[3] T. S. Eliot, 'Donne in Our Times.' *A Garland for Donne*, pp. 10–11.

virtue, whose heart was forever being torn on the brambles of love, might find in two or three experiences enough food for fifty poems and another fifty apophthegms. He was drawn to women like a moth to the candle flame, yet he went home to brood upon their frailty, their deception, their treacherous power over him, and to nurse his singed wings angrily.

He needed their intuitive appreciation, their stabilizing belief and devotion, yet he dreaded to be subjugated and enslaved. In fact he both loved and hated them, and his constant reiteration in the *Songs and Sonnets* that fear makes up no part of genuine love, only confirms this. Remember:

> 'And now good morrow to our waking souls,
> Which watch not one another out of fear;'

and:

> 'That love is weak, where fear's as strong as he;
> Tis not all spirit, pure and brave,
> If mixture it of Fear, Shame, Honour, have.'

Donne was at all times of a serious if witty cast of mind, with a nature troublously passionate: the one was 'subtle to plague' the other and held him in perpetual torment. With such a character, the emotion surrounding each amatory act, no matter how trivial, would be dramatized, heightened and intensified out of all proportion to the act's original significance, owing to the conflict over sex in his mind, bred by his youthful attitude to his mother and his absorption of the teaching of the Schoolmen. Being, too, of a secretive nature—('Wicked is not much worse than indiscreet')[1]—he would be apt to disclose his adventures cautiously and to discredit the description of them which his verse afforded but did not actually verify. But above all, his sensitivity which made him the artist that he was, indicated a mind as malleable as molten steel, which, when it is ready to receive an impression, takes it for better or worse with little modification.

[1] *An Anatomy of the World—The First Anniversary.*

6

The intimate household of the Lord Keeper Egerton at York House, in the Strand, consisted of Sir Thomas and his second wife, Elizabeth, her son Francis and her niece, Ann More. Lady Egerton, like her husband, had been married before, in fact twice before, and Francis was her son by her second husband, Sir John Wooley, of Pyrford in Surrey. Her brother was Sir George More of Losely, not far from Pyrford, and as Sir George was a widower with a large family of children he consented to lend Ann to the town household. The Lord Chancellor's sons by his first marriage, Thomas, knighted when on the Island Voyage with Donne, and John, the younger, who was six years Donne's senior, must often have been in and out of the great house, as well as a constantly fluctuating mass of eminent people who had business at Court.

Sir Thomas, the Lord Keeper, was an able, distinguished and learned man. His career was one of those which does not reveal its lapses and discouragements, but in retrospect seems to follow a full arc of growing glory. When Donne at twenty-six joined him as Secretary, Egerton was a man of fifty-eight. He had been called to the Bar in 1572, was appointed successively Governor, Lent Reader and Treasurer of Lincoln's Inn, Member of Parliament for Cheshire, the county of his birth, and Solicitor General. He had conducted the prosecution of some of the most eminent of the State's enemies, the religious martyrs,[1] had been appointed Attorney General, was promoted to the Bench as Master of the Rolls, and finally made Lord Keeper. The Queen admired and trusted him and he trod the slippery path of Court favour without suspicion or calumny. It was said that 'No man ever came to this dignity', (the position of Solicitor General) 'with more applause', and the Queen was known to have conferred

[1] Campion, Davison, the Earl of Arundel and Sir John Perrot.

the honour on him personally (despite the displeasure of Lord Burghley at her high-handedness) after hearing him plead in a case against the Crown. 'By my troth, he shall never plead against me again!,' she declared, and she consulted him repeatedly upon matters of both domestic and foreign policy.

One of Egerton's most endearing characteristics was his interest in young and rising men about him. He early recognized the talent of Bacon, who acknowledged his invariable care and fatherly consideration. Essex was another of his protégés and so warm was his friendship for this firebrand who nearly brought about his death, that an observer remarked, 'They love and join very honourably together'. To Donne, he showed grave courtesy and discretion, not 'accounting him to be so much his servant as to forget he was his friend' and 'appointing him a place at his own table to which he esteemed his company and discourse a great ornament'.[1]

In 1598/9 the Lord Keeper was occupied with a matter of singular importance—the remedying of abuses connected with the administration of the Clerkship of the Star Chamber, concerning which there had been complaints for some time past.[2] The reformation involved the question of Monopolies, or patents of privilege. In those days, when trade and industry began to grow too fast for health, a fierce scramble went on amongst courtiers—titled 'directors' and 'company promoters'—for the Royal patents. Such varied articles as starch, tin, brass farthings, books, printing and paper, came up for consideration and the unsound practice of Royal grants infected the trades and strangled poorer members of the Companies. Egerton was endeavouring to curtail the fees.

Upon the 9th of February, 1598, before the Queen, the Lords and Commons, the Lord Keeper addressed the Speaker, who on previous occasions had seen to it that bills for the reformation of offences were thrown out:

[1] Walton, p. 6.   [2] Grierson, vol. ii, pp. 104–5 and 126.

—'Touching the Monopolies, her Majesty hopeth that her dutiful and loving subjects will not take away her prerogative, which is the chiefest flower in her garden, and the principal and head pearl in her crown and diadem: but that they will rather leave that to her disposition.' [1]

Donne, as the Lord Keeper's trusted secretary, was both spectator and participant in these occupations and in his 5th *Satyre*, upon the bribing of Judges, reflects his employment. He asks if the Queen is aware of the state of things:

'Greatest and fairest Empress, know you this?'

Turning to his employer, the Lord Keeper, he says:

'You Sir, whose righteousness she loves, whom I
By having leave to serve, am most richly
For service paid, authoriz'd, now begin
To know and weed out this enormous sin.'

The whole question of the corruptibility of legal officers and the futility and wastefulness of legal proceedings troubles him:

'Oh, n'er may
Fair Law's white reverend name be strumpeted,
To warrant thefts: she is established
Recorder to Destiny, on earth, and she
Speaks Fate's words, . . .'

Here is enthusiasm, pride in his work and respect for his employer. It was an obvious relief for Donne to find an outlet for his energies in labour which combined intellect with humanity and which was neither pure scholastic searching nor mere physical prowess.

The Lord Keeper's mind was lucid and highly trained, yet his preferences were not entirely for dry legal facts, for he was recognized by poets and authors of the day as an admirer of literature, even an enthusiast. The praise which Ben Jonson, Daniel and Sylvester gave him cannot have been entirely perfunctory. Such a mind, discriminating, eager,

[1] Journal of Sir Simon d'Ewes, pp. 546–7 and 595–6.

yet tutored, akin to Donne's, yet superior in experience and clarity, was the very one to mould and influence him in his growing development. Donne recognized his debt to him: he loved and revered him. One of his biographers declares that he does 'not question that the most important influence to which Donne was ever subjected was that of Egerton, and that to the great sobriety of this lawyer we owe the radical change in the poet's outlook upon life and men'.[1] This may, or may not, be so. What is certain is that Donne's close association with Egerton had in it two other elements, bound in time to reveal themselves. The older man was the first whom he frankly regarded in the light of a father,[2] and he was also a consistent Protestant. No other person that we know of,—for his stepfather either antagonized, ignored or made no recorded impression on Donne's stubborn heart—fostered his interests, guided and admonished him so consistently and intimately. To be a member once more of a household headed by a man of ability and integrity, to share his work and his ambitions, to sit at his table, must have been warming and encouraging and we know that the Lord Keeper esteemed the conversation of Donne and, like the succeeding Sovereign, considered it an 'ornament'. Secondly, Egerton's Protestantism and his marked success at Court, must have stimulated, either consciously or unconsciously, the questioning, sifting, reasoning side of Donne's ambitious nature which hovered so long between Catholicism and the State Religion, between life in the Church or at Court.

In the year following his attempted reform of the Star Chamber abuses, Sir Thomas was employed as Commissioner for treating with the Dutch. Thus, in 1598, it is

[1] Gosse, vol. i, p. 94.

[2] Five months before he entered the Church Donne writes, at the age of forty-two, 'My Lord Chancellor gave me so noble and so ready a despatch, accompanied with so fatherly advice and remorse for my fortunes, that I am now like an alchemist delighted with discoveries by the way, though I attain not mine end.' Gosse, vol. ii, p. 49. Letter to Sir Henry Goodyer.

possible that Donne travelled to the Low Countries and enjoyed the magnificence and importance adorning the mission of a public servant from the heretical court, which was condemned and lampooned by the Catholic nations, and envied and wooed by the Protestant.

But events of a personal nature began to crowd upon the Lord Chancellor and sere his life. His two sons, with other of Donne's friends,[1] were both fighting under Essex in the Irish campaign, and in August of 1599, Sir Thomas, the elder son, was killed. In September he was buried with great solemnity in Chester Cathedral and Donne, as a fellow adventurer, friend, and servant of the father's household, bore the dead son's sword in the procession. In October, the Earl of Essex fleeing without authority from the barbarous and boggy land, was taken and confided to the Lord Keeper as a nettlesome prisoner, and early in 1600 Lady Egerton died.

The commitment of Essex into the Lord Keeper's hands brought with it anxiety and danger for his patron, and the great house in the Strand became an uncomfortable focus of curiosity and intrigue. Throughout the late summer of 1599 complaints of Essex's conduct of the Irish campaign had been rife at Court: Essex, hampered at every turn by the apparent distrust of the Queen, his enemy, Cecil, the Secretary of the Council, and other rivals at home, and by recalcitrant chieftains, casualties, desertion and disease in the rebellious country which he was attempting to bring to heel, wrote to Elizabeth long letters of expostulation, full of self-pity. 'Is it not known that from England I receive nothing but discomfort and soul's wounds?', was his cry, and in September he could endure it no longer but made his dramatic appearance and unskilful appeal to the Queen herself at Nonesuch Palace. Within twenty-four hours he had been

[1] Sir Charles Cornwallis, Sir Henry Goodyer, Sir Henry Wotton and Sir Thomas Roe.

committed to the custody of the Lord Keeper. The act was at once a compliment and a burden to Egerton and he can hardly have thanked Elizabeth for the quandary in which it placed him. Here was a man whom he had loved and fostered, to whom he had written letters of admonishment when he considered that Essex had erred, about whom now the wildest rumours tossed over London, thrust into his own saddened and disturbed home.

For some months Essex was gravely ill. He lay in the long rooms whose windows looked out on to the gardens stretching down to the water. The Queen's physicians examined him. The Queen herself paid him a visit, whether of condolence, curiosity or criticism no one knew, but he remained a prisoner. His intimate friends were forbidden to see him, even his wife, lately delivered of a daughter, was shut out from him. In June, nine months after his commitment to York House, a specially constituted Court was called, over which Egerton had the unpleasant duty of presiding. Essex was examined and deprived of all his offices.

Plot and counter-plot began to hatch, machinations concerning succession to the throne and anglings for the favour of the possible heir, James VI of Scotland. Despite the strict watch kept upon Essex, secret documents were insinuated into and drawn forth from York House, until Elizabeth, realizing the unpleasantness of Egerton's position relieved him by sending Essex, still a prisoner, to his own house further down the river.[1] How much of this hornet's nest did Donne observe? In how much of the buzzing did he intervene? The junior of Essex by only six years and his comrade on two voyages, his admirer at Court and possibly his personal votary, he cannot have failed to sympathize with

[1] York House stood at the bend of the river, where the water and the Strand running into Whitehall make an elbow. Citywards lay Durham House, which was Raleigh's and then the Savoy, Somerset and Arundel Houses and finally Leicester, or Essex, House by the Temple Stairs. (See Norden's Map of Westminster 1593.)

the unfortunate favourite whose character unfitted him for the posts of strategy into which ambition and a desire for the Queen's adulation threw him.

Meanwhile, in January 1600 Lady Egerton had died and it was not until October of the same year that Sir Thomas married again. Who was to sit at the head of his table and order his domestic affairs? The responsibility was an onerous one and it seems hardly credible that a young girl of sixteen could undertake it. Yet this is exactly what occurred, for Lady Egerton's niece stepped into the role allotted her. Her aunt had instructed her becomingly, Sir Thomas trusted her, her father, Sir George More, relied upon her to keep a place open for him at that hospitable and important house, and the young Secretary, thrown into her company, fell desperately in love with her.

What was the nature, the character, the appearance of Ann? Of none is there a record. Like a patient Griselda she remains aloof and unprotesting, a submissive accompaniment to her impetuous and discordant lover. She was twelve years younger than he and her youth and innocence held him more than the experience and sophistication of the great ladies at Court, or town hostesses. She fired in him that devotion and profound loyalty of which his soul was capable, and in his writings, as in a mirror, the new and more sincere love is evident.

The emotions of a poet may not be chronologically tabulated, nor need the material which he supplies be biographical, but it is generally agreed that *The Ecstasy*, the poem which speaks of the 'secession and suspension'[1] of the lovers' souls and their interanimation, was written to Ann. This poem, in which Donne displays some of his most intricate metaphysical lore—(the relation and interdependence of body and soul, their functions in the scholastic sense, the nature of spirit, and the influence of the heavenly bodies on

[1] Donne's Letter to Sir Thomas Lucy. Gosse, vol. i, p. 173.

F

man)[1]—is yet one of the greatest of love poems, revealing the early condition of love, when rapt stillness remains perfection, when words or movement are a violation, hastening inevitable division. No other succeeding lyric in English literature, unless it be Rossetti's *Silent Noon*, expresses this 'close-companioned inarticulate' state, which a modern poet would describe as one of 'anaesthetization', so exquisitely.

> 'As 'twixt two equal armies, Fate
>   Suspends uncertain victory,
> Our souls, (which to advance their state,
>   Were gone out,) hung 'twixt her, and me.
> And whilst our souls negotiate there,
>   We like sepulchral statues lay:
> All day, the same our postures were,
>   And we said nothing, all the day.'

The tenderness of the poem called *Song* implies that Ann was also its inspiration. This is the closing stanza:

> 'Let not thy divining heart
>   Forthink me any ill,
> Destiny may take thy part,
>   And may thy fears fulfil;
>   But think that we
>   Are but turned aside to sleep;
>   They who one another keep
>   Alive, ne'er parted be.'

There is no proof that the lovers' attraction drew them into intimacy, but what could be more natural? They must often have been alone together. For nine long months the house without a mistress sheltered their love like a benign and spreading tree. When the Lord Keeper lingered long at some tedious function, at which the attendance of his Secretary was not strictly required, when the torches and tapers flared low in the Gothic corridors and servants nodded, who is to

---

[1] Grierson, vol. ii, pp. 41–45, and Hughes, 'The Lineage of the Extasie,' *Modern Language Review*, xxvii, 1932.

disprove that Donne did not importune his Ann in some 'pale, latticed, moonlit room' in which:

'The carved angels, ever eager-eyed,
Stared, where upon their heads the cornice rests,
With hair blown back, and wings put crosswise on their breast.'[1]

The haste and secrecy surrounding the succeeding act in this drama cannot be accounted for unless one admits the possibility of such intimacy. Another trait in Donne's character makes this plausible. He was, in times of great emotional strain, liable to be concerned with squaring his own conscience, to the exclusion of outward appearances. If Ann and he had become involved, and Donne was honourably bent on setting matters aright, his first thoughts would be for her, and his second for the easing of his troubled mind. The opinion of relations or of high state dignitaries upon his action was of secondary importance. This same tendency is observable at a second crisis in his life,—when he was about to take Holy Orders. He was the victim of his emotions and powerful imagination and, as such, subject neither to reason nor idle persuasion.

7

Time crept forward. Sir Thomas was pleased with his brilliant, versatile secretary who was diligent, discreet and dependable. Who knows what projects he had in store for Donne's advancement or to what golden rung of the tall Court ladder the young man might climb should intellect rule rather than passion?

Yet there was much to be done. In 1600 the Lord Chancellor was employed in matters of financial diplomacy with the Danish ministers, attempting to gain a success similar to that which he had tasted with the Dutch. The troublesome business of Essex went on without satisfaction to anyone. Even

---

[1] Keats' *St. Agnes Eve.*

when the unfortunate Earl was set at liberty Elizabeth turned a stony ear to his humble petitions and Egerton did not care for the rumour that he was gathering about him a set of malcontents, devoted but dangerous, who might rise in Wales, where Essex had property, or even in London beneath the nose of the Sovereign. Then came the attempted rising, the failure of the citizens to rally, the blocking of Ludgate by the Queen's forces, Essex's flight down Friday Street to the river, and his capture and submission in his own house where Egerton went to plead with him and barely escaped with his life. Eleven days later the trial in which Egerton played a prominent part and Francis Bacon, the erstwhile friend, made the chief charges, took place and five days later Elizabeth, vacillating over her first decision, signed a second death warrant. The following day, the 25th of February, 1600, Essex was executed. Southampton was condemned but reprieved. As Captain of the Guard, Raleigh was forced to be present but it was too much for him and he retired to an inner room. Thus when, with double irony, Essex turned to beg for final reconciliation, there was no reply. If Donne was present the event left a peculiarly sharp and unpleasant impression on his sensitive mind, for the executioner, faltering at his work, failed to do it skilfully and struck at the brave, submissive head no less than three times.[1] The blows sent a kind of dull, sorrowing sickness through the minds of the people, half of whom had not believed that it was possible for Essex to be so ruthlessly destroyed. So great was the popularity of the Earl, who had fallen like Lucifer from high places,

[1] See *The Second Anniversary*:

> 'Or as sometimes in a beheaded man,
> Though at those two Red Seas, which freely ran,
> One from the trunk, another from the head,
> His soul be sailed, to her eternal bed,
> His eyes will twinkle, and his tongue will roll,
> As though he beckoned, and called back his soul,
> He grasps his hands, and he pulls up his feet,
> And seems to reach, and to step forth to meet
> His soul. . . .'

that public prayers had been offered for him in city churches: it was forbidden to publish ballads or broadsheets giving his career for fear of further risings, and the executioner was nearly torn limb from limb by a frenzied crowd.

The favourite's long imprisonment, illness, uncertain fate and final destruction had its repercussion on the public consciousness and the artists, as always, were sensitive to this restlessness, this sorrowful temper. Shakespeare had been obsessed with the inevitability of decay, with maturity fast overtaking nativity, 'once in the main of light.'

> 'How with this rage can beauty hold a plea
> When action is no stronger than a flower,
> O how shall summer's honey breath hold out
> Against the wreckful siege of battering days?'[1]

And now he was silent, producing nothing for two barren years.

Donne, too, reflected the distemper in a curious and repulsive poem, *The Progress of the Soul*,[2] which like a chasm, dark, dank, and unwholesome, gapingly reveals much in the divided mind of the man now nearing thirty. 'A strange and sombre explosion of spleen . . . bitter and sardonic . . . wantonly repulsive',[3] it shows Donne the student of obscure Hebrew writings, of the doctrines of Pythagoras and of immature science, the mother of 19th century evolution. It shows him weary, fretful and strained by his work for Egerton and by his own compelling nature which drove him to inner speculation and the ardours of love at one and the same time.

And herein lies the key to the poem, for although his intention was avowedly to ridicule heretics from Cain to Calvin in *The Progress* and to trace the habitations of the promiscuous soul from the apple of Eden down to 'this time when she is he whose life you shall find in the end of this book', Donne got hopelessly involved and could not finish the poem.

---

[1] *Sonnet* LXIII. [2] Not to be confused with the *First Anniversary*.
[3] Grierson, ii, pp. xvii–xx.

It is as if it left a bad taste in his mouth and he turned away from it, repelled, as we are. His attempts to foreshadow a theory of evolution objectively, which begin biologically, become tangled with his adherence to the Biblical legends of genesis and descent from Adam. His efforts to outwear his greed for perverse experience and his perverted interest in it end in satiety. In the battering of his moral conscience by self-habituation to filth, which resolves itself into the tolerant philosophy of the last three lines:

> 'There's nothing simply good, nor ill alone,
> Of every quality comparison,
>   The only measure is, and judge, opinion:'

he tries to escape from evil into good. But what comes out uppermost is his hatred of women.

The poem was written at the height of his deepest passion, that which was to culminate in his marriage. Why then, like Hamlet, must he revile the very thing which he adores? His polymorphic perversity, his religious tenacity, both become poisoned with the acid which burns and destroys corrosively. Thus, perhaps to his own astonishment, the heretic soul in her unscrupulous wanderings suddenly finds herself housed in Elizabeth, the Virgin Queen? The unavowed head of the Established Church appears to the young man, still partially Catholic in sympathy, not the paragon of sagacity and mental agility which others declare her, but in truth an arch-fiend, a she-wolf, the devourer who feeds upon favourites and drinks the blood of martyrs, rejoicing in this unholy ichor. His sullen agnosticism upon his pilgrimage from Rome breaks out in explosive irritation, in lampooning, in sceptical thrusts at courtiers, heretics, above all at the Queen, a daughter of fateful Eve.

Donne's violent misogyny may have sprung from his perverted love for his mother, a love which, like Hamlet's, got twisted from its natural heritage and was nourished on a false diet. But, whatever its origin, it forced him to draw woman as the evil influence affecting man, the destroyer, corrupter and insidious purveyor of life through hidden and sinister channels. He both loves and hates simultaneously. She who is the resolution of all his conflicts is, at the same time, their stimulator and awakener. She who comforts and reassures him yet tempts him with forbidden delights and sucks him under like a vortex of engulfing waters.

> 'So careless flowers strow'd on the waters face
> The curled whirlpools suck, smack and embrace,
> Yet drown them. . . .'[1]

he had written earlier, and now in *The Progress*:

> 'Man all at once was there by woman slain,
> And one by one we're here slain o'er again
> By them. The mother poison'd the well-head,
> The daughters here corrupt us, rivolets;
> No smallness scapes, no greatness breaks their nets;
> She thrust us out, and by them we are led
> Astray, from turning, to whence we are fled.
> Were prisoners judges, 'twould seem rigorous,
> She sinn'd, we bear; part of our pain is, thus
> To love them, whose fault to this painful love yoked us.'

Speaking, in the same poem, of the Soul's prenatal, prehuman experiences he speaks of her as having known 'treachery',

> 'Rapine, deceit, and lust, and ills enow
> To be a woman.'

She, who is inferior to man, since she has no soul—(and in *The Progress* the embryonic soul gets no further than a transmigration through the vegetable to the animal state)—is yet superior to him, since without her he cannot fulfil himself. 'The Idea of Woman', as he was later to confess to Ben Jonson,[2] haunted him,—the astral figure standing behind the

[1] Sixth Elegy. See also these lines from *An Anatomy of the World*:
> 'For that first marriage was our funeral:
> One woman at one blow, then kill'd us all
> And singly, one by one, they kill us now.'

[2] 'Conversations with Drummond of Hawthornden.'

very real and living one whose body tempted, tormented and delighted him.

In Ann, to whom he was consciously and outwardly loyal until her premature death, who was at once his resolution, his sovereign remedy, his sweet elixir without which life itself could barely be sustained, he found also, unconsciously, his destructive angel and the avenging one who brought about ruin. The servility of the letters which he was soon to write,[1] the crippling and utter dejection of spirit before his first reversal, reveal the self-torturing conflict which his Jesuit teachers had done much to foster, and had possibly originated in him, underlying the superficially successful and contented man.

Thus the intense desire to arrest the moment of perfection, to avert disintegration by some very personal act set like a seal upon his life, shortly betrayed itself.

8

Either the Lord Keeper regarded the attachment growing under his congested roof with benevolence or he was too immersed in public and private affairs to observe its seriousness. In October of 1601 he married for the third time. His wife was Alice, widow of Ferdinando, fifth Earl of Derby, who brought with her three unmarried daughters. The second of these, Frances, promptly married Sir Thomas's only surviving son, John, and subsequently became the first Countess of Bridgewater.

In November Sir Thomas received one of the few recorded rebuffs to his public career, for he came into collision with the Speaker of the House over some trifling matter of procedure and was forced to withdraw from the stand which he had adopted. He was possibly not in the best of humours to receive news of domestic difficulties.

[1] To Sir Thomas Egerton and Sir George More.

The arrival of a mistress for York House, as well as three presumptive mistresses, indicated that Ann More was exceeding the hospitality originally offered her, and about the same time her grandfather, old Sir William More of Loseley, who had kept the affairs of his estate with patriarchal fervour from the itching fingers of his ambitious son, died. When Parliament broke up for Christmas and when her father, who was Member of Parliament for Guildford in addition to his other duties, went back to Loseley, it was natural that Ann should return with him. Her mother had died some years before and again she would have to undertake the position of mistress of a house which Sovereigns and Princes visited.

In the 'booths' and bowers of York House courting and marriage contracts went forward, for Elizabeth Stanley, the Lord Keeper's second step-daughter, was engaged to Henry Hastings, fifth Earl of Huntingdon, and the wedding was to take place at the end of the month. Bridal preparations were garnished with whispered intimacies. What hopes were confided, what illusions discovered? Upon the susceptible heart of Ann More, already heavy with importunate passion, what effect had all this blossoming and intended fruition? Elizabeth was her junior, since she was only fifteen and her bridegroom little older. Did Ann unburden herself to the two sisters, one of whom was another Ann? If she shared her sweet torment with them, or if they with shining eyes observed it for her, and were drawn to her predicament, it goes far to explain their later interest and kind offices.

Unskilled and unwise in resisting advances, and besieged by the ardent and sophisticated Donne, how was she to withstand his Italianate fire? The thought of encroaching separation was a torment to the lovers and the 'faithful promises'[1] exchanged were inevitable if love were to be anything more to Donne than a repetition of mere passion.

The stumbling blocks to an open and happy termination of

[1] Walton, p. 7.

the love affair were Ann's minority and the disapproval of her father, for by now Sir George had received broad hints of the attachment and was greatly displeased. He had been unwise to leave his daughter so long unchaperoned in the rambling old house, yet he did not wish to pick a quarrel with his kinsman, that great man the Lord Keeper, with whom he had always been on terms of affectionate friendship. Francis Wooley, his stepson, may have been questioned and was doubtless discreet enough in his replies since he was not often at York House. Suspicion and anger simmered in Sir George's breast until at length he determined abruptly to put an end to the nonsense by removing Ann from York House. Yet the lovers would still be bound to see each other at a tantalizing distance, and like chafed and prevented souls to meet in proscribed secrecy, for Donne, as Secretary to the Lord Keeper, must be in almost constant attendance upon his master at Court and Ann, as the daughter of the future Lieutenant of the Tower and Chancellor of the Garter, would be likely to attend some Court entertainments.[1]

In Donne there lay a demon of distraction. His character was not single, not dual, but manifold, and now the passionate ruled supreme. Headstrong and unreasoning he suddenly committed an act of the gravest error, which was to involve him in years of penury and miserable reflection, for toward Christmas of 1601, he secretly married Ann More. She was seventeen and he twenty-nine. His old Trinity friend, Samuel Brooke, who had recently taken orders, performed the office; Christopher, without right, cheerfully gave the bride away and acted as a witness, and the mysterious second witness held his tongue. But the jubilation which the lovers must have felt at having outwitted their elders and made

---

[1] On pp. 20 and 22, Jessop calls Sir George More by the titles which he had not then received, and gives these offices as the cause of Ann's attendance at Court. More was not made Chancellor of the Garter until July 9th, 1611, and Lieutenant of the Tower until October, 1615. Gosse, on p. 89, vol. i, makes a similar error, based on Walton.

themselves one was short-lived indeed. Ann returned to Loseley and it became evident that her father would have to be enlightened. Possibly Sir George spoke of marrying Ann to someone else. She may even have thought herself to be with child. As a student of the Law, Donne must have known the gravity of his offences, first, that against the Canon Law in marrying a minor without the consent of her father, and second, the civil offence against the Common Law.[1] But it did not yet weigh heavy with him since he hoped for Sir George's approbation.

Who should bear the pregnant tidings? Why not the offender himself? A plea from Ann, a sudden disclosure or attack upon the character of Donne by a mischief-maker—something occurred which made it imperative to inform Sir George at once, and Donne was ill. He lay in lodgings 'by the Savoy' and someone else must be the equivocal messenger. What was the cause of Donne's removal from the palatial grandeur of York House? Sensing disapprobation upon the part of his employer at his rash act, had he changed quarters of his own volition, or because of open reprimand? Whatever the sequence of events Donne wrote to Sir George More upon the 2nd of February, informing him that he was his son-in-law. One of the highest peers of the realm, Henry Percy, ninth Earl of Northumberland, was chosen to carry the tidings and the author besought Sir George to use 'Nature, Reason, Wisdom and Christianity' towards both him (Donne) and his wife.

It was a vain wish. Donne, no less than other observers, knew Sir George to be a man 'full of passion' and poor Northumberland who bore the tidings must have had a choleric reception. There is something about deception which invariably angers the deceived, who feels that he has been outwitted, gulled and used unfairly, and the Earl was

---

[1] Jessop, p. 23, footnote: *Treatise relating to Infants.* W. Macpherson of the Inner Temple, 1847.

hardly the man to placate the deceived father, for his character was thoroughly out of harmony with that of the Master of Loseley. Sir George was an energetic, forceful, capable man, active and ready of speech. In addition to being a Member of Parliament for Guildford he was also High Sherrif of Surrey and Sussex and had recently accepted a grant of the Lordship of Godalming. The Queen had already paid Loseley four visits in his father's lifetime and Sir George had justifiable hopes of further indications of her, or her successor's, favour, both in the giving of offices and the conferring of honour by personal visits.

Northumberland was unpractical, theoretical, and inventive, in fact highly Paracelsan in character. A friend to Essex, Raleigh and to Donne, he was the last person, despite his exalted rank, to handle Sir George successfully. This vindictive and vituperative man, in the whiteheat of anger, proceeded to the Lord Chancellor and caused, first, the dismissal of Donne from his promising position as Secretary, and subsequently the imprisonment, not only of Donne, but of the two Brookes as well. Sir Thomas at first demurred and tried to dissuade his former kinsman from so heavy a punishment but eventually capitulated. As Walton quaintly puts it: 'And though Sir George were remembered' (reminded) 'that errors might be over-punished, and desired to forbear till second considerations might clear some scruples, yet he became restless until his suit was granted and the punishment executed.'[1]

The prisoners were not allowed to be near each other, Donne was flung into the Fleet and the Brookes into the Marshalsea.[2] To lie in prison in the days of Elizabeth was a more common occurrence than nowadays. Elizabeth Vernon had been consigned to the 'best apartment in the Fleet', three years before Donne's commitment, for

[1] Walton, p. 8.
[2] They stood in what are now Farringdon and Southwark Borough High Streets.

marrying the Earl of Southampton who was likewise imprisoned upon his return from France, for nothing more than her Majesty's displeasure. Raleigh had had the same experience. But it cannot at any time have been pleasant and to Donne with his sensitivity, his pride and irritability, with his new-sought contentment snatched from him and the heaviness of a ruined career lowering before him, it must have been particularly repellent.

He continued to do the only thing left to him, to write letters of appeal to Sir George More and Sir Thomas Egerton,[1] and to his wife from whom he was so cruelly separated. The first are extant, the last is not. Those to his father-in-law and former employer show becoming humility and genuine dejection: the one to Ann ends with a pun, which, execrable in taste as it may seem to the modern mind, rings with a forlorn finality:

'John Donne—Ann Donne—Undone.'[2]

To add to all this he was ill, so that at last his appeals were answered in measure, for he was allowed to go free from prison but was confined in chambers in the Strand. Here he remained for about ten days, writing further letters to More and Egerton as well as to Robert Cotton,[3] the political antiquary, from whom he hoped to get work. Christopher Brooke still lay in the Marshalsea and was prevented from going on circuit and performing his lucrative legal functions, much to his annoyance. Yet, while appealing to Sir Thomas Egerton to hasten his release he found occasion to plead courageously for his friend: 'Pardon me a word for Mr. Donne, my good Lord . . . who wants but fortune's hands and tongue to rear him up and set him out.'[4]

The rancour and hurt pride of Sir George urged him

[1] Letters dated February 11th and 12th, 1601/2.
[2] Walton, p. 9.
[3] Letters dated February 13th and 20th, 1601/2.
[4] Letter to Sir Thomas Egerton, February 25th, 1601/2. Gosse, i, p. 11a.

further and further in vengeful action. He now caused a commission to be set up to report upon the validity of the so-called marriage, hoping, possibly, to prove lack of cohabitation and consequent nullity. This was too much for the dignity of the Lord Keeper and he in turn vented his displeasure upon Donne. But at length Sir George, having made himself and his family sufficiently ridiculous, changed his tune, and regretting his past intemperance and possibly fearing an end of his relations with the Lord Keeper, now asked him to reinstate Donne. Yet despite the pleading of his new wife and her three daughters, all of whom remained constant in their friendship for the young man who had erred so foolishly and yet so humanly, the Lord Keeper remained adamant. He did not permit personal feeling to cloud the the clarity of his judgment. As a public servant of the Crown, in one of the highest positions of the State, he could not afford to take back into his service a young man about whom there had been public scandal, and to his former brother-in-law he replied that: 'Though he was unfeignedly sorry for what he had done, it was yet inconsistent with his place and credit to discharge and re-admit servants at the request of passionate petitioners.'[1] Donne was left with the cold solace of knowing that Sir Thomas had described him as a friend and a Secretary, 'fitter to serve a King than a subject.'[2]

It was indeed a time of barrenness. The country still smarted under the loss of Essex and the seemingly capricious acts of the Queen. For Donne, who had wasted his inheritance and rejected the favours of fortune thrown in his lap, there was little hope of employment, unless by long years of working up a practice at the Bar or receiving private commissions for work of a literary kind.

Added to his difficulties was the fact that he was now a marked man at whom each new and prospective employer would point a finger, enquiring why the Lord Keeper had

[1] Walton, p. 10.   [2] Walton, p. 8.

dismissed him? Was it only because of his amorous indiscretion? or did something more lie beneath it? Had he been inefficient or untrustworthy as a Secretary? Was there any question of his religious inclinations making him a dangerous enemy to the State? That there was something unpleasant afoot we know because in his letter to Sir George More on the 13th of February he opens with the statement that the charges laid to him 'of having deceived some gentlewoman before, and that *of loving a corrupt religion*, are vanished and smoked away'.[1] In another letter to him in March, he says: 'I languish and rust dangerously. From seeking preferments abroad my love and conscience restrain me: from hoping for them here, my Lord's disgracings cut me off.'[2] And he in turn pleads for the Brookes. To the Lord Keeper his tone is more open and less penitential. . . .'I have some bridle now upon me more than by my marriage. . . . To seek preferment here with any but your Lordship were a madness. Every great man to whom I shall address any such suit will silently dispute the case, and say, 'Would my Lord Keeper so disgraciously have imprisoned him and flung him away if he had not done some other great fault of which we hear not?' So that to the burden of my true weaknesses I shall have this addition of this very prejudicial suspicion that I am worse than I hope your Lordship doth think me, or would that the world should think.'[3]

It was not until the 27th of April, 1602, that the Ecclesiastical Court confirmed his marriage. Even then some other obstructions prevented the couple from coming together. 'He was forced to get possession of Ann by a long and restless suit in law.'[4] But even if the law and an irate parent allowed them to set up house together, what were they to live upon? Sir George refused to grant a marriage portion, or an allowance. His expenses in keeping up Loseley on the scale of

[1] Gosse, i, p. 106.
[2] Gosse, i, p. 113.
[3] Letter dated March 1st, 1601/2. Gosse i, p. 115.
[4] Walton, p. 9.

magnificence which he required must have been enormous, and, in addition, he had lately paid out the sum of £800 (the modern equivalent of which would be about £8,000) for the wardship of young Edward Herbert, later to become first Lord Herbert of Cherbury and a confirmed friend of Donne. Thus the divided lovers,—'they, who were more used to confer favours than receive them,'[1] had before them the very real task of building up a marriage already smutched by scandal and criticism, weakened by financial insecurity and unproven by time and temperament.

The shadow of gloomy cynicism which lay across Jacobean London had begun to shift uneasily, not at Elizabeth's death in 1603, but earlier, with the death of Essex in 1601, and in Donne's life the personal dejection coincided with the national.

[1] Walton, p. 10.

CHAPTER III

ADJUSTMENT AND RECONCILIATION

> '. . . But up unto the watch-tower get,
> And see all things despoil'd of fallacies;
> Thou shalt not peep through lattices of eyes,
> Nor hear through labyrinths of ears, nor learn
> By circuit, or collections to discern.'
>
> *Second Anniversary.*

I

The Queen, virile and demonstrative to the end, danced her way with feverish defiance to the grave. In 1600 the French ambassador describes her as dancing 'gayement et de belle disposition':[1] in 1601, three months after the beheading of Essex, she went a-maying at Highgate, and in May of 1602, soon after Donne's release from prison, she 'mayed' again at Lewisham. In August of the same year, upon the first three days of the month, Sir Thomas Egerton entertained her at great expense at his newly-bought country seat, Harvil, or Harefield, in Middlesex. Donne, now facing a new and straitened life and longing to seek preferment at Court, must have paused to meditate with saddened thought upon his late position and the nearness of that amazing feminine vitalizer, the dancer of galliards, to his former employer.

However, at Christmas, the Queen began to show signs 'of human infirmitie'[2] and in March she died, leaving behind her a rich wardrobe of some odd thousands of gowns, which in a few months Anne of Denmark began to cut up for use in court masques. The Earl of Northumberland, Lucy, Coun-

[1] P. P. Laffleur de Kermaingant. *Mission de Jean de Thumery*, i, p. 415.
[2] Sir John Harington.

tess of Bedford, and other of Donne's friends, went forth to meet the new King from Scotland, and Donne's star, like that of other malcontents under Elizabeth, shone fitfully but with more determined brightness.

At some time, after vexatious litigation had ceased, Sir George More's temper had cooled, and Donne and Ann had come together, fortune, or the more sound and enticing sides of his nature, evoked for Donne the offer of a home. For Ann's cousin, young Francis Wolley, who had been on the Island Voyage with him and watched them both struggling up the 'tentatious' path of clandestine matrimony, came to the rescue. His father had lately died and Francis, succeeding to the baronetcy and Surrey estates, welcomed them to Pyrford Park.

Here Donne lived for more than two years and Ann bore two of her children. Here, the new Sovereign, shortly after his accession, paid Sir Francis an official visit whilst on his way to Ann's father, at Loseley. The canny eye of James may early have discerned something of promise in the maturing features of Donne and one would give much to be able to throw light upon such passing meetings. In 1610, the hospitable and generous Sir Francis died but the Donnes had left Pyrford before this event, for in 1605, Donne took an unpretentious house in Mitcham.

Two of Ann's sisters lived nearby, Lady Carew at the Manor in Mitcham and Lady Grymes in Camberwell. Sir Julius Caesar, an influential Court favourite and a good friend to Donne, also lived there. Perhaps he, or perhaps Ann's relations, persuaded the poet that if he wished to succeed in obtaining Court favour it was wise for him to live nearer the centre of things, not too far from Town. At Mitcham the Donnes remained for five years and Ann, the pattern of passive obedience and fruitfulness, bore an equal number of babies. The house in which they lived stood well on into the nineteenth century and it is a pity that it does not still exist to bear out Donne's description of it as his 'thin little house'. He also took rooms in Whitehall, doubtless in one of the wings of the old palaces, fast becoming outmoded and beginning to resemble nests or warrens, peopled by student or courtier 'bachelors' whose business made it necessary for them to remain in town, especially when the Court lodged nearby, although Ann remained at Mitcham, secure from fog, smoke, plague, noise and city expenses. For Donne was not a country lover. City born and city bred, the descendant of Court attendants and a Court aspirant himself, the country was to him little better than a wilderness. In an early literary *débat* which he shared with some of his friends[1] he ridicules the barrenness of Court, Country and City alike but writes with particular tedium of the 'country's dulness'. In his letters he speaks again of the 'barbarousness and insipid dulness of the country', and declares: 'I that live in the country without stupefying, am not in darkness, but in shadow, which is not light, but a pallid, waterish, and diluted one.'[2]

Although he embellishes the *Devotions* with decorative similes about the dunging, liming or burning of the land, and the pruning of fruit trees, he does it with the air of a student observer rather than the keen land-owner, gardener or farmer with an inherited knowledge. The splendour of Loseley, built of the stones of old Waverley Abbey, and the dignified grandeur of Pyrford Park, may have helped him to support the tedium of country life with something like affability, but when he found himself cramped in an unpretentious house with a growing family, growing expenses and the damps and vapours of an ill-drained cellar seeping into his aching bones, a depression with very real and obvious causes took serious hold on him.

[1] See Grierson, vol. ii, p. 140. *Verse Letter* to Sir Henry Wotton.
[2] Letter to Sir Henry Goodyer, Mitcham 1609. Gosse, vol. i, p. 219.

2

While living at Mitcham Donne was commissioned to
work for Thomas Morton. The English church had especial
need just then of trained thinkers and clever casuists, men of
learning who spoke with conviction, champions of the faith
against the brilliant Catholic and Jesuit opponents who saw
new hope of success in a country somewhat dormant and
lethargic after the opening of the century, upon the succession
of a King whose religious tendencies were as yet not altogether clear. Morton was ten years Donne's senior and
destined to hold, first, the Deanery of Gloucester, and subsequently the Bishopric of Durham, which, since the north
was for long a stubborn citadel of Romanism, was not an easy
post to fill. Like Donne he was a Cambridge man, with a
reputation for scholarship and, like him, inclined to moderation rather than harshness in religious matters. He was quick
to appreciate the genius of Donne, trained up by Jesuit
tutors, whose arts and weapons he might use with poisonous
effect against their originators. He recognized a mind which
was dogged in the extreme, not satisfied with superficial conclusions, certain only of its ground when it had sifted out the
whole mass of doctrine and learning, relentless in its legal
force and cunning in its devious and intricate subtlety. Not
for Donne, 'unscholarlike arguings . . . contradictions of
himself . . . silly ridiculous triflings, extreme flatteries . . .
the neglecting of better and more obvious answers, or of
letting slip some enormous advantages which the other gave
and he spies not.'[1]

Morton was noted for his suavity in argument and clemency in punishment. Elizabeth, in confronting the ever-vexed
question of recusancy and the stamping out of Catholicism,
had been particularly perturbed by the stubborn persistence
of northern Romanists and with her usual perspicacity had

[1] Donne's Letter to Sir Henry Goodyer. *Letters*, 1651, p. 163.

realized that harsher and ever harsher methods did not diminish the evil but only increased it. She had therefore advised especial leniency towards the recusants in those parts and Morton carried out her policy with tact. The new King likewise advocated 'that uniformity which we desire may be wrought by clemency and by weight of reason, and not by rigour of law',[1] and, appreciating the talents and persuasive ability of Morton, whose civility the Jesuits readily acknowledged, encouraged him. So far Morton had conducted the best part of his arguments by 'oral discourse and debate'.[2] But if the invisible opponent, who made use of a flood of printed controversy which followed the relaxing of press censorship and an increased facility in printing, were to be successfully parried, the contest must be carried forward in written, not oral debate, and it was in this that Donne became indispensable to Morton. The controversial volumes and pamphlets—and among them was an analysis of the causes of the Gunpowder Plot—were issued under Morton's name without reference to his collaborator.

Such was the force and appositeness of Morton's work that the celebrated Robert Parsons himself thought fit to dispute it. Donne's sifting of his 1,400 authors and his study of the Civil and Canon Law, which he had carried on since his marriage, began to tell their weight.

For some years Morton had been in the service of the Earls of Huntingdon. The most recent holder of this title was the young peer who had married Elizabeth Stanley, from York House. It is possible that she augmented Morton's belief in Donne's exceptional ability and aptitude for the controversial work, but his merits must have been sufficiently known to the circle of living scholars to do without this personal recommendation.

Throughout his life his capacity for friendship was marked. If he had need of feminine society and appreciation he yet

[1] Gosse, vol. i, p. 148.   [2] Gosse, vol. i, p. 149.

had staunch friends of his own sex to whom he gave as much as he received. Chief among these was Sir Henry Goodyer of Polesworth in Warwickshire, and Sir Henry Wotton, ambassador. It was to Goodyer that Donne, exultant at his liberation from the Fleet, had written inquiring the way to Polesworth:[1] to Goodyer that he wrote almost weekly from Mitcham: and later in life, of the intended publication of his poems, of his new debts, of the illnesses and death of his children, and of the manner of writing his Sermons. In short we owe to this friendship the few intimate revelations of domesticity and character which the cautious Donne permitted himself, and Goodyer must have had much sweetness and openness of nature to so affect his difficult intellectual friend. His chief weakness was too great an openhandedness, for, having inherited rich estates, he lived far beyond his means and found himself like many another extravagant Jacobean in straitened circumstances towards the close of his life. Donne, forseeing such a possibility, cautioned him lovingly and tactfully in a Verse Letter. To be a Member for Parliament and Gentleman of the Privy Chamber was all very well but such posts, while complimentary, were apt to drain, rather than fill, the pocket. Despite his moral counselling Donne admits to Goodyer, in a prose letter, that 'we who have been accustomed to one another are like in this, that we love not business', and in another to the more adventurous Wotton, that he avoids business like the plague itself. The ghost of his father must have frowned disapprovingly over his shoulder when he wrote such words to his friends.

This latter friend was his old companion of Hart Hall and the Cadiz and Island Voyages, who, by the time that Donne was working for Morton, had been one of the private secretaries of Lord Essex and was well launched on his brilliant

[1] Letter to Sir Henry Wotton, 23rd February, 1601/2. Gosse, vol. i, p. 110.

career of diplomatist. Thus an increasing number of friends
revolved about Donne like attendant satellites. Although he
declared that he had 'but a short roll of friends writ in his
heart', his other statement, that 'Friendship was his second
religion' comes nearer to the truth.

In 1605/6 a permit was issued to several titled people and
to one, 'John Donne,' to travel for a period of three years[1] but
there is nothing to prove that this individual was not the
Captain Donne who flits confusingly across Elizabethan State
papers, or another usurper of the name.

I am inclined to deny the likelihood of travel at this date.
Everything in Donne's melancholy mental state tends to dis-
prove it. Foreign travel, always a stimulant to one of his
mercurial and susceptible nature would have alleviated or
removed this but instead, we find no such dissipation, only
an intensification of the mood, and two serious preoccupations
which would further strain the already distempered mind—
Donne's consideration of Morton's generous offer made to
aid him in accepting the Church as his calling, and the writing
of three long prose works, *Biathanatos, Pseudo-Martyr* and
Ignatius His Conclave.

3

In June, 1607, Thomas Morton received his first preferment—the Deanery of Gloucester, to be held in plurality with
the living of Long Marston, in Yorkshire, which he had
obtained from one of the Huntingdons nine years before.
With true generosity he determined to give the latter to
Donne. What better tribute could he pay his collaborator
and editor? What finer gift could he make to a friend than
such a benefice? Bishop Morton was still alive when Walton
wrote his *Life of Donne* and provided him with an account of
his offer:

[1] February 16th, 1605/6. Domestic State Papers. See Gosse, i, p. 151.

'He' (Morton) 'sent to Mr. Donne and entreated to borrow an hour of his time for a conference the next day. After their meeting there was not many minutes passed before he spake to him to this purpose:

"The occasion of sending for you is to propose to you what I have often revolved in my own thought since I last saw you: which, nevertheless, I will not declare but upon this condition, that you shall not return me a present answer, but forbear three days, and bestow some part of that time in fasting and prayer: and after a serious consideration of what I shall propose, then return to me with your answer. Deny me not . . . for it is the effect of a true love, which I would gladly pay as a debt due for yours to me." [1]

Donne agreed and Morton continued:

"I know your education and abilities: I know your expectation of a state employment: and I know your fitness for it: and I know, too, the many delays and contingencies that attend court promises; and let me tell you, that my love, begot by our long friendship and your merits, hath prompted me to such an inquisition after your present temporal estate, as makes me no stranger to your necessities; which I know to be such as your generous spirit could not bear, if it were not supported by a pious patience. You know I have formerly persuaded you to waive your court hopes and enter into holy orders: which I now again persuade you to embrace, with this reason added to my former request: . . ." '

He then explained to Donne how he had been preferred but that the emoluments from the Deanery, which were equal to those of the Yorkshire living, would be sufficient for his needs: that he had already discussed the proposition of yielding the latter to Donne with his patron, the young Earl of Huntingdon, and that his Lordship was agreed.

' "Remember", he added, "that no man's education or parts make him too good for this employment, which is to be an ambassador for the God of glory. . . . Make me no present answer; but remember your promise, and return to me the third day with your resolution."

At the hearing of this, Mr. Donne's faint breath and perplexed countenance gave a visible testimony of an inward conflict: but he

[1] Walton, pp. 12–14.

performed his promise, and departed without returning an answer. . . .'

Morton had put the matter persuasively. He had appealed to Donne's ambition, by tactfully acknowledging his preference for state and secular appointment, and in using the simile of a churchman being an '*ambassador* for the God of glory'. Poet and dialectician, Donne would note the use of words and the implied compliment. He would also be grateful to Morton for giving him time to balance the matter with weights of impeccable accuracy in the scales of his heart and mind. Where it was a matter of conscience he was not to be hurried, and Morton, working beside him day by day, watching the younger man's persistence, integrity and delicacy of adjustment in sifting intellectual argument, summed him up with understanding and left the decision to his better nature, 'if God should incline his heart to embrace this motion.'[1]

The three days which should form a hiatus between the old life and the new, if he accepted the offer, must have been days full of agonizing indecision. For Donne was now thirty-five, married and the father of half a dozen children: he had run through the greater part, if not all, of his patrimony, had involved himself in unsatisfactory relationships with his father-in-law and former employer, and for some reason or other the King, to whom all applications for advancement were known, stubbornly refused to foster any unless they lay in line with his own wishes, which were that Donne should enter the Church. By agreeing with Morton and the King, he had everything to gain. Both would have been flattered and pleased, preferment upon preferment might have fallen upon him like warm, encouraging, spring sunshine and he might still shape his talents while yet they were young and pliable. If, on the other hand, he refused, he incurred the charges of ingratitude, obstinacy and suspicion: such an offer, from an exceptionally generous friend, might never be repeated, the

[1] Walton, p. 13.

King's sanction and the co-operation of an influential patron might never again be forthcoming: the ecclesiastical path might be blocked, in addition to the secular, and the prospect of living, of mere existence, be bleak indeed. To refuse the wishes of one's Sovereign was a rash step in itself, but it incurred the additional gravity of suspicion as to the rejector's religious beliefs. Elizabeth's drastic treatment of recusants had not entirely pruned Catholicism from the land: the old bogey of Spain as an arch-enemy, an arch-conspirator with the Pope and Rome, remained even after the death of Philip. The Gunpowder Plot had shocked men into a fresh realization of danger soon after James' accession, and he himself was bitterly disillusioned to find later that a large number of his courtiers were in Spanish pay. The laws against recusants were therefore re-enforced with pleas from the pusillanimous, but tolerant, James that they be not too harshly enforced. As late as at the time of his marriage Donne had had to try to clear himself to his father-in-law of the worst of charges,—that of following in the footsteps of his Catholic ancestors,—and, if he continued in his apparent obduracy, his refusal to accept a very obvious piece of worldly and ecclesiastical advancement might be interpreted very unpleasantly indeed, despite his work for Morton under the aegis of the King.

Did he remain in town to consider the proposition or go down to Mitcham to discuss it with Ann and his friends and relations? His opinion of women as anything more than passive, obedient wives, or (when fortune had endowed them with talents, beauty and position) charming patronesses, or flames with which to light his physical and poetic fire, would not incline him to feminine discussion, and since he was one to work and study much alone he probably came to a resolution only after solitary consideration.

In three days time he gave his answer to Morton.

'Since I saw you I have been faithful to my promise, and have meditated much of your great kindness, which has been such as would exceed even my gratitude: but that it cannot do: and more I cannot return you: and I do that with a heart full of humility and thanks, though I may not accept of your offer.

But, Sir, my refusal is not for that I think myself too good for that calling, for which kings, if they think so, are not good enough: nor for that my education and learning, though not eminent may not, being assisted with God's grace and humility, render me in some measure fit for it: but I dare make so dear a friend as you are my confessor. Some irregularities of my life have been so visible to some men, that though I have, I thank God, made my peace with Him by penitential resolutions against them, and, by the assistance of His grace, banished them from my affections: yet this, which God knows to be so, is not so visible to men, as to free me from their censures, and, it may be, that sacred calling from a dishonour.

And besides, whereas it is determined by the best of casuists that God's glory should be the first end, and a maintenance the second motive to embrace that calling; and though each man may propose to himself both together; yet the first may not be put last without a violation of conscience, which he that searches the heart will judge. And truly, my present condition is such that if I ask my own conscience whether it be reconcilable to that rule, it is at this time so perplexed about it, that I can neither give you nor myself an answer. You know, Sir, who says, *Happy is that man whose conscience doth not accuse him for that thing which he does*. To these, I might add other reasons which dissuade me: but I crave your favour that I may forbear to express them, and thankfully decline your offer.'[1]

Morton had not been quite discerning enough. The complexities of character and the profound influence of the unreasoning unconscious upon the more easily adaptable conscious mind, were unknown to our ancestors three centuries and more ago. Had Morton been astute enough to paint life in the Church for Donne in the sombre, parchment colours of a late Mantegna, or with the horrible, torturing details of Circignani, had he pointed out to Donne the danger, the difculties, the urgent necessity for his soul's salvation in accepting preferment in the Established Church it is probable that Donne would have wavered less and acceded earlier. For his

[1] Walton, p. 14.

basic neurosis of martyrdom, fostered by his Jesuit training, hampered him at every favourable turn in his career. It attracted him to the painful, the repellent and suffering side of life; it called for emotional crises. It distracted him from the serene and purposeful pursuit of matters in hand, such as his position with Egerton and his courting of Ann, (which, had he proceeded patiently, might have been considered favourably by her father), and forced him to refuse Morton's offer which would have alleviated life not only for him but for those whom he loved.

One of his biographers has described him as a man whose crises were always intellectual,[1] but this is only partial truth. Donne was highly emotional as well as intellectual: the intellect, complex, original and strong, strove to control the emotions, which were in turn tormented by the intellect. The endearing simplicity of one half of his nature (and his conscientious consideration of the good Bishop's offer sprang from this source) was antagonistic to the self-condemnatory pride of the other, with which it was doomed forever to live. The balance of the nature swings violently from joy to dejection, from passion to recrimination, from action to melancholy pensiveness, and the vital force which drives him forward is blocked by that which is hostile to life itself.

This may explain why we hear so little of Ann in his life. Once acquiescent, and always submissive, captured at a a stroke and never recalcitrant, she ceased to attract him with the mind. He owed her repose, trusting fidelity, and a revaluation of the spiritual qualities of woman, but her very normality, her innate simplicity was so alien to his own constant and absorbing conflict that she, possibly, could never comprehend him, nor he share with her the deeper problems of his inner battle.

[1] Gosse, vol. i, p. 161. 'When he halts, when he plunges, it is the brain which steers him.' He calls *Biathanatos* 'one of the most poignant relics of Donne's intellectual career'.

4

For his honest and conscientious refusal to go into the Church at this juncture Donne has been heavily censured. Critics have read into the decision a worldliness, a meanness of character which was never his. Donne was an open lover, an honest hater if need be, but above all a *sincere*, if intricate, thinker, and he did not believe himself good enough for the Church at this stage in his growth. He admits his perplexity, and that very perplexity implies the presence of conflict but also of latent seed and future flowering. But for the time being he was quite definite in his refusal.

To call him a 'pretendiente', a mere worldling and hanger-on at Court, who only accepted the Church when all other professions were closed to him, is idle criticism if one enquires into the avenues for advancement in Elizabethan and Jacobean days. A courtier of distinction in one of the professions open to gentlemen—the Army, the Church, the revenue or the law (and more especially the diplomatic service to which Donne aspired)—was forced to adopt the practice of place-hunting. He had to furnish himself with Court dress, carry letters of introduction upon his person, and with what money he could muster, seek accomodation near one of the palaces, and wait in the ante-rooms of ministers, through which some observant courtier might pass. To dine with favourites, to attend the social gatherings of patronesses, and certain Court functions, was inevitable if one hoped for notice and promotion.

Many courtiers impoverished themselves and, like Goodyer, sacrificed their inherited estates in their efforts to outshow the more fortunate, who had obtained fresh lucrative offices or royal favour. Men of breeding and position begged for petty, even menial, offices connected with the Court for the sake of small salaries. Long waiting was sometimes rewarded: influence sometimes availed: grants of office or estates sometimes ensued: very often nothing occurred. It must be remembered, too, that Donne came of those accustomed to wait upon the Court, and it was therefore natural for him to seek employment there.

Nevertheless, the tedium and irritation involved in suing for Court preferment was recognized and deplored by the very men forced to endure it. Shakespeare cries out against it in Hamlet's phrase 'the insolence of office', and Spenser, like Donne, knew it well:

> 'Full little knowest thou that hast not tried
> What hell it is in suing long to bide:
> To lose good days, that might be better spent;
> To waste long nights in pensive discontent,
> To speed today, to be put back to-morrow:
> To feed on hope, to pine with fear and sorrow;
> To fret thy soul with crosses and with cares;
> To eat thy heart through comfortless despairs;
> To fawn, to crouch, to wait, to ride, to run,
> To spend, to give, to want, to be undone.'[1]

This leads to the interesting question why did Donne never succeed in obtaining the positions of state for which he angled. About this time, so desperate was he for success in any field, that he considered the possibility of escape from the old life into a startling new. He had tried for an appointment in the Queen's household, had aspired to the position of Secretary for Ireland, had suffered unrealized hopes of being sent on an embassy to Venice or the Low Countries, but all to no purpose. Now he applied for an appointment in the newly-founded Colony of Virginia which, after the earlier tentative settlements of Raleigh and his successors, had at length, in 1607, begun to flourish.

To Ann, nurtured in comparative luxury, and with her brood of delicate fledglings, the suggestion must have been a nightmare. The journey in a small ship to unknown, inhospit-

[1]Spenser's *Mother Hubbard's Tale*, 1591.

able shores, far from all those she knew and loved, would be an intolerable adventure. Fortunately for her the projected journey never materialized.

Was it simply ill-fortune dogging the proud footsteps of Donne? Or was there something in his character which prevented the realization of his ambitions? Friends and biographers all agree in describing his charm, and the merits of his intellect, but his irresolution, his complexity, his stubborn honesty and agnostic inclinations all stood in his way, barring him from worldly success. Men are invariably suspicious of one who, talented but highly original in thought, wishes to follow conventional paths. They dislike a gifted person and shield themselves from him as though he might rob them of their complacency. Donne's 'technique' of life was not that of the unthinking subscriber or the insincere devotee. Individual and always impassioned, one of those 'who find it hard to run in harness',[1] it was irksome and distasteful to him to follow the beaten track and to tread in the footsteps of others.

Full of endearing charm to those whom he loved and admired about him, he may have been disdainful, casual, even hurtful to those whom he looked down upon. The gentle, amenable, Tobias side of his nature had its counterpart in a black, Lucifer pride, and beneath, unseen to all but the most penetrating of observers, was the old, repugnant circling of thought, like a cancer nourishing itself from that which at the same time it seeks to destroy, contributing nothing to the constructive side of the nature. Hamlet, caught in the same terrible web of indecision, spinning in ever widening circles of devouring vortices, made those of simpler, more direct calibre around him distrustful, even of his sanity. And it was this discord which held the talented Donne at its mercy, preventing him from blossoming freely in young manhood, delaying his maturity, hindering him from obtaining worldly advancement or accepting ecclesiastical preferment until he was over forty.

[1] Jessop, p. 61.

5

Donne sought for the post in Virginia in 1609 and shortly afterwards Sir George More, softened by the persuasive words of Sir Francis Wooley, who died in the following year, or impressed by Donne's integrity and assiduity, was induced to pay a belated dowry. At last the straitened circumstances were somewhat relaxed.

But before this might be, in the cramped year of 1608, much sorrow came to the Donnes. The letters which survive tell us of the illnesses which attacked the entire family: for Donne there was neuralgic pain which drew his head 'so much awry that mine eye can not follow mine hand', fevers of a malarial sort and signs of future gastric trouble: for Ann, the difficult bearing of children while others lay ill and nearly dying. It was the year's low ebb, the 'world's whole sap' was sunk. To Sir Henry Goodyer Donne poured out his misery in a manner less restrained than that to any other friend:

'And the reason why I did not send an answer to your last week's letter was because it then found me under too great a sadness and at present is thus with me. There is no one person but myself well of the family: I have already lost half a child, and with that mischance of hers, my wife is fallen into such a discomposure as would afflict her too extremely, but that the sickness of all her other children stupefies her; of one of which, in good faith I have not much hope; and these meet with a fortune so ill-provided for physic and such relief, that if God should ease us with burials, I know not how to perform even that: but I flatter myself with this hope, that I am dying too; for I can not waste faster than by such griefs. . . .

From my Hospital at Mitcham,
August 10*th*   JOHN DONNE.'

Even the lighter picture, rare as a glimpse into domesticity, is tinged with the restless gloom which hung over all Donne's thoughts:

'I write from the fire side in my Parler, and in the noise of three gamesome children; and by the side of her, whom because I have transplanted into a wretched fortune, I must labour to disguise that from her by all such honest devices, as giving her my company, and discourse, therefore I steal from her, all the time which I give this letter, and it is therefore that I take so short a list and gallop so fast over it. . . .'[1]

The reproaches of a nature recoiling upon itself are acid indeed: add to this a fretful, ambitious, thwarted inclination and the burden becomes intolerable. There is no outlet for powers which eat their own generator:

> 'They are the mills which grind you, yet you are
> The wind which drives them; and a wasteful war
> Is fought against you, and you fight it.'[2]

In writing of Donne's disabilities it is interesting to note what a physician has said on this subject:

'Donne seems to have been inclined to dwell upon his own illnesses and their symptoms, to consider what they indicated in the past or promised in the future. . . . He had probably no great physical vigour, and was throughout life in that condition of mental and nervous instability which we speak of as neurotic. This led him to dwell upon the ancient discussion as to the nature of health. . . . A man of sound mind and nerves will not be disturbed by such discussions, but will eat his meals, take his exercise, and sleep soundly, careless of what his state may be called by physicians or metaphysicians. . . . Such a person as St. Francis of Assisi will suffer illness without dwelling on it, will drive it from his thoughts and say nothing of it in his writings. The neurotic person dwells to himself and to others on his own feelings and illnesses, is gratified by sympathy and enjoys his own feeling for himself. . . .

This condition is, however, in some of its degrees, compatible with regard for others and the maintenance of friendships, as it was in Donne's case. It often gives a false unity to the morbid conditions of a patient throughout life. In his own idea, such a patient has never been well, and therefore the various occasional attacks . . . from which few men are free are by him felt to be manifestations of one lifelong diseased condition, though often they are as isolated in origin as similar attacks in a man of generally robust health. . . .

[1] *A Vuestra Merced*, Hayward, p. 457.   [2] *5th Satyre*.

H

Behind all is the neurotic constitution which makes the man himself his own lifelong pathological study, and so, in his descriptions, gives a unity of origin to all his illnesses, apparent to him, but not present so far as morbid anatomy is concerned. . . .'[1]

6

Mental strain was another source of melancholia, for the brain which overworks seeks to ease itself by further labour, running in a repetitive fashion and thus burrowing into a second and more serious stage of aridity. Donne's work for Morton had been hairsplitting and exacting, to the point of nightmare, and the whole result, the entire efflux, came out in the writing of *Biathanatos*, the treatise against life itself. The learned men to whom Donne submitted it felt that the earnest piece of jet writing must be full of flaws: with microscopic eyes they scrutinized it but could not detect the fallacious threads.

Biathanatos was a dangerous study. Even in the twentieth century a vindication of suicide would be received with outraged sentiments and voices raised in vociferous protest. How much more delicate must the handling be, before so-called freedom of thought and speech were permitted. The fact that the treatise was meant to be an honest scientific enquiry into the grounds upon which theologians and lawyers condemned self-extinction as mortal sin, and an unlawful act, would not prevent carping critics and fanatics from fastening upon *Biathanatos* as unholy and vicious meat. Donne had already touched upon the theme in prose in his *Paradoxes*— 'Only Cowards dare Die' and 'That all Things Kill Themselves' and in verse, in the *Third Satyre*, in which he condemned it.

[1] In writing his *Life and Letters of Donne*, Sir Edmund Gosse sent excerpts from Donne's writings to Dr. Norman Moore, F.R.C.P. and Lecturer on the Principles and Practice of Medicine to St. Bartholomew's Hospital, who diagnosed Donne's health and causes of death. (Appendix E. Gosse, vol. ii, p. 373.)

The *Paradoxes*, and the poems had been his method of airing his quandaries, and the themes—the inconstancy of women, life under the shadow of mortality, the interrelation of body and soul—were treated with lyric fire, gibing wit, levity or cynicism, as mood and medium meted. Passion redeemed where doctrine and mere cleverness cloyed, but in this, his second prose work and the first of any length, the author was wholly serious. Some argue that he intended to publish *Biathanatos*,[1] others that it was never his intention.[2] His statement in the Preface varies with that made in later letters, as in one to Sir Henry Goodyer, in which he declares he 'never purposed to print it'.[3] My own opinion is that he courageously set out with the idea of possible publication, but as he advanced he realized the severity of censure and punishment awaiting him if he did so; that the work was mainly a prop for his own support, to exonerate him in the eyes of his intimate friends should he ever sink so low as to succumb to the temptation to destroy himself. He 'forbade it both the press and the fire':[4] in other words he had enough common sense to refrain from flaunting it before the eyes of the ecclesiastical censors, yet treasured it as a self-explanatory document upon which he had spent great time and heart-wringing thought. He must also have been conscious that it was a curiosity, that no-one else had so far written anything similar and it was like him to be attracted to the 'steepy, slippery, narrow and obscure.'[5]

The manuscript was not printed in his lifetime. Eleven years after he wrote it he sent a copy to his friends, Sir Robert Ker and Lord Herbert of Cherbury with a letter in which he states that he had sent it to 'some particular friends in both Universities but that not many eyes had read it or no hand

[1] Simpson, p. 154.   [4] Letter to Sir Robert Ker, April 1619.
[2] Gosse, vol. i, p. 258.   [5] *Biathanatos*.
[3] Jessop, quoting Donne, p. 97.

hath passed upon it to copy it'.[1] Donne's son determined to publish it, with little regard for his father's discretion, and the book was licensed for the press in 1644, thirteen years after Donne's death.[2]

For us, its interest lies, not in casuistical brilliance or scholastic learning, nor in Donne's defence to himself of possible action, but in the light which it throws on his abiding neurosis. For long he had dwelt upon and tried to reconcile the problem of life versus death,—more particularly, life versus the so-called holy death of martyrdom, (very often voluntary) and the condemned but equally voluntary one of suicide. Wherein lay the difference? Was it merely a difference in opinion, of attitude, or of uncharitable censure? He set to work to segregate Truth and as usual, the way with him was to 'wrastle', to 'debate and vex it' and he 'abstained not for fear of misinterpretation from the undertaking'.[3] He uses again the simile of the sieve, declaring that there be four sorts of reader: 'Spunges, which attract all without distinguishing; Hour-glasses, which receive and pour out as fast; Bags, which retain only the dregs of the spices, and let the wine escape; and Sieves, which retain the best only.'[4] The 'cribrating, re-cribrating and post-cribrating' process went on, the intellect fretting the emotional soreness beneath.

In the first Part there is a curious reference to Sir Thomas More's consideration of suicide in *Utopia*. For there, 'the priests and magistrates did use to exhort men afflicted with incurable diseases to kill themselves, and that they were obeyed as the interpreters of God's will; but they who killed themselves without giving an account of their reasons to them, were cast out unburied.' This reinforces the texture of his heredity, of his descent from 'the men of suppressed and afflicted religion, accustomed to the despite of death', and from the men of learning querying the problems of evil.

---

[1] *Letters*, 1651, p. 21. Before his going into Germany.　　[2] Simpson, p. 149.
[3] *Biathanatos*—Preface to.　　　　[4] *Biathanatos*—Preface to.

In the second Part, Donne makes a statement which at first appears ridiculous—that the harsh condemnation of suicide by English law is due to the inordinate desire for death in the nation. That there had been, and still existed, a tremendous pull deathwards, a national disregard for life as valuable, no-one can deny. Even foreigners noted this. The Italian astronomer, Cardano, remarked in 1552, that 'the English care little or not at all for death', and this was not entirely a eulogy of English courage.

When suffering is contemplated as the portion of normal life, and when the contemplation is filled rather with curiosity than with compassion or active pity, the emotions become easily blunted. Repulsion is replaced by indifference and indifference by actual interest, heightened to mental enjoyment. The heart has been stifled by the rapacious mind, and an age inured to slow torture, burnings at the stake, hangings, drawings and quarterings, or the condemned being hauled away to the scaffold and gallows as pleasurable spectacles, has lost its native springs of tenderness. At the same time the subject of death begins to hold a fascination for men who are morbidly attracted by the mystery. How best to die,—with what courage, what effrontery, what artlessness, what carelessness,—concerns them: what lies hereafter, the refiner's fire, torpidity, quiescence, or the sun-breathing air of Paradise, in comparison to which this world is a mere prologue of imitation and artificiality—these are the questions which vex and torment the mind.

Shakespeare's *Hamlet* had, when Donne wrote his *Biathanatos*, been enacted six or seven years and the famous soliloquy may have been only too familiar to him. But he could not condense the quandary into a few lines. Donne had been attempting throughout his life to strangle an aspect of himself, hostile to his own life and health, and now, by airing it and dissipating its force, he cleared his own mind and heart.

The whole prose work is, in epitome, a plea for charity, for self-examination, for truth, for the journey towards peace, for the suspension of criticism and moral condemnation. 'Their very severity proceeds from a self guiltiness . . . it is the nature of stiff wickedness, to think that of others which they themselves deserve, and it is all the comfort the guilty have, not to find any innocent.'[1]

In it Donne, the Protestant, stands out clearly at last, declaring the right to personal reasoning, which may be upheld against accepted and dictated opinion. Like Descartes, he began to question what had been handed down as sacred and immutable, determining to throw it aside and build anew on his own foundations, not like the 'uncharitable mis-interpreter' who 'unthriftily demolishes his own house and repairs not another, losing without profit or gain to any',[2] but soundly and carefully. It did not agree with the sensitive man, of whom Walton speaks, that his natural tenderness and charity should be extinguished by a doctrine of hell-fire and torturing condemnation. The revolt which *Biathanatos* typifies was as much a personal one against this unsatisfactory warfare, waging internecine struggle within the breast of John Donne, as against the depressing moral doctrines of the day. The God of the Old Testament, revengeful, hating; God the Father, hatching out miserable sinners, God the Enemy, and God the Traitor, creating pitiful beings doomed before birth, as against the God of true Charity, Lovingkindness and Mercy, tolerant to all sinners, comprehending temptation, whose chiefest advocate was Christ, the great experimenter in the handling of love, this is the inner problem of the work which has been dismissed as a mere example of pedantry and theological casuistry, handed down from the dialecticians of the Middle Ages. It is a bridge from Catholicism to Protestantism, and as such, a record of the transitional stage in Donne's own soul. Which was to triumph, the spiritual democracy of Christian law, or the feudal tyranny of the doc-

[1] *Biathanatos*—Preface to.   [2] *Ibid.*

trines of the Middle Ages? Donne the Scholastic, compound
of theory and intellect, or Donne the Christian, actively concerning himself with human temptation, weakness and
reconciliation?

In our own times, had he been able to dispense with his
superfluity of learning, Donne would have made a first-rate
novelist. He had all the interest in character and in the springs
of action; we know that he kept for many years examples of
'cases of conscience that had concerned his friends, with his
observations and solutions of them'.[1] He would have 'analysed with morbid and relentless skill'[2] the frailities of his
protagonists, but since he was above all a man who lived fully,
avidly and passionately, not 'cloistered in contemplative seclusion',[2] he would have sympathized with their predicaments
and carried his readers forward, as later he carried his audiences under the cross of old St. Paul's, in a fever of curiosity
and partisanship.

7

The origin of *Pseudo-Martyr* was somewhat less personal
and secretive. It was well known that King James, although
he was not as fastidious about his public ablutions as witnesses might wish,—('His skin was as soft as tafta sarsnet,
which felt so because he never washt his hands, onlie rubbed
his fingers' ends slightly with the wet end of a napkin'[3])—
was more than fastidious about his table conversations. He
liked being read to while he ate but preferred to be 'ever in
chase about some disputable doubts, which he would wind
and turn about with the most stabbing objections that ever I
heard. His table was a trial of Wits'.[4] This pedant of a Sovereign therefore surrounded himself at meal times with men
of learning who had to survive a kind of 'viva voce examin-

[1] Walton, p. 62.   [2] Simpson, p. 157.
[3] Rye, p. 277. Quoting Sir James Balfour's *Annales of Scotland*, ii, 108.
[4] *Life of the Lord Keeper Williams*, Hacket, p. 38.

ation',[1] a severe test for those who had not ready tongues and primed minds. At one of these oral debates Donne was present, introduced, it is thought, by his friend, Lord Hay, afterwards Earl of Carlisle, whom Donne tells us that he met through Francis Bacon. A dispute concerning the Oaths of Supremacy and Allegiance arose and the King adroitly engaged Donne in a discussion of the reasons 'usually urged against the taking of those Oaths'. He 'apprehended such a clearness and validity in his stating the questions, and his answers to them, that his Majesty commanded him to bestow some time in drawing the arguments into a method and then to write his answers to them: and having done that, not to send, but to be his own messenger, and bring them to him'.[2] This he accomplished in the short time of six weeks.

But the swiftness with which Donne complied is not so astonishing if one realizes that the subject was one after his own heart. The Oaths of Allegiance and Supremacy had been the cup of bitter hemlock which his forbears had been asked to drink and which he himself had barely evaded with serpentine sinuosity as a student at the Universities; his whole life had hung upon its dangerous lips. His work with Thomas Morton had familiarized him with erudite and obscure advocates for and against the points in dispute between Papacy and the English Church, and *Biathanatos* was stamped with a face similar to that of *Pseudo-Martyr*, the coin of royal command. In fact, the one was the obverse of the other, for *Biathanatos* argues that self-destruction is wanton and unlawful, with certain exceptions depending upon the general good or the glory of God, and *Pseudo-Martyr* that the martyr's death, urged by the Jesuits, is only another form of wasteful and wicked self-annihilation not profiting the community or pleasing God. Self-inflicted death is the theme of both works, played upon in different keys, the first considered from the point of view of the individual and the second from

[1] Jessop, p. 69.   [2] Walton, pp. 23–24.

that of the loyal and conscientious citizen. 'Who but a mono-maniac would read *Pseudo-Martyr* through?' asks Jessop in a deprecatory mood,[1] yet at that time, when controversy was the breath of life for the established Church, for prelates and divines, for their Jesuit and Catholic opponents, it was an invaluable production, so forceful and so closely reasoned that not a single combatant came forth to dispute it.

The title was not original, for Bacon had used the term in 1583 when he wrote of Campion. With truth and humility Campion had declared at his trial that from matters of state and policy of the realm he did 'gladly sequester and estrange his thoughts', but Bacon, prosecuting furiously, without proof, denied such innocence and added . . . 'whereby may appear what trust is to be given to the words of such *Pseudo-Martyrs*.'[2]

It was the first of Donne's published works and it brought with it the conferring of his Master's degree from Oxford University in April of the year of publication (1610). Con-vocation permitted him to take the degree while duly acknow-ledging that he had previously failed to take his B.A., but this was a pure technicality since it must have been well known that Donne had attended both Universities and fulfilled the ordinary requirements.

A limited public received the work well. It was far too in-tellectual and casuistical to be read by the masses and was not intended for them: it never ran into a second edition and was never reprinted or translated, but, excepting for one attack of negligible force, it received praise for its moderation and general scope. Possibly Morton's benign influence came to bear but the fact that Donne, of all people, was able to stand like a Colossus with one foot in the Catholic camp in which

[1] Letter to Evelyn Simpson. See n. page 166, *Study of the Prose Works of John Donne*.

[2] 'Execution of Justice in England for Maintenance of Public and Christian Peace against certain Stirrers of Sedition. December 1583.'

he was bred and the other in the Protestant, to which he inclined, engendered moderation and thoughtfulness in those
whose minds, like his, had been tossed upon the fractious
waves of indecision, but who, unlike him, had not the time,
knowledge or ability to 'survey and digest the whole body of
Divinity controverted between ours and the Roman Church'.[1]
The reasoning side of his nature which loved a scientific approach, and which his years at Cambridge had done much to
foster, helped Donne to approach the thorny problem with
this unimpassioned ingenuity, none the less sincere for its
lack of warmth.

Only once does he allow the emotion, underlying the whole
theme so close to his heart, to carry him away into a flood of
words, comparable to the finest passages in the King James
Version of the Bible, which was at that very time being
patiently compiled by a band of forty-nine scholars, amongst
whom was Donne's good friend, John King, the future
Bishop of London. (Donne did not, of course, take part in the
undertaking since he was not yet in Holy Orders.)

'I call to witness against you, those whose testimony God
himself hath accepted. Speak then and testify, O you glorious and
triumphant Army of Martyrs, who enjoy now a permanent
triumph in Heaven, which knew the voice of your Shepherd, and
stayed till he called, and went then with all alacrity. . . .

That which Christian religion hath added to the old philosophy,
which was to do no wrong, is in this point no more than this, to
keep our mind in an habitual preparation of suffering wrong, but
not to urge and provoke and importune affliction so much as to
make those punishments just, which otherwise had been wrong-
fully inflicted upon us. We are *not* sent into this world *to suffer*,
but *to do*, and to perform the offices of society required by our
several callings. . . .'[2]

[1] *Pseudo-Martyr*, Preface.

[2] *Pseudo-Martyr*. The full titles of these works are: 'Biathanatos, a
Declaration of that Paradox or Thesis, that Self-Homicide is not so Naturally Sinne that it may never be otherwise, Wherein the Nature and the
Extent of all these Lawes, which seem to be violated by this Act, are diligently Surveyed,' and 'Pseudo-Martyr, Wherein out of Certaine Proposi-

Thus did he remain loyal to the glorious company who had suffered for their consciences like a shadowy army 'behind, around, before, about' him, and yet clear, with equivocal ingenuity, the springs of his own natural conscience which told him that the life-force was good, that men need not vex, torment and destroy themselves for man-made doctrines; and thus he strengthened his own hesitant irresolution.

8

Ignatius His Conclave is quite a different kettle of fish. The three prose works are all remarkable if only for one thing —that they are all books on religious themes, written by a layman who rigidly refused to go into the Church. *Biathanatos* was a serious justification by Donne, to himself, of the 'greatest and most hazardous of all cases of conscience,'[1] *Pseudo-Martyr* was a temperate plea written, if not expressly by royal command, at least for the eye of the Sovereign, whereas *Ignatius* is the most daring piece of invective and scurrility. It is 'a squib . . . composed of bitter jests and skirmishings'[2] hurled in particular at the Jesuits; 'a fierce little diatribe.'[3] In it, Donne returns to the old vein of satire and one feels that it is a relief to him to gibe at, and to ridicule the aggressive and provocative set which stood for ambitious intolerance and ultimate supremacy. He tosses his jests about, throwing them up mischievously as a sea-lion tosses its food in play, either from sheer delight or from an excess of nervous energy which it dispels in this manner. Vitality was coming back to Donne, after his spirits had been to 'the bed's foot,' and mental health succeeded the period of narrow gloom in which he had studied both the 'steepy and slippery'[4] as well as 'the

---

tions and Gradations, this Conclusion is evicted: That Those which are of the Romane Religion in This Kingdome, may and Ought to Take The Oath of Allegiance.'

[1] Jessop, p. 62.   [2] Gosse, i, p. 254.
[3] Jessop, p. 68.   [4] *Biathanatos.*

stony and sullen'.[1] The writing was shortly to be followed by more verse, his youthful medium, and thus the moods, emotional variations, and channels for their expression, interplayed and overlapped. This interplay, this overlapping, is only another proof of the co-existence in Donne of the serious and sportive, the ecclesiastical and secular, the poetic and sterner prosaic, running side by side and developing unequally.

Ignatius displays Donne's attraction to the new and expanding thought around him, for it is here (as well as in *The First Anniversary*) that he shows us most fully his interest in astronomy. It appeared in 1611, in both Latin and English, and is chiefly interesting because of this concern, exceptional in Jacobean literature. Galileo and Kepler were then just rising to open fame and Donne even prophesies the official condemnation of the Copernican theory by the Church of Rome and the punishment of Galileo. Copernicus, Tycho Brahe, Paracelsus and Machiavelli in turn, with other eminent characters, wander through the chambers of Hell, disputing with Lucifer, and the satire ends in a riot, caused by Ignatius Loyola, who has lately been beatified, attempting to dispossess one of the Popes of his seat.

The cloud of martyrs began to shadow Donne's mind less and less with their significance:

'Lucifer . . . observed . . . that all his troops, which were many, subtle and busy, set up their bristles, grumbled, and compacted themselves into one body, gathered, produced and urged all their evidence, whatsoever they had done, or suffered. There, the English Legion . . . which Campion led . . . was fiercer than all the rest. And as though there had been such a second martyrdom to have been suffered or as though they might have put off their Immortalities, they offered themselves to any employment.'

The holy ones whom Donne had been brought up to reverence and emulate have now become not only powerless over him, but actually something which he can ridicule: their

[1] *Pseudo-Martyr*, Preface.

LUCY, COUNTESS OF BEDFORD

seat is not heaven, among the blest, nor the penumbra of Purgatory, but Hell itself. Much as one may regret this rather tasteless show of spleen—and Donne, the supreme egotist, was markedly insensitive to others in his writing, making puns in his sermons, coarse allegations in his love poems and cynical asides in the midst of ecstasy—the treatment is indicative of the final dethronement of the martyrs, at least as an intellectual influence in his life. Emotionally he was never to be anything but their prisoner, pursued with inquisitorial violence.

9

Upon this scene of gloomy introspection and intolerably learned effusion there comes the softening influence of one of the loveliest of Jacobean patronesses, Lucy, Countess of Bedford. She was the daughter of John Harington of Exton in Rutland, and had married Edward Russell, third Earl of Bedford, before she was twenty.[1] In 1608 she would therefore be about thirty-three and Donne thirty-five. She had been a lady-in-waiting under Queen Elizabeth, had gone north to welcome the new King and Queen, and had been made Lady of the Chamber upon their accession. Like the goddesses, she had beauty, talent and position, but what was more unusual in court favourites, a serious side to her nature, breaking out now and again into avowedly religious expression. The elaborate Masques, for which Daniel and Ben Jonson wrote and Inigo Jones designed, claimed her as an actress and the Spanish Ambassador especially desired her presence at courtly entertainments.[2] No-one, more than Queen Elizabeth herself, had had so much literary homage paid to her, for Lucy was the 'crowning rose' of verse throughout late Elizabethan and early Jacobean days and it speaks well for her that she did not incur hatred and malice from her rivals for her universal admiration. Jonson, Daniel, Drayton, Florio and

[1] In 1594.   [2] In 1603. Grierson, vol. ii, p. 153.

Donne were all her protégés in an age when the reputable poet disdained to write for mere monetary remuneration, and her approbation meant much to those who proffered their verses.

The making of gardens, as well as of verse, was one of her happiest ways of refreshing herself. Those at Twickenham, where she lived in a manner only rivalled by royalty, inspired one of Donne's best known lyrics and Sir William Temple, no mean judge, commended those she made in her next home, Moor Park in Hertfordshire.[1]

As early as the year of his marriage Donne was writing of her to his friend Goodyer, mentioning the death of her only son. He knew and worshipped her distantly but a closer intimacy sprang up between them in the Mitcham days, when Donne's constricted mind and circumstances pled for the recreation she could give. At Twickenham he found ease, wealth, courtly manners, mental stimulation from fellow poets, and, above all, the thing which he could never be long without, admiration and compassion from a feminine source. The women whom the maturing man admired were all great ladies, but not mere 'painted, frizzled, powdered vizards'.[2] They had the beauty, intelligence, sympathy and aristocratic mien which he needed as a complement to his own gifts and bearing. Although his poems to them carry the stamp of the conventional adoration of the admirer, they bear, as well, a personal note of gratitude and implication of pleasant restoring intimacy. The two women whom he admired the most had also a strain of goodness, of essential seriousness and worth which fed him.

To the Countess of Bedford he writes:

> 'the reasons why you are lov'd by all
> Grow infinite.'

He calls her 'good' and speaks of the natural *Balsamum*, or healing compound, which nourishes her and wards off evil

---

[1] She went here in 1617. Grierson, vol. ii, p. 153.
[2] Birch's *Court and Times of James the 1st*, vol. i, p. 162.

around her. This is equivalent to a spiritual good, an autonomous wisdom directing her thoughts and actions, which maintains its balance and influences her to useful and pleasant being. The question of whether good might overcome evil was one of Donne's everlasting preoccupations, handled early in the *Paradoxes*, and later in the *Sermons*, at the extremities of his life:

'Something there is in the Soul of man too, that hath some proportion and analogy to this Balsamum of the Body . . . she hath a perfume, a fragrancy, a sweet savour in her-self . . . a natural and untaught hatred, and detestation of that which is evil.'[1]

In his second *Verse Letter* to the Countess, as in the first, the relative merits of good and evil arise, with reference to the 'entangling labyrinths of Schools' of religion and philosophy, and Donne declares that he finds the lady 'all record and prophecy', which even this paragon of women must have found it difficult to emulate. In two other *Verse Letters* addressed to her he indulges in some of his most difficult erudition, for when Donne was moved the intellect was heightened and sharpened by the emotions which fired it. But it is in the *Nocturnal on Saint Lucy's Day*, written four years later when she was desperately ill, that he sings the Countess' praise most profoundly, and the measure of his gloom at her expected death is the measure of his devotion to her. It is impossible to read this annihilating poem without feeling the sincerity underlying the scholastic doctrines handled in it: the sable pall which hangs over it is steeped in negation and misery.

How Donne met her does not matter. It may have been at Court before his marriage, it may have been through the offices of Henry Goodyer, who was later attached to her household, or most likely of all, through her first cousin, Lady Huntingdon, who was married while Donne was at York House. She remained steadfast to him in adversity, some-

[1] *Sermons 80*, 51.

times paying his debts in the courtly but unsatisfactory fashion of the period, (since payments could not be counted on by the petitioner,) and in August 1608 she stood god-mother to a daughter of Donne's who took her name.

Her talent in writing was considerable. If, as some think, she wrote the elegy, 'Death be not proud, thy hand gave not this blow,'[1] she was an apt pupil of her more competent protégé, but 'her religion', therein expressed, 'was of a simpler, more pietistic cast than Donne's own in its earlier phase.'[2]

Lady Huntingdon's conjectured part in influencing the Lord Keeper to be lenient with Donne at the time of his marriage has already been touched on. She had, like Lady Bedford, the 'commandment of high birth', but perhaps not her 'persuasive eloquence of beauty' or the 'advantage of the furniture of arts and languages' to such a degree.[3] She too, was a Court favourite, and a patroness of arts and letters and she, too, wrote frequently to Donne.

Next to the Countess of Bedford, Magdalen Herbert must count as the most influential of Donne's feminine friends. The mother of Edward Herbert, afterwards Lord Herbert of Cherbury, and George Herbert, the poet, she was shortly to be married to a staid young man, nearly half her age, Sir John Danvers. Donne met her, either through her eldest son, who had been a ward of Sir George More's, or through the Lord Keeper who may have sent him on business to her home in Oxfordshire. In 1608 she was living in town. One imagines her as having a sweet, grave bearing, for the Ninth *Elegy*, written to her about this time,[4] begins:

'No Spring, nor Summer Beauty hath such grace,
As I have seen in one Autumnal face':

[1], [2] Grierson, vol. ii, p. 153.

[3] Letter from Donne to Lady Bedford, 1608–1614. Nonesuch Edition, p. 461.

[4] See Grierson, vol. ii, pp. 62–63.

and later, in the same poem he describes her expression:

> 'Here, where still Evening is; not noon, nor night;
> Where no voluptuousness, yet all delight.
> In all her words, unto all hearers fit,
> You may at Revels, you at Council, sit.'

Unlike the Countess of Bedford, Magdalen Herbert had a great many children and her facility in handling them may have attracted Donne as a mirror of Ann's behaviour, reflected in a different setting. He was on easier terms of intimacy with her than with his other patronesses and paid her a warm and genuine compliment when he wrote:

> 'This day I came to town, and to the best part of it, your house.'[1]

10

In March 1608/9 Donne's probing and self-examination culminated in his first religious poems. A group of sonnets called *La Corona*, a longer poem called *Upon The Annunciation and Passion*, *The Litany*, and possibly *The Cross* were all written about this time, their 'intellectual, tormented, wire-drawn style'[2] indicating the tortuous path Donne was treading on his ascent to self-reconciliation. He sent the Sonnets, including one specifically addressed to her, to Magdalen Herbert and to a young man of poetic ability, who became another of his patrons, the Earl of Dorset, whose bride was a first cousin of Edward Russell, Earl of Bedford. This was nearly six years before Donne took Holy Orders. What was the incentive of the poems besides illness and introspection? Surely, the growth of the seed lying naked and foetal within.

Donne assures us in the *Pseudo-Martyr* that he had been able to take his stand upon religious matters only after much study, humility and prayer. The first outcome of these pains was the effusion in both prose and verse of an astringent,

[1] Letter, July 23rd, 1607.   [2] Grierson, vol. ii, pp. 225–229.

I

somewhat barren style, akin to the roughened temper of his mind which attempted to portray itself before the man was emotionally and intellectually harmonized. The tasteless conceits, the sensuous phraseology show that their author had not reached spiritual fusion. The fire did not yet burn clear and intense, there was green wood and stubborn fuel to be consumed, before the embers should give out their full heat.

What was Donne's inheritance in English devotional writing? He had behind him the whole mass of Middle English verse and prose from the Conquest down to the fifteenth century—legends of the lives of the saints, pious tales of the miracles, prophetic writings, homilies, visions, and visits to the underworld, the works of religious information and instruction, allegories, proverbs and precepts, translations and paraphrases of the Bible, dialogues and debates, religious lyrics, hymns and prayers, the miracle plays and moralities and especially, standing out like monoliths from the scree of anonymous pieces, the work of Langland, Rolle, Wycliffe, Gower and Chaucer. Between the death of Chaucer and Donne's birth came Lydgate, Dunbar, Malory, with his loving concern for the Grail theme, and the Oxford reformers, amongst them Sir Thomas More. From the Pre-Conquest work of Bede and Caedmon to Donne's collateral ancestor is a far cry, covering the best part of a thousand years. What influence and inspiration did Donne draw from these literary forefathers of his? Scarcely any, it would seem. The man who stood in the age of shifting emphasis from Catholic to Protestant thought, a transitional experimenter, turns his back upon this heritage. He pays no heed to the work of contemporaries or near forerunners such as the gentle Catholic, Southwell, or Giles Fletcher. Instead, he looks to the Church fathers and to Spain for his influence.

II

But between the tentative, strangled efforts visible in the first sacred poems, and the sensuous ecstasy of the later lay much experience.

In 1610, Donne became acquainted with a Suffolk man of wealth, Sir Robert Drury, who had been knighted by Essex at the age of seventeen at the siege of Rouen, and who, serving in the Low Countries, had distinguished himself by bringing off Sir Francis Vere from the field when his horse had been shot under him. Courtier, traveller and Member of Parliament, he had married Francis Bacon's niece. Lady Drury and her brother, Sir Edmund Bacon, were patrons, both of Donne's rival satirist, Joseph Hall, and of Donne's great friend, Sir Henry Wotton.

Sir Robert and Lady Drury had an only child, a daughter, already destined in their minds to become the wife of Prince Henry, and, possibly, future Queen of England. But at fifteen Elizabeth died and her death moved Donne to write for her first a *Funeral Elegy*, in the following year, *An Anatomy of the World* (or *The First Anniversary*), and twelve months later *Of the Progress of the Soul* (or *Second Anniversary*). These extraordinary poems, which Ben Jonson told Donne, 'it had been something if it had been written of the Virgin Marie', and that they were 'profane and full of blasphemies',[1] which in their excessive imagery and ingeniousness offended his former patronesses, were given to the father. Sir Robert in his unrestrained pride and grief was touched: he admired Donne for the very extravagance of his eulogies. Here was a man, a poet of note, a courtier and traveller, the father of daughters, like himself, who understood the magnitude of his loss and commemorated his child in unmatched verse. Not being a poet himself he did not know how the minds and hearts of poets worked: he could not, I am certain,

[1] *Conversations with Drummond of Hawthornden*, 3.

have understood Donne when he assured Ben Jonson that, in the *Anniversaries*, he 'described the Idea of Woman, and not as she was',[1] nor have comprehended the subtle phrases which Donne used in *Verse Letters* to the Countess of Bedford and others to explain away his apparent inconstancy.

But the amazing fact is that Donne had, as far as we know, never seen Elizabeth Drury. His extravagant praises of her were not those of a realist, or a lover, or actual admirer, and his former patronesses were foolish to interpret the *Anniversaries* in this light. They were the poems of an idealist, and he expressly says so. With open eyes he transformed the abstract feeling which he had for the dead child into homage towards an ideal beauty. When Michelangelo wrote:

'The love wherewith I love thee hath no heart',

or a modern poet:

> 'Love not as do the flesh-imprisoned men
> Whose dreams are of a bitter-bought caress. . . .
> But love thou nothing thou wouldst love the less
> If henceforth ever hidden from thy ken.
> Love but the formless and eternal Whole. . . .'[2]

it does not mean that they were heartless or incapable of human passion, but rather that, for the moment, they were not idolators, but worshippers of a vision emanating from past experience and emotion. In these poems Donne did not, as in his early love poems, class himself with those who love only that she loves again'. He was done with adolescence, passion, and the longing for reciprocation. His mind went constantly deeper, away from love, away from distracting passion, to the root of life and truth and essential being, and the formal, despairing laments over Elizabeth Drury were but a frame upon which to train the profuse growth of his own mental germin-

---

[1] *Conversations with Drummond of Hawthornden*, 3.

[2] Santayana, Sonnet VI.

ation. The world is, he declares, 'a lame cripple,' 'a dry cinder,' 'an ugly monster', 'a wan ghost,' or 'fragmentary rubbidge not worth a thought,' always prefaced by the reiterated statement of the heavy fact of death, thus:

> 'She, she is dead; she's dead: when thou knowest this
> Thou knowest how trifling poor a thing man is. . . .'

Elizabeth Drury's death and the barrenness of the world are mere pegs upon which to hang all manner of things which interest Donne—his scholastic knowledge, his struggling philosophy, his nascent religion and admonitions to his own soul, as well as his keen observation of all that was new and startling in current science. As early as 1609 he had written to Sir Henry Goodyer of 'the new astronomy'; he had spoken freely of the sensational revolution in the heavens in *Ignatius*, and now the recent discoveries of Kepler and Galileo are echoed once more in the *Anniversaries*. No other seventeenth-century poet, with the exception of Fulke Greville shows such an appreciation of their significance.[1]

Here and there are passages of beauty, such as the description of Paradise in the *First Anninersary*, or in the *Second*, the lines:

> 'Think then, my soul, that death is but a groom,
> Which brings a taper to the outward room,
> Whence thou spiest first a little glimmering light,
> And after brings it nearer to thy sight:
> For such approaches doth Heaven make in death.'

But on the whole, as poetry, the *Anniversaries* break down. They are 'an astonishing constellation of absurdities and beauties, of profound thoughts and maddening conceits'.[2] What had become of the lyric poet? The mistress of his youth was merging into that of his age—Poetry into Divinity,

[1] See 'Donne and His Age' by Theodore Spencer in *A Garland for Donne*, p. 196, and Evelyn Simpson's 'Donne's Paradoxes and Problems' in the same, p. 42.

[2] Gosse, i, p. 275.

is Donne's description of the metamorphosis. Spontaneity
and passion were giving place to learning, querying, and a
search for a new philosophy of life which might soothe and
stabilize. He began to woo another world in disillusionment
of this. Much as one may regret the loss of the early
passionate intensity, the character of the seed sown, the
rising of the sap, the direction of the current all pointed to
the necessity for this painful, rather arid period before the
full ripening should be apparent. The magnificent note of
authority in the closing lines is strangely prophetic:

> 'Thou art the Proclamation; and I am
> The Trumpet, at whose voice the people came.'

12

Sir Robert Drury was both flattered and touched and his
gratitude took the very practical form of offering Donne and
his family a home in palatial quarters in Drury Lane. Here,
surrounded by gardens, and looking out on Temple Bar,
Donne found himself at last installed in affluence, living not
only rent-free, but with a man reputed to be of sympathetic
nature, who shared his 'joys and sorrows and was also a
cherisher of his studies'.[1]

No doubt the man of wealth, tiring of the advantages
brought by means and position, unanchored in life by the
sudden shock of his daughter's death, looked to Donne for
philosophy, for religion even—something which would en-
able him to support grief and the loss of the realization of his
ambitions which must have played an absorbing part in his
worldly outlook. In the autumn of 1611, more than a year
after Elizabeth's death, Sir Robert determined to travel and
begged Donne to acccompany him and Lady Drury. The
decision was a sudden one and Walton relates with touching
simplicity the disastrous effect which it had upon Ann:

[1] Walton, p. 18.

'. . . this desire was suddenly made known to his wife, who was then with child, and otherwise under so dangerous a habit of body, as to her health, that she professed an unwillingness to allow him any absence from her; saying, *Her divining soul boded her some ill in his absence*; and therefore desired him not to leave her. This made Mr. Donne lay aside all thoughts of the journey, and really to resolve against it. But Sir Robert became restless in his persuasions for it, and Mr. Donne was so generous as to think he had sold his liberty, when he received so many charitable kindnesses from him, and told his wife so; who did therefore, with an unwilling willingness, give a faint consent to the journey, which was proposed to be but for two months; for about that time they determined their return. Within a few days after this resolve, the ambassador, Sir Robert, and Mr. Donne, left London, and were, the twelfth day, got all safe to Paris. Two days after their arrival there, Mr. Donne was left alone in that room, in which Sir Robert, and he, and some other friends had dined together. To this place Sir Robert returned within half an hour; and as he left, so he found, Mr. Donne alone; but in such an ecstasy, and so altered as to his looks, as amazed Sir Robert to behold him; insomuch, that he earnestly desired Mr. Donne to declare what had befallen him in the short time of his absence. To which Mr. Donne was not able to make a present answer; but, after a long and perplexed pause, did at last say, 'I have seen a dreadful vision since I saw you; I have seen my dear wife pass twice by me through this room, with her hair hanging about her shoulders, and a dead child in her arms: this I have seen since I saw you.' To which Sir Robert replied, 'Sure, Sir, you have slept since I saw you; and this is the result of some melancholy dream, which I desire you to forget, for you are now awake.' To which Mr. Donne's reply was, 'I cannot be surer that I now live, than that I have not slept since I saw you: and I am as sure that at her second appearing she stopped, and looked me in the face, and vanished.' Rest and sleep had not altered Mr. Donne's opinion the next day; for he then affirmed this vision with a more deliberate, and so confirmed a confidence, that he inclined Sir Robert to a faint belief that the vision was true,—It is truly said that desire and doubt have no rest; and it proved so with Sir Robert; for he immediately sent a servant to Drewry-house, with a charge to hasten back, and to bring him word, whether Mrs. Donne were alive; and if alive, in what condition she was as to her health. The twelfth day the messenger returned with this account—That he found, and left, Mrs. Donne very sad, and sick in her bed; and that, after a long and dangerous labour, she had been delivered of a dead child. And, upon examination, the abortion proved to be the same day, and about the very hour, that Mr. Donne affirmed he saw her pass by him in his chamber.

This is a relation that will beget some wonder; and it well may, for most of our world are at present possessed of an opinion that visions and miracles are ceased. And though it is most certain, that two lutes being both strung and tuned to an equal pitch, and then one played upon, the other, that is not touched, being laid upon a table at a fit distance, will, like an echo to a trumpet, warble a faint audible harmony in answer to the same tune; yet many will not believe there is any such thing as a sympathy of souls: and I am well pleased that every reader do enjoy his own opinion.'[1]

This experience resembles Ben Jonson's 'vision' at the time of his son's death some years before (1603).

'When the King came into England, at that time the pest was in London, he (Ben Jonson) being in the country at Sir Robert Cotton's house with old Camden, he saw in a vision his eldest son, then a child and at London, appear unto him with the mark of a bloody cross on his forehead as if he had been cut with a sword, at which, amazed, he prayed unto God, and in the morning he came to Mr. Camden's chamber to tell him, who persuaded him that it was but an apprehension of his fantasy at which he should not be dejected. In the meantime comes there letters from his wife of the death of that boy in the plague. He appeared to him, he said, of a manly shape and of that growth that he thinks he shall be at the resurrection.'[2]

One is left to wonder whether the intuitive powers of our ancestors were more highly developed or whether we more readily discount and explain away such phenomena. It will be remembered that Sir Robert Cotton was the antiquarian to whom Donne appealed for work, when imprisoned after his marriage, two years before Ben lost the boy of seven, whom he called the 'child of his right hand', and his 'best piece of poetry'.

[1] Walton, pp. 18–20.
[2] *Conversations with Drummond of Hawthornden*, 13.

Thus Donne's child conceived in opulence and relaxation from worry fared less well than those more grudgingly born, for it died at birth and Ann lay at the gates of death. It was a period of agonizing suspense for Donne. Separated from his wife for the first time in many years, he felt more closely drawn to her than he had been for some time past when his own dejected state had preoccupied him. Her premonition at parting, the distance from London to Paris, the long time necessary for the sending and receiving of messages, must have been wearing factors. He writes restrainedly to a friend:

'I have received no syllable, neither from herself nor by any other, how my wife hath passed her danger; nor do I know whether I am increased by the birth of a child, or diminished by the loss of a wife.'[1]

He wrote many letters to draw himself from his sorrow and to remain in touch with English friends whom he begs to keep him in good favour with his prime patroness, Lucy, Countess of Bedford. From Amiens, where the Drurys delayed some time, he spoke of political, religious and courtly matters. It was a tedious period, despite the distractions of foreign travel, for he remained unsatisfied in his future prospects and in the harnessing of his ability to outward and gratifying ends.

'I am now in the afternoon of my life, and then it is unwholesome to sleep. It is ill to look back, or give over in a course; but worse never to set out.'[2]

While still at Amiens he determined to write to his old friend Thomas Morton and ask his advice about adopting the practice of Law:

'. . . whether, taking the degree of Doctor in that profession . . . it might not be conducible and advantageous unto him to practise at home in the Arches, London. Unto whom the Dean then returned him answer, that in his judgment, he thought the Ministry

---

[1] To Sir G. F., April 1612. Gosse, i, p. 305.
[2] Letter to my Lord George Herbert, Nov. 1611. Gosse i, p. 283.

in the Church of God would be safer, and fitter for him: whereupon he desisted from further prosecution of those studies.'[1]

One more narcotic was thereupon abandoned.

Much against his wishes and while he was still on the Continent with his patrons, in 1611 and 1612 the *Anniversaries* were published. None of his other poems had yet been formally printed and the publication did not enhance his reputation either as poet or theologian.

In Paris, in the spring of 1612, Donne suffered one of his attacks of intestinal disorder, but the unhappy trio continued their travels. From Spa they passed to Maastricht, Cleves, Louvain and the Palatinate, destined to become the home of the Princess Elizabeth, to which he would return seven years later.

In July he was in a hurry to be home. He speaks of 'sneaking into London about the end of August' with obvious relish, and of 'running fast through Antwerp and some parts of Holland' before he can return.[2] At last, in September the Drurys were back in London and the eleven months of tedium, of discomfort, of altered sights and sounds, of enforced separation from his wife, of the writing of apologetic Verse Letters to his patrons and chronicle letters to his friends, of illness, of inward contemplation and of anticipation were ended.

Two months later both Donne and the nation were plunged into grief: the country by the loss of a true favourite, and Donne by the almost fatal illness of Lucy, Countess of Bedford.

13

The only children of James the 1st and Anne of Denmark to survive to maturity were Henry, Elizabeth and Charles. Prince Henry grew easily into manhood without any of those

[1] Richard Baddily, Secretary to the Bishop of Durham, in *The Life of Dr. Thomas Morton*. See Simpson, p. 25.
[2] Letter to George Gerrard, July 1612.

apparent hesitancies and deferential tendencies which marked the early years of the younger Charles. Gifted with a sincere and thoughtful character, Henry, who had been created Prince of Wales in 1610, was the favourite of the people. He tilted and rode at the ring, was a keen player of tennis and showed agility in dancing, but he stood low in the eyes of his royal father because he did not care for hunting. Even in adolescence the Prince showed a discerning mind and writers of experience treated him with deference and relished his judgment. Ben Jonson dedicated his *Masque of Queens* to him, having furnished it at his request; and Chapman, his *Iliad*: Sir Walter Raleigh comforted himself in his imprisonment with the Prince's interest in his *History of the World*. Drayton, and Donne's vagabond friend Coryat, who had walked half over the globe and then hung up his shoes in his native Somerset church, were his protégés, as well as the Admiral's Company of Players.

To him the Puritans, of whom his father was afraid since their extreme views might carry the control of church affairs out of his hands, looked for leadership. The contest between Anglicanism and Puritanism threatened to take as bitter a place in seventeenth century public life as that between Catholicism and Protestantism had done in the preceding century. But the ambitions of the Puritan party and royal match-makers at home and abroad were disappointed in November of 1612, for at the age of eighteen Prince Henry died. The funeral ceremonies were long and upon them were lavished all the ornamentation and drama known to the period. Donne was amongst those contributing Funeral Elegies. At this sombre form of expression he was not a novice, since the one for the royal victim was his fifth. His friend Edward Herbert added another, and Donne's excuse for his own lamentable production was that he wrote it 'to match Sir Edward's in obscureness'.[1]

[1] *Conversations with Drummond of Hawthornden*, 7.

Although some suspected Rochester, the King's favourite, of having poisoned the Prince, the real cause of his death was typhoid fever,—'that common complaint of an age of bad drains.'[1] The same vile illness attacked Lucy, Countess of Bedford, in the month of Prince Henry's death.

'My Lady Bedford, last night about one of the clock, became suddenly, and has continued ever since, speechless, and is past all hopes, though yet alive,'[2]

wrote Donne's friend, the young Earl of Dorset, at the end of November. The severity of the seizure indicates that she had been ill some time before this letter was written; the fever was virulent and the attack severe and prolonged. In December her life might still have been despaired of. Donne's dejection is mirrored in the following poem, written upon the shortest day of the year:

A Nocturnal upon S. Lucy's Day,
being the shortest day.

'Tis the year's midnight, and it is the day's,
Lucy's, who scarce seven hours herself unmasks,
   The Sun is spent, and now his flasks
   Send forth light squibs, no constant rays;
     The world's whole sap is sunk:
The general balm th'hydroptique earth hath drunk,
Whither, as to the bed's-feet, life is shrunk,
Dead and interr'd; yet all these seem to laugh,
Compar'd with me, who am their Epitaph.

Study me then, you who shall lovers be
At the next world, that is, at the next Spring:
   For I am every dead thing,
   In whom love wrought new Alchemy.
     For his art did express
A quintessence even from nothingness,
From dull privations, and lean emptiness,
He ruin'd me, and I am re-begot
Of absence, darkness, death; things which are not.

---

[1] Grierson, vol. ii, p. 10.   [2] Quoted by Grierson, vol. ii, p. 10.

All others, from all things, draw all that's good,
Life, soul, form, spirit, whence they being have;
   I, by love's limbec, am the grave
   Of all, that's nothing. Oft a flood
     Have we two wept, and so
Drown'd the whole world, us two; oft did we grow
To be two Chaoses, when we did show
Care to ought else; and often absences
Withdrew our souls, and made us carcases.

But I am by her death, (which word wrongs her)
Of the first nothing, the Elixir grown;
   Were I a man, that I were one,
   I needs must know; I should prefer,
     If I were any beast,
Some ends, some means; Yea plants, yea stones detest,
And love; All, all some properties invest;
If I an ordinary nothing were,
As shadow, a light, and body must be here.

But I am None; nor will my Sun renew.
You lovers, for whose sake, the lesser Sun
   At this time to the Goat is run
   To fetch new lust, and give it you,
     Enjoy your summer all;
Since she enjoys her long night's festival,
Let me prepare towards her, and let me call
This hour her Vigil, and her Eve, since this
Both the year's, and the day's deep midnight is.

Fortunately Lucy recovered and was well enough to attend the royal wedding in February of 1613. Her illness had altered her and courtiers noted her grave manner and reformation in attire, as well as the fact that she forebore painting, 'which makes her look strange amongst so many vizards, which together with their frizzled, powdered, hair makes them look all alike, so that you can scant know one from another at first view.'[1] The Countess of Bedford had the courage of her convictions and was great enough to defy convention.

Upon St. Valentine's Day a national event of felicity

---

[1] Birch, *Court and Times of James 1st*, vol. i, p. 262.

beckoned citizens to London. This was the marriage of Princess Elizabeth to Frederick, the Count Palatine.

The bride was not a stranger to Donne, and was more than a name or royal figurehead. Shortly after the accession of her father, she had been committed to the care of Sir John and Lady Harington, the parents of Lucy, Countess of Bedford. Sir John, later Lord Harington, had had the foresight to entertain the King in a sumptuous manner upon his journey south and the festivities, the banquets, and above all the good sport provided impressed the Scotsman used to more parsimonious ways in a crabbed life in Edinburgh. His method of rewarding his host was to entrust his daughter to him. But Sir John had more than tact and lavishness to commend him. He was an example of the staunch old Elizabethan gentry, uniting personal dignity with mental independence, 'a spirit of devoted loyalty to the most clear integrity' and disregard for his own safety when that of his royal charge was in danger. At the time of the Gunpowder Plot certain men of treacherous character attempted to abduct the Princess but Sir John, getting wind of the plot in advance, hid her away in the country. As a young woman of beauty and promise she set up a court of her own at Kew, near the palatial establishment of Sir John's daughter, Lucy, at Twickenham. Now, upon the marriage of the Princess, Lord Harington and his wife were to accompany her to her new home over the sea, through continental capitals en route to the Rhine, a journey which was to cost him his life.

Donne may often have spoken with the Princess Elizabeth, either at Court or at Twickenham and he may, when in Bohemia the previous year, have been concerned with details of the approaching betrothal. Sir Robert Drury's part in these negotiations is not abundantly clear.

In London, all was gaiety and extravagance. The bells of the churches rang lustily, bonfires were lit in many streets, down which the voices of pedlars, selling popular broadsides with details of the royal pedigrees, rang: the spring tides were up and the Thames at its best height to assist in the spectacular water pageant arranged by John Taylor, the water-boatman and poet.

The wedding celebrations covered days. Upon Thursday the 11th, the Master Gunner of England performed upon the Thames shore:

'many skilful and ingenious exploits with great bumbards, shooting up artificial balls of fire into the aire, which flew up in one whole fierie ball, and in their falling, dispersed into divers streams like rainbowes in many innumerable fires. After all which was discharged a great peale of chambers. . . .'

Upon the Friday,

'His Highness gave cause of forebearance, with some rest to the engineers for their great toyle the night before. Moreover, it was thought convenient that a whole day's preparation should be made in providing against Saturday's pastimes.'

Upon the Saturday a water pageant, or sea-fight, was displayed between 'Turkish and Christian gallies and friggots, all being artifically trimmed and rigged, well manned and furnished with great ordinance and musquettier' . . . so that after this 'delightful battle' had lasted three hours,

'to the great contentment of all the beholders, the victory inclining to neither side, all being opposed foes and combined friends, all victors, all triumphers, none to be vanquished and therefore no conquerors . . . the drums, trumpets, flutes and guns filling the air with repercussive acclamations . . . command was given that the retreat should be sounded upon on both sides. And thus these Princely recreations were accomplished and finished.

Finally, upon Shrove Sunday the marriage ceremony took place, 'between eleven and twelve of the clock.' The bridegroom, dressed in white, 'richly beset with pearl and gold,' was followed by the 'batchelery of the nation, paranymphs in sumptuous habiliments'. The bride, who was preceded by Lord Harington and followed by Lady Harington, was clothed in white satin, her amber hair hanging in plaits, braided with gold, pearls and diamonds, and upon her head 'a crown of refined gold, so thick beset with pearls and diamonds that they stood like shining pinnacles'.[1]

At the end of the long ceremony,

'divers of the Lords brought bowls with wine, spiced hippocras and wafers. . . . An health was begun to the prosperity of the marriage out of a great gold bowl by the Prince Palatinate and answered by the Princess. . . . Then was joy given by the King and Queen.'

Upon the return of the pair from the Chapel, six of the Palgrave's country gallants, clad in crimson velvet thick with gold lace, presented them with a flourish upon silver trumpets, 'flourishing so delightfully that it greatly rejoiced the whole court.'

'And then all fell to dancing, masking and revelling, which continued all the day and part of the night in great pleasure.'

The masks and revels continued through Shrove Monday and Shrove Tuesday in the banqueting hall at Whitehall, hung from top to toe with fine Arras depicting the trouncing of the Spanish Armada, while jousting and tourneying were engaged in by day. A rivalry was set up between the various dramatic performers. Players of the Inns of Court vied with each other: Sir Francis Bacon contrived for them, Beaumont, Chapman and Campion wracked their poetic brains for them. *The Tempest* was amongst plays performed: 'performers came on horseback and in fine chariots, or upon richly decorated boats and barges...until the King was so wearied and sleepy with sitting up almost two whole nights . . . that he had no edge to it!'

A flood of wedding songs, such as might hardly 'be compressed into a folio volume' was the order of the day. Those poets who had but lately lamented the death of the bride's elder brother now burst obligingly into more joyous song and

---

[1] The quotations above are from the *Progresses and Processions of James the 1st*, vol. ii, pp. 527 *et seqs*. 828. Nichols.

amongst them, Donne. For a man whose mind was ever concerned with antitheses, both Funeral Elegy and Epithalamion would seem to be his best medium for expression— negation, annihilation, the corruption of the body and the persistent activity of the loathsome worm,—and contrasted, in colours of enticing brilliance, the idea of physical union, the creation of new and mysterious life, the imagery of nakedness, living, sentient, lovely flesh, the perfection of the human body which he seems to touch, almost to stroke as he considers it, in the same graphic, lingering way that he hangs over and considers an abstract idea.[1] The opening stanza of this Epithalamion, although not typically Donnian, is a lovely thing, reminding one of Spenser in his most delicately embroidered passages or Chaucer in the *Parliament of Foules*.

'Hail Bishop Valentine, whose day this is,
    All the Air is thy Diocese,
    And all the chirping Choristers
And other birds are thy Parishioners,
    Thou marriest every year
The Lyric Lark, and the grave whispering Dove,
The Sparrow that neglects his life for love,
The Household Bird, with the red stomacher,
    Thou mak'st the black-bird speed as soon,
As doth the Goldfinch, or the Halcyon;
The husband cock looks out, and straight is sped,
And meets his wife, which brings her feather-bed.
This day more cheerfully than ever shine,
This day, which might inflame thy-self, Old Valentine.'

As in the *Lincoln's Inn Epithalamion*, written when he was a student, Donne had drawn the musicians and dancers tired with their 'pleasing labours', so now he portrays:

'The masquers come too late, and I think, will stay,
Like Fairies, till the Cock crow them away.'

For the Jacobean, theatrical splendour replaced the earlier enjoyment of music unadorned, which the citizen of Eliz-

[1] See T. S. Eliot in 'Donne in Our Time', in *A Garland for Donne*. 'He feels an idea almost as if it were something he could stroke and touch.'

K

abeth's day had indulged in. It is good to think of Donne, so much of whose inner life was distracted by dark torment, refreshing himself with masques and music. As a young man he rated music as one of the chief sensual delights. 'I see her', he says, speaking of the soul, 'often solaced with beauties which she sees through mine eyes and with music which through mine ears she hears.'[1] And four years before his death, in the Funeral Sermon which he prepared with especial love for Magdalen Herbert, he used a charming simile to explain the discrepancy in age between her and her husband:

'For as the wire-tuning of an instrument makes higher and lower strings of one sound, so the inequality of their years was reduced.'

I do not think that Donne was a musical man. His rhythm, except in the fine lyric passages, is too abrupt, too close-packed, too weighted with thought to flow freely and un-trammelled, but like every Elizabethan gentleman he had a superficial knowledge of the structure of music and of current instruments.

Something of the old pageantry, the old gaiety of Eliz-abeth's days, had come back to Donne and to the city with the royal wedding, but with so much extravagance that the Puritans were justly scandalized. It was not until April that the bridal pair passed over into Germany, fêted and ban-queted on their long journey.

14

In the same month, Donne set out for Montgomeryshire to visit his friends the Herberts. He rode northwest from London to Warwick, putting up first with Sir Henry Goodyer in his monastic home of Polesworth in which Donne's rival

[1] *Paradoxes and Problems*, XI. 'That the Gifts of the Body are better than those of the Mind.' Hayward, p. 345.

and contemporary, Drayton, had lived when in the service of Sir Henry's father. He then rode due west into Wales. As he rode he composed a divine poem called 'Good Friday', ... 'impressive and comparatively simple' until 'a spasm of his disease of style caught him. ... Nothing could be more odious; yet, such was the taste of the day that no doubt, when he read these verses that evening in Montgomery Castle, the noble Herberts were not merely astonished, but charmed and edified.'[1]

This visit in the spring of the year was a happy interlude. Donne, like others of his time, was not of an antiquarian turn of mind. We hear nothing of the gaunt castle, now only a ruin, rising from its bold escarpment, dominating the little village running towards it up the hill, nor of the wooded knoll under whose loam a British camp lies, nor of the ancient serpent-like dyke which Offa, King of the Mercians, built and the Welsh rose to destroy in a night. The historic and picturesque did not appeal to him: the outward and visible world held him less than the mysterious invisible mind of man. In the gracious Magdalen Herbert and her two sons, one destined to be that odd mixture of coxcomb-courtier and philosopher, the other a poet and divine, Donne found absorbing company. The mood which had prevailed upon him while riding westward continued and *The Primrose*, *The Blossom*, *The Damp* and possibly *The Funeral* and *The Relique*, which repeatedly recur close to each other in various manuscripts, probably had their inspiration in Wales.

They are difficult poems to appreciate, full of contradictions—their background an apparently conservative, conventional relationship interrupted by a little more than solid friendship, a little less than heady passion: they are, like their maker, bundles of mysticism, cynicism, appealing simplicity and scornful rejection, and the tone of the Petrarchan lover is here and there broken outright. Occasionally lines

[1] Gosse, vol. i, p. 267.

with the old spearlike directness occur, relieving the abstruse-
ness, as:

> 'Naked you've odds enough of any man'

and:

> 'A bracelet of bright hair about the bone'

Or in lines of human wisdom:

> 'A naked thinking heart, that makes no show,
> Is to a woman, but a kind of ghost'—

the young poet speaks again.

Some lines in the first stanza of the 'Primrose' in which he
says:

> '. . . their form and their infinity
> Make a terrestrial Galaxy,
> As the small stars do in the sky:'

are the nearest that Donne comes to natural descriptive work
but for all their simplicity one feels in them an artificial quality as if they did not rise smoothly in the mind. The thoughts,
the words, seem incised like marqueterie, built up like mosaic,
or simply sewn on, like appliqué work on a woman's robe.
The age of Wordsworthian appreciation, of Thomson's
'Seasons' and Shenstone's 'Schoolmistress', of Gray and
William Collins, was still more than a century and a half removed, but Chaucer and Spenser and the Madrigalists had
written with enchanting delicacy of pastoral scenes, which
did not appeal to the rebel Donne.

Thus one is impressed, in retrospect, with the 'graphic'
quality of his verse. The short lines are packed hard like the
sharp, inlaid lines of an engraver, rather than the flowing
ones of a painter.

> 'I like a spyed spy shook'

and:

> 'Being double dead, going, and bidding go,'

and:

> 'Men leave behind them that which their sin shows,
> And are as thieves trac'd, which rob when it snows.'

and lastly:

> '. . . And though his face be as ill
> As theirs which in old hangings whip Christ . . .'

are examples of this compressed style.

His reference to Dürer, whose macabre realism was like his own, indicates a knowledge of the German school of engravers, and his constant references to coins, to the circle, to charts, maps and compasses, while part of the current interest of the times, is exceptional in literature and shows his concern for precision, line and relief. He seldom mentions the beauties of nature in a sympathetic manner, and the charming gaiety of Herrick is quite foreign to him.

His two poet friends of the succeeding generation, Henry King and George Herbert, and Jeremy Taylor, his successor as 'the most eloquent of English divines', all write of flowers with an appealing gentleness, rare indeed in Donne.

Here is King, in his *Contemplation upon Flowers*:

> 'Brave flowers—that I could gallant it like you
>   And be as little vain!
> You come abroad, and make a harmless show,
>   And to your beds of earth again.
> You are not proud: you know your birth:
> For your embroider'd garments are from earth.'

Here is Herbert:

> 'I got me flowers to straw Thy way,
>   I got me boughs off many a tree;
> But Thou wast up by break of day,
>   And brought'st Thy sweets along with Thee.'

and finally, Jeremy Taylor:[1]

'But so have I seen a rose newly springing from the clefts of its hood, and at first, it was as fair as the morning, and full with the dew of heaven, as a lamb's fleece; but when a ruder breath had forced open its virgin modesty, and dismantled its too youthful and unripe retirements, it began to put on darkness, and to decline to softness and the symptoms of a sickly age; it bowed the head

[1] *The Rule and Exercises of Holy Dying.*

and broke its stalk; and, at night, having lost some of its leaves and all its beauty, it fell into the portion of weeds and outworn faces. The same is the portion of every man and woman.'

Now here is Donne in verse:

> 'I had not taught thee then, the Alphabet
> Of flowers, how they devisefully being set
> And bound up, might with speechless secrecy
> Deliver errands mutely, and mutually....'[1]

and in prose:

> 'That Soul, that ... as a flower at sun-rising conceives a sense of God, in every beam of his, and spreads and dilates itself towards him, in a thankfulness, in every small blessing that he sheds upon her; that Soul, that as a flower at the sun's declining, contracts and gathers in, and shuts up herself, as though she had received a blow, whensoever she hears her Saviour wounded by an oath, or blasphemy, or execration; ... prays sometimes when it does not know that it prays.'[2]

This is more like Vaughan than Herrick, and Donne, like his Welsh follower, was concerned with the flower as a symbol, with its shadowings of divinity, not with its own beauty. *The Blossom*, portions of the Royal *Epithalamion*, and *The Progress of the Soul* are exceptions to this rule, but on the whole, the ductileness of gold, the orbits of the sun, stars and planets, the course of the rough stream-head, interest his mind more than mere floral softness and rural prettiness. It has been argued that this is because Donne sickened of the Elizabethan tendency to sentimentalize and idealize, and that he wished to be 'spare, counter, original, strange'.[3] I do not think that it was entirely a conscious revolt. His Jesuit training with its continental, rather than English bias, inclined him to these interests, but the structure of his mind was such that this only emphasized the original tendency.

In the note-books of Leonardo da Vinci there are, in ad-

---

[1] *Elegy* VII.   [2] Sermon IX.   [3] Gerard Manley Hopkins, *Pied Beauty*.

dition to the drawings of flowers and grasses, sketches of rock-strata, of whirlwinds and falling mountains, of architectural problems, of the angle of a falling shadow and of the frets, jets and currents of water. These are akin to Donne's interests and are what, if he had expressed his genius in painting rather than writing, he might have given us.

He had the observant eye of a painter and an appreciation of the old masters in advance of his time. As proof of this we have his references to Dürer and Hilliard, and some lines in the *Litany* which show a feeling for the work of sculptors and woodcarvers. In his will, before he bequeaths anything to his aged mother, or his children, Donne hastens to apportion his paintings. He makes as many as seventeen separate bequests of these and indicates that there were other unapportioned paintings. We know that his friend Sir Henry Wotton, while ambassador to the Court at Venice, bought paintings for Charles the Ist and for the Duke of Buckingham. Possibly Donne instigated Wotton to buy for him too, or while on his travels, Donne may have bought for himself. Walton tells us that Donne knew the painters Fulgentio and Paolo personally, but as Gosse remarks, Englishmen of the Jacobean age were interested in the subject rather than the painter of a picture. This is borne out by the fact that Donne does not attach the name of a single artist to any of the paintings which he wills.

In the *First Anniversary* he speaks of the elements of Beauty—Colour and Proportion:

> 'When Nature was most busy, the first week
> Swadling the new born earth, God seemed to like
> That she should sport herself sometimes, and play:
> To mingle, and vary colours every day:
> And then, as though she could not make enow,
> Himself his various rainbow did allow.'

He constantly shows an interest in light and the quality of light, which varies when a taper is brought into a room, or

when the sun 'strikes obliquely'.[1] He watches how a shadow
may vary in intensity according to the substance of the body
from which it is cast—'For our shadow upon clay will be
dirty, and in a garden green, and flowery.'[2] He speaks of a
'growing and full constant light', of the wan light of the moon,
of the dazzling light of the Sun. 'Through-light' and
'through-shine' are favourite adjectives of his, indicating his
feeling for translucency and opaque light. True, he never tires
of speaking of the Sun with a mystical meaning. Yet though
we accept Donne's scholastic and metaphysical use of light,
shadows and darkness, as symbols of spiritual clarity or
obscuration, though we recognize the psychological significance, there still remains this keen, painter-like perception of,
and preoccupation with, their character and essential nature.

The 'Welsh' poems are testimony of his lasting affection
for Magdalen Herbert whose gravity was tempered by a
delicate humour—(what Walton calls her 'great and harmless
wit')[3]—who although twice married and the mother of ten
children, was still adorable. It was a strange coincidence that
had made the choleric Sir George More, of Loseley, both
guardian of her eldest son, Edward, the future Lord Herbert
of Cherbury, and father-in-law of Donne, and it is one more
tribute to Donne's endearing and enticing character that both
Lady Herbert and her young sons took pleasure in his company.

The visit to Wales had been a respite from his circle of
thought attendant upon Court ambitions or entry into the
Church, and from the painful consideration of the delicacy of
his wife, but it culminated upon his return in a severe illness,
'a combination of gastric and rheumatic disorders,'[4] threatening him with blindness. Ann bore another child in August,
little Nicholas, who only lived fifteen months. In fact, it was
another desperate year, like that of 1608 at Mitcham. Sick-

---

[1] *Second Anniversary* and *Essays in Divinity*.

[2] Letter to Sir Henry Goodyer, 1609. Gosse, i, p. 219.

[3] Life of George Herbert.   [4] Gosse, ii, p. 5.

ness overtook the children one after another, and finally two of them succumbed.

'I have paid death one of my children for my ransom,'[1]

is Donne's dignified and restrained way of announcing the fact of his own survival.

Others in his circle suffered in the same year. Lucy, Countess of Bedford, lost her only brother, Lord Harington. Whilst travelling on the Continent he had contracted some form of poisoning and had struggled home to his sister's house at Twickenham only to die, at the age of twenty-two. The barony then became extinct. The *Funeral Elegy* which Donne wrote for Lord Harington was long but sincere and it closed with the sombre determination to write poetry no more. The statement of the intention is indicative of the mood of sterility which bound him in this painful time when he was 'unapparelling', yet about to 'enlarge' his heart and mind.

The Countess of Bedford was touched by Donne's tribute and although involved in an expensive suit-at-law, she showed her affection by contributing a sum towards his ever recurrent debts. One has to admit that he was not very gracious in his acceptance, since he complained in a letter to Wotton that he had hoped for more!

The extremes of meanness and extravagance were exemplified in Donne as in many Elizabethans, including the Queen herself.

'With all his revolt against the spirit of the time, Donne was a true Elizabethan in his passionate friendships, his acts of sudden generosity, and also in his fits of meanness and his moments of selfish calculating ambition. We see him repeating court gossip, making bad jokes, bewailing his poverty, criticizing his contemporaries, or at other times offering tender sympathy and meditating on the profoundest mysteries of life.'[2]

In later life he haggled over the income from livings which he ought to have abandoned with a good grace upon receiving

[1] Letter to Sir Robert Ker, May 1614.　　[2] Simpson, p. 270.

higher preferments: he quarrelled with his son-in-law over the promised gift of some linen and a useless pony: yet he spent his fortune without apparent premeditation, took in his aged mother, for whom he had no deep affection, and gave to old friends when in need. He was interested in commercial ventures whilst getting into debt at his new deanery, yet he admits that he hates business and is repelled by the mercenary attitude of his showman son-in-law. Even when near his deathbed Donne combines this odd mixture of sanctity and worldliness, for he speaks with gratitude of having been able to repay some of those who had substantially befriended him in earlier years, almost in the same breath that he ponders upon his soul's leavetaking.

15

In these critical months when death, illness, penury and a harrowing lack of advancement conspired against Donne to bring him to the nadir of grief, he must often have turned aside to regard the fortunes of his friends, and it is an odd coincidence that many of them were going through a time of strain, unemployment, or preparation for a new kind of life, just as he himself was doing.

First there were his Hart Hall friends, chief of whom was Sir Henry Wotton, who, in the years 1613 and 1614, had fallen on an equally unproductive period. His career, which had promised favourably, beginning with his Secretaryship to Essex, his insinuation into the graces of James in the Scottish court, his knighthood and ambassadorship to Venice, had suddenly stopped short in abrupt disgrace. For he had been recalled to England and coolly received by the King because of a chance line written in jest on the Continent nearly ten years earlier. Upon the death of Lord Salisbury he became a candidate for the position of Secretary to the King, but the months were as barren as those for poor Donne and he sought employment in vain. It was not until August of 1614 that he was sent to negotiate with the French and Dutch, and not until 1616 that he was properly reinstated as an ambassador. The contemporary criticism that Wotton's obsequious bearing diminished his reputation during his unemployment, and his method of re-ingratiating himself into Royal favour, are interesting. We have grown accustomed to overlooking the servility of phrase and bearing in the Jacobean courtier as a necessary characteristic of those who sought advancement. Influence was paramount. The power of the Sovereign was greater than nowadays, political parties had not yet come into being, the aristocracy, especially the current favourites, were practically omnipotent. The Court was riddled with rivalry, jealousy and constant intrigue. The comment that Wotton was too obsequious was obviously made by a rival but it nevertheless throws light on Donne's unsuccessful importunity and suggests that he too may have suffered from an excess of adulatory words and importunate phrases. Wotton's insinuation into royal favour a second time was due to his championship of the King's right to lay impositions upon merchandise entering the country, without first appealing to Parliament. He had the wit and ingenuity to flatter James in the current argument. Donne, as writer and legal authority, might have used similar methods but these would have involved tampering with his conscience. He might attempt to influence by charm, by a recital of merit, or by downright flattery, but he was slow to advance himself by definite action.

Of Donne's friends of the Cambridge days, the Brookes stand out pre-eminent. Samuel, who had married him to Ann More, was now an august Doctor of Divinity and had had the honour of being chosen Chaplain to Prince Henry. Like Donne, he became Chaplain to James the Ist as well, and subsequently to Charles the Ist. In 1613, three Latin plays which he had written were performed before the King at Cambridge. Christopher had twice stood as Member of Parliament for York, and, in 1614, was appointed Bencher and Summer Reader at Lincoln's Inn. When, two years later, Donne was made Reader in Divinity to the Benchers of his old Inn, these two were once more drawn together. One or the other must often have looked up at the windows of the chamber they had shared, and wondered at the strange and diverse experiences each had known since those halcyon days.

Of the group which had set out for adventure so rapaciously eighteen years earlier, on the Cadiz and Island Voyages, many were gone or were suffering grievous punishment. Sir Francis Wooley and young Sir Thomas Egerton were dead, as well as headstrong Essex. Raleigh had been imprisoned for eleven wearisome years and, in 1614, had issued from the Tower his ambitious *History of the World*. The King might be offended, archbishops might attempt to suppress the book, but the magnificent courage of a man who, disgraced, ruined and imprisoned, could calmly set about considering the origins of races and their order of progress, no man could ever touch. They might cramp the body, used to exploration and adventure, but they could not clip the wings of his imagination.

Donne's old employer, Sir Thomas Egerton, now Baron Ellesmere, Lord Chancellor, and Chancellor of Oxford University, was nearing the end of his busy life. Bacon, with whom Donne had often been in close touch in those years of state work and diplomacy, was shortly to see the extinction of his political influence with the dissolution of the 'Addled Parliament' in this very year.

The Earl of Northumberland, who had been Donne's emissary to Sir George More at Loseley, accused of complicity in the Gunpowder Plot, was also imprisoned in the Tower. His solitude, like that of Raleigh's, was broken by the visits of scholars, and what little exercise they might 'take upon the prison leads' was enlivened by scientific and philosophical discussions. Raleigh's imprisonment lasted thirteen, and Northumberland's fifteen, years.

Sir Henry Goodyer had lately lost his wife and Sir Thomas Roe, whom Donne calls 'dear Tom' in an unusually simple manner, having formerly served Queen Elizabeth as Esquire of the Body, was in this same year preparing to leave England on 'a long and hazardous mission. He had served in Parliament for a short time and was now appointed to represent James the Ist at the court of the Emperor Jehanghir at Agra, and to protect there the interests of the infant East India Company. He sailed in 1615.'[1]

Perhaps the most adventurous and unfortunate of Donne's friends was Rowland Woodward, who had accompanied Sir Henry Wotton upon his first embassy to Venice. Wotton tells us that Woodward was proficient in the French, Italian and Spanish languages, 'whereof he spoke the last best,'[2] and this doubtless endeared him to Donne whose enthusiasm for Spanish was unfailing. Woodward had been sent on ticklish errands to Milan and dangerous ones to England. His reward for the former was imprisonment by the Inquisition. In 1606 he carried papers from Venice to Lord Salisbury but was attacked by robbers and nearly killed. His despatches, stained and torn, which passed through the hands of Henry IV of France, may be seen in the Record Office today.[3] In 1608 he took service with 'my Lord of London', that is, Dr. John King, Bishop of London, who had been Chaplain to Sir Thomas Egerton when Donne had been Secretary, and who was shortly to ordain the poet.

16

The insecurity of his position as a guest of Sir Robert Drury, as a sycophant of the King's favourite, Rochester, and a dependant of his irascible old father-in-law, Sir George

[1] Gosse, vol. ii, p. 67.

[2] *Life and Letters of Sir Henry Wotton*, Logan Pearsall Smith, Clarendon Press, 1907, vol. i, p. 326.

[3] Pearsall Smith, vol. i, pp. 365 and 372.

More, gnawed at Donne's mind and weighed upon his spirit. When the Countess of Bedford, involved in endless extravagances of her own, found it impossible to pay off the whole of his debts, Donne turned to her cousin, the Countess of Huntingdon, and that charming lady came to the rescue. It was she who, as Elizabeth Stanley, had formed one of the constellation of consoling stars at York House and who, possibly, had pleaded for the acceptance of his marriage. But over all his nights and days hung the recurrent dissatisfaction, growing into repulsion, with court and worldly affairs.

He was obsessed, like Bacon, with the vanity and uselessness of seeking preferment and, like Bacon, he groaned in spirit.

'The rising into place is laborious, and by pains men come to greater pains, and it is sometimes base: and by indignities men come to dignities.'[1]

In August he wrote in a *Verse Letter* to the Countess of Salisbury:

'. . . he that would be good, is thought by all
A monster, or at best fantastical:'

He was oppressed, too, with a sense of fleeting time and oncoming age, of a life wasted and maladjusted to its powers and environment:

'And I, as giddy travellers must do,
Which stray or sleep all day, and having lost
Light and strength, dark and tired, must then ride post.'[2]

His 'in-mate soule', which lodged within him but had not yet possessed him, longed for 're-housing', and thirsted with an 'insatiate thirst'. It could not, however, in quietness and confidence hear God still 'pleading his safe precontract'. Self-depreciation, stagnation, and an inward dry-rot had set in as new evils to be combated and it was easier for Donne to write to his friend, 'to thy-self be approved', than to perform this very necessary piece of mental hygiene. The self-made

[1] Bacon's Essay on *Great Place*.   [2] *Verse Letter* to Mr. Basil Brooke.

hell which occupied the inner galleries of his mind, and which
he admitted was but a privation of Christian light, was both
the cause and result of the galling fortune which aggravated
it. For fourteen long years, as long as the imprisonment of
Raleigh and Northumberland, he had been free, as they were
not, to go and come, yet immured in a windowless vault of the
spirit, a tantalizing cage such as an inquisitor might fashion,
in which he could neither stretch to the fullness of his power
nor lie in a dreamless, restoring sleep.

> 'And as our bodies, so our minds are crampt:
> 'Tis shrinking, not close-weaving that hath thus,
> In mind, and body both bedwarfed us.'[1]

'The ravelled sleeve of care' hung ever upon his arm and, like
the garments which Penelope wove so fruitlessly, never
warmed his chillness of heart. Indecision and hope deferred
had made his heart sick.

> 'Pregnant again with the old twins, Hope and Fear,'

he writes, and like Ann, patiently carrying and nourishing a
child only to bring it forth stillborn, Donne was broken and
deluded.

'Believe me, I do not cast into the account of my years, these
last five which I have lived no otherwise than as nights slept out,
which are indeed a part of time—which the body steals from the
mind—rather than a part of life, which cannot live but it must feel
itself alive. God Almighty awake me! And in the meantime I
think that even this sleep I am in, is but a troubled one. I have not
forgotten that in a letter of yours you asked me once whether we
should be fine gentlemen still? . . . still idlers, without aims or
ends? . . .'[2]

His appeal to God to rouse him is echoed again and again
during these years.

> 'Up, up, my drowsy Soul, where thy new ear,
> Shall in the Angels' songs no discord hear,'

[1] *An Anatomy of the World: The First Anniversary.*
[2] To Sir Henry Wotton. Jessop, p. 86.

or:

'. . . But up unto the watch-tower get'

written two years before, are echoes in verse of his self-stirring.

Misfortune drew him and Ann together. In one of the simplest of his letters he writes to his brother-in-law:

'We are condemned to this desert of London for all this summer, for it is company, not houses, which distinguishes between cities and deserts. When I begin to apprehend that, even to myself, who can relieve myself upon books, solitariness was a little burdenous, I believe it would be much more so to my wife, if she were left alone. So much company, therefore, as I am, she shall not want; and we had not one another at so cheap a rate, as that we should ever be weary of one another. . . .'[1]

In other letters he writes of her courage, of how she would not permit herself a respite, ill as she was, until she had done all she could for her invalid husband, and speaks of her sensitivity, touching yet dangerous, to his own moods. Identification with the beloved was all too easy for gentle Ann More.

17

Throughout this tedious time Donne sought relief in books and the making of books, 'trying all things, assenting to the force of reason and convincement.'[2] He busied himself with the study of Oriental languages, and towards the close of the year he began the *Essays in Divinity*—awkward and ingenious as a whole but rising to magnificence in the prayers—and considered the publication of his secular verse.

His last *Epithalamion*, written for the marriage of Lord Somerset and Lady Essex in December of 1613, has since caused Donne's name to be mixed in an unsavoury Jacobean affair. At the age of thirteen, Frances Howard, daughter of

---

[1] Letter to his brother-in-law, Sir Robert More, 10th August, 1614.
[2] Milton, *Areopagitica*.

the Earl of Suffolk, was married to the third Earl of Essex, at the especial wish of King James. The young Earl, not much older than his bride, was then sent abroad to travel, but upon his return he found that his wife, who had taken a lover, refused to live with him. This lover was the King's new favourite, Robert Carr, created Viscount Rochester in 1611, and the King, perhaps regretting the child marriage and anxious to placate Rochester, set to work to justify divorcing Lady Essex and speedily remarrying her. Commissioners were appointed to look into the case, the highest prelates of the land were petitioned for advice and the whole affair became town-talk despite the fact that the proceedings were nominally secret. Rochester was created Earl of Somerset so that his rank might match his future wife's, the couple were married, and those who before had reviled Lady Essex now paid open court to her. So far, the lady's indiscretions were not particularly culpable but she turned murderess as well. Her victim was Sir Thomas Overbury, a friend of Carr's who had opposed his marriage. The King was forced into condemnation and both Somerset and his wife were thrown into prison. The Countess's agents were hanged, and she was condemned, but reprieved after a sensational trial in which witchcraft and the devil himself appeared to play a part.

Unfortunately for Donne's reputation in posterity, one of the commissioners who tried the case for divorce was Sir Daniel Donne, D.C.L., who has become confused with the poet, and the fact that Donne wrote a wedding song seemed to implicate him further. His letters show that he was agreeable to lending a hand in promoting the divorce which he accepted as a foregone conclusion since, before the decree was made absolute, he was busy polishing his marriage ode. But in writing an Epithalamion Donne is 'no more blameworthy than Ben Jonson or Campion, who wrote similar poems for the same occasion. Nothing was then known of the murder.

. . . Even the saintly Bishop Andrews had acquiesced in the
divorce, the King and whole court favoured the marriage. It
was not until 1615 that the truth came to light. . . .'[1]

The *Epithalamion* is full of delightful passages, welcome
after the laboured *Anniversaries*, and here again we have
the anomaly of seeing the poet revive in the coming prelate.

> 'Nature's instinct draws to the warmer clime
> Even small birds, who by that courage dare,
> In numerous fleets, sail through their Sea, the air.
> What, delicacy can in fields appear,
> Whil'st Flora herself doth a freeze jerkin wear?
> Whil'st winds do all the trees and hedges strip
> Of leaves, to furnish rods enough to whip
> Thy madness from thee; and all springs by frost
> Have taken cold, and their sweet murmur lost.'

The eleven stages of the *Epithalamion* follow: the bridegroom is bidden, in language reminiscent of 'Hark! Hark!
the Lark', to outrun 'the red foaming horses' of the Sun, and
the bride to 'powder her radiant hair', until the omnipresence
of love is drawn in the lovely lines:

> 'Thou art not gone, being gone; where e'er thou art,
> Thou leav'st in him thy watchful eyes, in him thy loving heart.'

One regrets that the *Epithalamion* was not written for
more worthy people and feels that to say to Somerset that:

> '. . . the heart of man
> Is an epitome of God's great book
> Of creatures . . .'

or:

> '. . . so is he still at home
> That doth, abroad, to honest actions come',

was wasted wisdom.

If, however, he wished for advancement, it seemed absolutely essential for Donne to pay homage to Lord Roches-

---

[1] Simpson, p. 31. In his article in the D.N.B. Jessop also points out the
error.

ter. The poet was now forty-two years old, an authority on law but not a lawyer, a frequenter of the Court but not a courtier, an author on religious matters yet not a prelate, a dabbler in science yet not a scientist, he was 'nobody and nothing still.'[1] Rochester had the King's ear; Donne's friend, Lord Hay, the future Earl of Carlisle, had the ear of Rochester, who like a giant cuckoo had ousted all other birds from the royal nest. Either in 1611 or 1612 Donne had approached the favourite through Lord Hay. In his letters he placed himself under the protection of Rochester and at last declared his intentions of taking Holy Orders. Still the worldly side of his nature clamoured for attention, for in other letters he begs for a diplomatic appointment to the Dutch States or to the Court at Venice. When twelve months had straggled by and nothing had come of his application, Donne, who had been employed by Rochester in some matters of whose nature we have no clear proof, approached him again.[2] In his first letter of appeal he refers to the struggle he has had in reaching a decision and states his determination.

'For, having obeyed at last, after much debatement within me, the inspirations (as I hope) of the Spirit of God, and resolved to make my profession Divinity; I make account, that I do but tell your Lordship, what God hath told me, which is, that it is in this course, if in any, that my service may be of use to this Church and State.'

In the second he pitifully reminds the Earl that a twelve-month has elapsed:—'I am now a year older and broken with some sickness.' He begs either for encouragement or flat discouragement, so that he may either hope or 'pursue his first purpose' and 'abandon all'.

It is impossible not to regard some of the expressions in these letters as servile, but one must remember both the idiom and custom of the day, and that a man hard pressed by time and conscience, impatient of delay and interrupted

[1] Gosse, vol. ii, p. 3.
[2] The two undated letters may be found in Gosse, vol. ii, p. 20 and p. 41.

decision, sometimes greases the wheels of his chariot until the axle-trees drip. But an addded cause for discouragement followed. Somerset's influence began to wane. A new favourite rose to oust him, and it was significant that Ben Jonson busied himself with a new Masque in which *Mr. Villiers* was to take part. The Court must often have seemed to Donne to be occupied with extravagance and vanity irrespective of men's gaunt pockets and cracking hearts.

Suddenly Donne was summoned to the King's favourite palace which the Sovereign had exchanged with Sir Robert Cecil for Hatfield, and at which he died.

'The Earl of Somerset . . . being then at Theobald's with the King, where one of the clerks of the council died that night, posted a messenger for Mr. Donne to come to him immediately and at Mr. Donne's coming said;

"Mr. Donne, to testify the reality of my affection, and my purpose to prefer you, stay in this garden till I go up to the King, and bring you word that you are clerk of the council. Doubt not my doing this, for I know the King loves you, and know the King will not deny me."

But the King gave a positive denial to all requests, and, having a discerning spirit, replied, "I know Mr. Donne is a learned man, has the abilities of a learned divine, and will prove a powerful preacher; and my desire is to prefer him that way, and in that way I will deny you nothing for him." After that time . . . the King descended to a persuasion almost to solicitation of him to enter into sacred orders, which though he then denied not, yet he deferred for almost three years.'[1]

The date of this dramatic interview, in the palatial gardens upon which the Lord Treasurer had been in the habit of spending about £100 a week, is not clear. Whether it occurred, as Gosse thinks, in November of 1614, or as Walton implies, three years before his submission in January 1614/5, that is, in 1611 when Donne first wrote to Somerset, does not ultimately matter. That the King was at Newmarket

[1] Walton, p. 24.

late in 1614 and that Donne visited him there concerning his
future office is evident from a letter from Donne to his old
father-in-law, now Lieutenant of the Tower.

'I returned not till yesternight from my expensive journey to
Newmarket, where I have received from the King as good allowance and encouragement to pursue my purpose as I could desire.'[1]

He goes on to explain a rift in the lute which he had
discerned whilst there—the differences between the Lord
Chamberlain, Somerset, and 'my Lord of Canterbury',
Archbishop Abbot, who as Donne's new master, should he
enter the church, it behoved him to placate. Donne warily
begins to trim his sails to the new wind. He begs Sir George
to 'discern the Archbishop's inclination towards him' and to
find out whether the Archbishop 'have any conjecture upon
my relation to my Lord Chamberlain, which is very likely to
have come to his knowledge since my going, by reason of his
Lordship's more open avowing me than before'.

His old friends, especially John King, Bishop of London,
and the Lord Chancellor, Baron Ellesmere, when they heard
of his decision, encouraged him warmly, and at length, after
wrestling and debating for so long a time, John Donne was
ordained. The exact date of his ordination has only recently
come to light in a letter to Sir Edward Herbert, signed 'Your
very humble chapleyn, J. Donne', and dated '23rd January
1614/5 which was the very day wherein I took orders'.[2]

At the last moment before his ordination his friends were
forced to dissuade him from issuing his love poems. Very
likely he thought it best to publish them in proper form, since
so many of them had been handed round in manuscript,

---

[1] Letter to Sir George More, Dec. 1614, Gosse, ii, p. 60.

[2] The letter to Edward Herbert was printed for the first time in the
Nonesuch *Donne* in 1929, by permission of the Earl of Powis, among
whose Herbert MSS, while under examination at the Record Office, it
was discovered. The finder, Mr. C. S. Ratcliff, communicated the discovery to Mr. Hayward, thereby adding 'one small and hitherto unknown
fact to Donne's biography'. See Hayward, pp. 466-786.

copied, imitated and plagiarized. But the intention was more significant. 'I must do this as a valediction to the world before I take orders,' he declared and he was determined to dedicate the volume to Rochester, then Lord Chamberlain.

It was like Donne to be so engrossed in his own attitude to his 'conversion' that it obscured for him the attitude of others. It was urgent for him to stand well with the Archbishop of Canterbury, Abbot, and since amatory verse was looked down upon as the doubtful effervescence of youth, and since the Archbishop and Lord Chamberlain were bitter enemies, nothing could have prejudiced Donne more in Abbot's eyes. Like Herrick, who, after he had entered the church, wrote with faint regret of 'his unbaptized rhymes', Donne later censured himself for having written his exquisite love poems. How much of this censure was conventional, and how much deeply sincere, only those who study the age and the enigma of Donne's character can judge. But the fact that, at this moment, he was concerned with the drama of setting a seal upon his new endeavours and of breaking with the past so naïvely and disadvantageously, throws a strong light upon the causes of his ill-fortune up to the present.

The decision can not have been made because he hoped for financial benefit from the publication, for Donne expressly states that he intends to pay for this.

'One more thing I must tell you, but so softly that I am loth to hear myself. . . . It is that I am brought to a necessity of printing my poems, and addressing them to my Lord Chamberlain. This I mean to do forthwith, not for much public view, but at mine own cost, a few copies. I apprehend some incongruities in the resolution, and I know what I shall suffer from many interpretations; but I am at an end of much considering that, and if I were as startling in that kind as ever I was, yet in this particular I am under an unescapable necessity, as I shall let you perceive when I see you. By this occasion I am made a rhapsoder of mine own rags, and that cost me more diligence to seek them than it did to make them.'[1]

[1] Gosse, II. p. 68. Letter to Sir Henry Goodyer, December 20, 1614.

Donne says that he appreciates the anachronistic temper of his intention: he says that he realizes the false inferences which will be deduced from his action, but the matter is so urgent in his own mind that these outward currents do not appear to govern him. However, no record of the issue has ever been found and it has therefore been assumed that Goodyer, the Countess of Bedford, or his ecclesiastical friends persuaded him of the inadvisability of publication.

Now at last the tedious business of seeking for place and sueing for grace was over. Now all was changed. The decision and accomplished act of his having entered the Church cleansed and fortified the man. After the long struggle, the relinquishment and the submission, came new life and a new way of thought. He was marvellously and painfully enlarged. The 'winding stair'[1] which had confused him and which, in his nightmare states, had seemed to mount without an ending, had led at last to an ante-chamber filled with a soft, 'through-shine' light, looking on to pleasant fields. The 'starveling soul' was 'bountifully fed' and after the 'banquet' she set about 'saying her grace'.

[1] Bacon's simile.

CHAPTER IV

FULFILMENT AND FRUITION

'Heaven is as near, and present to her face,
As colours are, and objects, in a room
Where darkness was before, when Tapers come.'
Second Anniversary.

'You know I have never imprisoned the word Religion: not straightening it friarly . . . nor immuring it in a Rome, or a Geneva; they are all virtual beams of one Sun . . . connatural pieces of one circle. Religion is Christianity.'

Donne's *Letter to Sir H. R.*

I

The village of Paddington lay, in the early seventeenth century, at a distance of four or five miles from the westernmost boundaries of London proper and was noted for its watercourse, which ran 'to James-head on the hill'.[1] Here, in a small church falling into ruin, Donne preached his first sermon and his choice of an audience indicates his hesitancy and humility. There is no record of the text he chose, or of what he said, of his manner of speech, or of how his congregation responded to him. Perhaps one of his constant friends, or Ann, faithful in encouragement, was present to hearten him. Perhaps a member of that small, unrecorded congregation followed the future Dean's career with prophecy and amazement, living to tremble beneath the dramatic fire which was to pour from the pulpit of old Saint Paul's in another decade.

Soon after this tentative flight and three months after his ordination, in the spring of the year, Donne preached before the Queen in her palace at Greenwich, which Inigo Jones was altering with such ingenuity. This is Donne's first surviving sermon. Then he preached before the King at Whitehall,

[1] Stowe, p. 17.

which might have unnerved a less confident man. For the Sermon in the time of James reached its highest and most complicated form, rising to peculiar perfection. There was nothing haphazard or spontaneous in either preparation or delivery. We know something of Donne's method from his letters and from Walton—how he carefully prepared the heads of his discourse, giving the sources in the margin and making copious notes, and committing his meditations to memory: how, when all was performed at last, there was not even a welcome respite, for as soon as one sermon was finished he began the selection of a new text and the tremendous preparation of another.[1] Other dignitaries, jealous perhaps of the growing or even assured success of rival talent, courtiers, scholars and politicians, lay in wait to trip up the preacher on the thorns of doctrinal differences which multiplied and abounded as Puritanism grew, Catholicism revived, and Anglicanism split into hostile camps. Twice in his ecclesiastical career, Donne was forced to endure the humiliation of suspicion and suspension from royal favour through this very occurrence.

That Donne always realized the responsibility attaching to his work is evident from a letter he wrote towards the close of his life to a lady who begged him to install a young friend in a London living:

'Goes there no more to the giving a scholar a Church in London but that he was a young gentleman's schoolmaster? You know the *ticklishness* of London pulpits, and how ill it would become me to place in a London Church one that were not both a *strong* and a *sound* man.'[2]

King James was immeasurably pleased with the protégé whom he had marked as a winner years ago and who had eluded him with all the tenacity and wiliness of a shy, stub-

[1] See 'John Donne and Contemporary Preachers', John Sparrow. *Essays and Studies*, Oxford, Clarendon Press, vol. VII. 1921. Also Simpson, p. 239.

[2] Letter to Mrs. Cockayne, January 1630/1. Italics mine.

born, highspirited horse, determined upon running other courses. In April 1615, immediately after the sermon at Whitehall, the King insisted that both Universities should confer upon Donne the degree of Doctor of Divinity, not without disagreeable remonstrance from the autocratic Cambridge heads who declared Donne and his co-recipients to be: '*filios noctis et tenebriones*, that sought thus to come in at the window when there was a gate open.'[1] The King was actually forced to plead with the Vice-Chancellor like any petitioning courtier, until he threatened him with a mandate which the Vice-Chancellor dared not disregard.

In the same year, abundant in its favours to Donne, through the graciousness of the Benchers of Lincoln's Inn and then of the King, he received the livings of Keyston in Huntingdon and Sevenoaks in Kent, which meant that his income was substantially increased but that, according to the custom of the day, he was neither forced to live in these parishes nor to do very much work connected with them. Finally the King appointed Donne one of his Chaplains.

In the autumn of the ensuing year, 1616, Donne was appointed Reader in Divinity to the Benchers of Lincoln's Inn, a position felicitous for both Benchers and Preacher, for his listeners, many of them old acquaintances, valued their preacher and the place was, for Donne, filled with memories of happier, less responsible days. The post was not without its arduous side since it entailed delivering two Sermons every Sunday during term, and one on every other, to an exacting and learned congregation. This, in addition to his work as Chaplain to His Majesty, made heavy demands on mind, voice and general health, but at all times Donne seems to have relished preaching at Lincoln's Inn and the Benchers 'added courtesies . . . so many and so freely, as if they meant their gratitude should exceed his merits'.[2] One of the stipula-

---

[1] Nicholls, vol. iii, p. 60.   [2] Walton, p. 31.

tions attached to the position was that the Reader should have 'fair and newly furnished lodgings' and thus Donne might once more sleep beneath the rooftree which had secured him safe from wind and weather thirty years earlier. (He remained Reader until 1622, when his work as Dean of St. Paul's caused him to give up the appointment.)

The year of this felicitous appointment was that in which the new Chapel of Lincoln's Inn was begun. The architect was Inigo Jones, the Welshman who quarrelled with Donne's friend, rough Ben Jonson, and whom Donne had often met for revels and gaiety at 'The Mermaid' or 'Mitre'. Now they were joined in holier work for the corner stone of Inigo's chapel was laid by Donne. In his sermons to the Benchers Donne was less ceremonious than in those to his Cathedral or Court audiences. He addressed his legal friends with candour and humour, and in a manner almost personal. He tells them how he loves the Psalms of David, the Epistles of Paul, and the prophet Ezekiel,[1] whose greatness 'is in his extraordinary depth and mysteriousness': of his travels abroad—how, once, when he lay in a rambling old house in Germany which stretched skyward, tier upon tier like a great honeycomb:

'I asked who lay over my head, they told me a family of Anabaptists; And who over theirs? Another family of Anabaptists; and another family of Anabaptists over theirs; and the whole house was a nest of these boxes; several artificers; all Anabaptists . . . yet for some collateral differences, they detested one another, and, though many of them were near in blood and alliance to one another, yet the son would ex-communicate the father in the room above him, and the Nephew the Uncle.'[2]

I cannot believe that Donne used this simile to point his hatred of hostile sects without a smile. It is so vivid and ironic.

[1] The wheels of Ezekiel fascinated Donne, as well as Jeremy Taylor, and it is possible that Donne's circular desk at the Deanery was made with these in mind.

[2] *Fifty Sermons*. No. 21. Preached at Lincoln's Inn.

In the same year Shakespeare died. Donne, 'close and secret,' never once mentions him. Proud, haughty and aloof, he threads his way through the galaxy of literary talent without so much as a glance or acknowledgment for his contemporaries. He condescends to doff his cap to Dante and to Rabelais to whose 'dark intensity' and 'blunt grossness'[1] he owed so much in style and feeling, and indirectly, to the dead Marlowe in his second *Satyre*. Yet, such is the similarity between the scepticism of Hamlet, who may stand for his creator, and Donne, in his *Progress of the Soul*, that one suspects that Donne and Shakespeare's paths at some time crossed. Hamlet's misogyny, his deep dejection, his sensing of the world's infection and his desire, as Donne puts it, 'to be none of it,' the questioning of his very faculties, are all mirrored, if a mirroring it be and not an independent image of despondency, in this and a succeeding poem of Donne's, *the First Anniversary*.

The concluding lines of *The Progress*,

> 'There's nothing simply good, nor ill alone
> Of every quality comparison,
> The only measure is, and judge, opinion.'

reminiscent of Hamlet's more famous statement, make one wonder whether Shakespeare influenced Donne, or Donne Shakespeare, or whether, by some odd coincidence of current thought, both reflected the earlier Nashe.[2] A version of *Hamlet*, recognized as Shakespeare's, was in existence before 1602. *The Progress* was written in 1601.[3]

Another pair of lines bears a marked resemblance to one of Shakespeare's. In *Romeo and Juliet*, for the composition of which the latest date is generally held to be 1596, Juliet com-

---

[1] F. L. Lucas, in his Review in *The New Statesman*, Nov. 1, 1924.

[2] 'So that our opinion . . . gives the name of good or ill to everything.' *Works*, ed. McKerrow, iii, p. 332.

[3] For Hamlet and Donne, see Theodore Spencer, 'Donne and His Age.' in *A Garland for Donne*, pp. 187 *et seq.*, and George Williamson, 'The Libertine Donne,' p. 288, *Philological Quarterly*, xiii, July 3rd, 1934.

plains to her lover of his impetuosity, and declares his love to
be:

> 'Too like the lightning which doth cease to be
> Ere one can say "It lightens" . . .'

Donne, speaking of one of the migrations of the fickle soul
says:

> 'As lightning, which one scarce dares say he saw,
> Tis so soon gone . . .
>
> . . . swiftly she flew.'

This superficial verbal similarity has a deeper counterpart
and Hamlet's creator and the author of *The Progress* were
probably closer to one another than has yet been proven.[1]

In July 1617, Donne preached in that loveliest of Elizabethan manor houses, Knole, before the Earl of Dorset,
who became his patron, and to whom, eventually, he owed
the living of St. Dunstan's in the West. But before this, in
March, one of the most important milestones in his ecclesiastical career was raised—his first sermon at Paul's Cross. The
occasion was the King's Day and Donne had been commanded to preach by the Sovereign himself. The Archbishop
of Canterbury, the Lord Keeper (Francis Bacon), the Lord
Privy Seal, the Earls of Arundel and Southampton, the
Master of the Rolls, (Sir Julius Caesar, Donne's host and
friend at Mitcham), his staunch friend Lord Hay, and 'divers
other great men' were present to hear a man whose career
some of them had followed with cynicism and others with
conviction and affection. The Sermon was surprisingly
summed up as 'dainty' and was 'exceeding well liked for that
Dr. Donne did Queen Elizabeth right and held himself close
to the text without flattering the time too much'.[2] In other
words, it was well balanced, tactful and not tedious.

[1] See also Donne's letter to Sir Henry Goodyer, in 1609, (Hayward,
p. 459) in which he compares court life to 'a garment made of remnants,
a life ravelled out into ends', with Macbeth's soliloquy, Act ii, Sc. 2., Cir.
1606. And Chapter V ensuing.

[2] Nicholls, vol. iii, p. 267. 1617.

Paul's Cross, a simple wooden structure, hexagonal in shape and roofed with lead, which stood on the stone steps of the original thirteenth century cross in the angle made by the nave and transept of the old Cathedral, was a place hallowed by every association connected with national religious development for the past three centuries. Sermons here had been interrupted by riders bearing the news of a rebel defeat: Kings themselves had been criticized by the audacious preacher who barely escaped with his life: here, Latimer had been 'coughed down' by angry opponents: here, Jewell had uttered his famous challenge to Rome, and here the Spanish King, encircled by a guard of four hundred horsemen, had come to hear Bishop Gardiner. Here Bishop Hooker had preached in scarlet robes falling to his feet, and here the persecuted and pious, sometimes before a crowd of 20,000 people, were forced to recant and disown their faith, amongst them John Heywood, Donne's grandfather. Here, since it was the chief London burial ground, the dead were brought for public interment: here the congregation, disapproving of the words of the preacher, might drown his voice with discordant noises, or hurl squibs of paper bearing scurrilous words into the 'chamber' were he stood. Here, later, he might read the open condemnation of all he had said, insultingly posted upon the Cross.[1] But the single admiration with which good preachers were listened to tempted all kinds of talent to this metropolitan theatre—young Puritans from the country, eager to gain a London hearing, men of the new school which recommended 'inspired', extempore speaking, much looked down upon by Donne and contrasting strangely with the learned and ordered dignity of the Sermons of the Anglican divines, higher in social standing. Thus, within two years of his ordination Donne, so long an apparent failure, found himself preaching to the highest in the land, in the centre of the

[1] Paul's Cross was pulled down, together with Charing Cross and Cheapside in 1643 by order of Parliament. See Neal's *History of the Puritans*, iii, p. 39, and Willmot's *Jeremy Taylor*, pp. 44–50.

capital and at the very hub of the ecclesiastical life of the country. He was indeed 'the Trumpet at whose voice the people came', a moulder of public opinion, whose doctrines, ideas and philosophy were attractive to his cultivated contemporaries and acceptable to the majority of his listeners.

2

In the middle of all this long-delayed plenty and happiness, rich and full like a harvest day, the forked lightning suddenly struck. Death, which Donne himself was to court and woo in an agony of analysis, placation and melodramatic propitiation, took away his wife from him at the early age of thirty-three, just as she bore him her twelfth child. The light went out of his life and shutting himself away, even from his children, he strove to overcome his grief. 'We had not one another at so cheap a rate as that we should ever be wearye of one another,' and 'So much company as I am she shall not want', had been his testimony to his love for her when she was alive and now in an anguish of spirit he sublimated his love and epitomized his sorrow in the *Holy Sonnets*.

> 'Since she whom I lov'd hath paid her last debt
> To nature, and to hers, and my good is dead,
> And her Soul early into heaven ravished,
> Wholly on heavenly things my mind is set.
> Here the admiring her my mind did whet
> To seek thee God; so streams do shew their head;
> But though I have found thee, and thou my thirst hast fed,
> A holy thirsty dropsy melts me yet. . . .'[1]

Who knows through what anguish Ann passed at each delivery since, when she was only six years old, her mother, also called Ann, had likewise died in childbed. It seemed that the motto of the Mores—*Morus tarde moriens morum cito moriturum*—above the rebus of a mulberry tree, implying that the family stock should, like the tree, be of long endurance,

[1] *Holy Sonnets*, XVII.

but that individual descendants, like the fruit, might be subject to early decay, was fulfilled.[1]

As a young man Donne had written with appealing simplicity:

> 'Oh do not die, for I shall hate
> All women so, when thou art gone,
> That thee I shall not celebrate,
> When I remember thou wast one.'[2]

At the same time he had questioned if women had souls, possibly with his tongue in his cheek.[3] He had concurred with a man, who, like him, had been at Trinity and who, in the very pulpit which Donne was to ornament, had declared that:

> 'If a man would marry, it were a thousand to one but he should light upon a bad one . . . and if he should chance to find a good one, yet he were not sure to hold her so. For women are like a cowl full of snakes, amongst which there is one eel, and a thousand to one, if a man happen upon the eel, and get it with his hand, all he has gotten is a wet eel by the tail.'[4]

It was the age of witchcraft, of the public denunciation, revilement, torture and destruction of woman. The Virgin had, in the hearts of many Englishmen, been dethroned, scoffed at and spat upon. Yet individual love, fidelity and charity remained triumphant, and the measure of Donne's grief at the loss of his wife was the measure of his need for her, and his appreciation of her unprotesting worth.

It was also the measure of his capacity for remorse, for somewhere, deep in the recesses of his heart, he must have felt that he had killed her. He had used her selfishly for constant delight and propagation, with scarcely an interval for recovery. He had destroyed the very thing he loved in a fury

---

[1] *Loseley MSS*, (p. xv). Edited by A. J. Kempe.

[2] *A Fever*.

[3] *Loseley MSS*, p. 489. Ann Donne's grandfather, Sir William More, received a request from the Bishop of Winchester, three years before Donne's birth, to look into the assertion by a neighbour that women were thus lacking in spiritual appurtenance.

[4] *Jacobean Journal*, G. B. Harrison, p. 13.

of devitalizing fire. 'Now the consequences of his insatiable egoism stared him in the face, and even he could scarcely avoid drawing damaging conclusions. He had dragged his wife away from ease, to plunge her into poverty, and from life he had hurried her unsparingly to death.'[1]

His fear and his hatred of women worked like a subtle poison to undermine and sap the more healthy, courteous and constructive love, and remorse was the constant shadow and companion of his enjoyment. If a woman rebuffed the Jack Donne of the *Songs and Sonnets* and *Elegies*, he hated her with almost venomous hatred. The rebuff recoiled upon him, proving to him his own instability and worthlessness. Thus, when later he came to woo his God, in accents as pleading, as impassioned and as violent as those in which he had courted mortal woman, and the divine voice failed to answer, he reviled both himself as the pleader, and his God, as deaf and inattentive.

'Thus man, that might be his pleasure, is his rod,
And is his devil that might be his God.'

A year before the death of his wife his sister Anne[2] had also died. In the only surviving letter from Donne to his mother, written just after his sister's death, one senses, above all the perfunctoriness of the writing, the constrained almost laboured tone. His mother had by now married for the third time[3] and they had long been strangers to one another spiritually. His denial of all that Elizabeth Donne had held vital to life, the perilous danger in which she must have believed his soul to lie, when he began to loosen himself from the Catholic church and the guiding reins of her principles, doubtless alienated mother and son. It is even possible that she re-

[1] Fausset, p. 229.

[2] Anne Donne, Donne's only surviving sister married first, Avery Copley, a Yorkshire Catholic, from whose family the American painter Copley was descended, and secondly William Lyly, of London, gentleman.

[3] A gentleman called Rainsford or Raynsforth, probably of the Catholic family in the north.

M

garded him as a worthless heretic in the honourable position which he held in the Established Church, little comprehending the agony of indecision and conscientious sifting he had undergone before accepting it. To such a breadth does the alienation appear to have grown that Donne, in this very letter, says: '*All those children*, (for whose maintenance my father's industry provided and for whose education you were so carefully and so chargeably diligent) *He hath now taken from you.*'[1]

Did he regard himself as a changeling, or lost irredeemably to her as a son? Towards the close he breaks out: 'And, for God's sake pardon those negligences, which I have heretofore used towards you . . . and assist me . . . to do all my duties, especially those that belong to you.' He offers her protection and provision, and indeed he looked after her until the day he died, (for she outlived him), with proper devotion, but it sprang more from a sense of duty than from the heart.

3

The sonnet form, which Donne had used but sparingly before, now moulded his more profound, less urgent thought, which, in young manhood had poured out in that amazing variety of line and form, startling in its very directness, and which in middle-age had emerged in the long, laboured *Funeral Elegies* and *Anniversaries*, with their 'scrapheaps of scholastic rubbish'.[2] In words as impassioned as those formerly addressed to his mistresses he besieged his invisible God and, just as the earlier love poems are threaded with metaphysical and religious thought, so now the Divine are couched in amorous language. The sensuousness of feeling is akin to ecstasy, like that of Donne's successor, Crashaw, but

[1] Letter to his Mother, 1616. Hayward, p. 471. Italics mine.
[2] Desmond MacCarthy, *Criticism*, p. 61.

always there is the note of striving, of vain and frantic struggling to bridge the chasm lying dark and immeasurable between his soul and God. It is this consciousness of the bridgeless chasm, which Milton, too, used all his thunder to emphasize, which prevents Donne from becoming a true mystic.

> 'Except Thou rise and for Thine own work fight,
> Oh I shall soon despair, when I do see
> That Thou lov'st mankind well, yet wilt not choose me,
> And Satan hates me, yet is loth to lose me.'[1]

He calls his Soul 'my black soul' and likens her to a pilgrim,

> '. . . which abroad hath done
> Treason and durst not turn to whence he is fled,
> Or like a thief, which till death's doom be read,
> Wisheth himself delivered from prison;
> But damn'd and hal'd to execution,
> Wisheth that still he might be imprisoned.'[2]

The image of his exiled forebears and of the condemned man being led away to the gallows, or the stake, haunts even these poems addressed to God, or his soul. Remorse gnaws at the heart of Donne, like the worm of corruption which he could not forget, and so he runs the endless circle of repenting, begging for forgiveness, lending himself anew to thoughts, perhaps actions, which he condemns as sinful, and repenting afresh in excruciating bouts of contrition. 'Teach me how to repent,' he implores, and declares 'I think it mercy if Thou wilt forget'.

In the most magnificently brazen of all the *Holy Sonnets* he beseeches his Deity in much the same manner as he might an Inquisitorial gaoler:

> 'Batter my heart, three person'd God; for, you
> As yet, but knock, breath, shine, and seek to mend;
> That I may rise, and stand, o'erthrow me, and bend
> Your force, to break, blow, burn and make me new.

[1] *Holy Sonnets*, II.   [2] *Holy Sonnets*, IV.

> I, like an usurpt town, to another due,
> Labour to admit you, but Oh, to no end,
> Reason, your viceroy in me, me should defend,
> But is captiv'd and proves weak or untrue.
> Yet dearly I love you, and would be loved fain,
> But am betroth'd unto your enemy:
> Divorce me, untie, or break that knot again,
> Take me to you, imprison me, for I,
> Except you enthral me, never shall be free,
> Nor ever chaste, except you ravish me.'[1]

The symbols of the beseiged town, imprisonment, legal restraint and physical violence, are all employed to emphasize the mental torment.

Donne's debt to the Spanish mystics, all of whom died in his boyhood, has been carefully studied by scholars.[2] In some aspects of his thought he was completely un-English but he had not, as a young man, inclined to Italy alone for his broadening influence like so many of the Elizabethans,[3] but also to Spain, whose trends of thought had long been familiar to his ancestors. Sir Thomas More had counted as one of his greatest friends Luis Vives, tutor to Mary Tudor: his grandfather, John Heywood, had been one of the translators of the Spanish *Celestina* whose success would now be described as sensational: his uncles, constantly in touch with the continental seminaries, who looked to Spain as well as to Rome for support, doubtless early taught him a love of Spanish literature. At Oxford he had encountered the Spanish professor Corrano, busiest of all the Spanish reformers, who angered the great Philip by disseminating Protestant literature under his very nose in Spain. He may even have been chosen to go on the expedition to Cadiz and the Azores because of his knowledge

---

[1] *Holy Sonnets*, XIV.

[2] See Miss Ramsay's thesis on *Donne's Mediaevalism*, which deals with his especial debt to St. Theresa and St. Philip Nerius.

[3] For Donne's debt to the Italian mediaeval poets and neo-platonists see Signor Mario Praz, 'Donne's Relation to the Poetry of His Time,' *A Garland for Donne*, and Hughes, *The Lineage of 'The Extasie'*.

of Spanish and we know that, among his friends, Wotton, Woodward, Herbert and Ben Jonson were all proficient in that language.

Upon returning to England he would have come in contact with Antonio Perez, the protégé of Essex and, for a time, the pet of the 'greatest literary set in England, which sat under the shade of Essex and the Bacons'.[1] Perez's 'bittersweet epigrams' were the fashion in England and all the young bloods who followed the footsteps of the splendid Earl sought to imitate the quips and absurdities of Master Antonio, at whose affected manners they laughed.

Here is a letter written by Perez to Lady Rich, one of the beauties of the day, to whom Donne later wrote a *Verse Letter*:

'I have been so troubled not to have the dog's-skin gloves your ladyship desires, that, pending the time when they shall arrive, I have resolved to sacrifice myself to your service, and flay a piece of my own skin from the most tender part of my body, if such an uncouth carcase as mine can have any tender skin. To this length can love and the wish to serve a lady be carried, that man should flay himself to make gloves for his lady. But in my case this is as nothing, for even the soul will skin itself for the person it loves. . . .'[2]

And then Perez, for two or three pages continues to ring the tiresome changes upon dogs, skins and souls.

Donne was too deep a scholar, too great an Aristotelian, too sincere a theologian to write flippantly of the soul, except in a satirical outburst, but there is in his work something of this wearisome play upon themes, phrases and words, admired in Elizabeth's day but offensive to modern ears, and which Donne along with other authors of the day inherited from Spanish sources.

Donne's youthful choice of a Spanish motto for his por-

[1] Martin Hume, *Spanish Influence upon English Literature*, pp. 62 and 243.

[2] Ibid., p. 273.

trait by Hilliard was followed by dabs of Spanish on the MSS which he sent to his friends. He uses the words endearingly, almost as a proof of especial affection and intimacy. Such tags, Oriental in their origin, were popular in England until the end of the seventeenth century and formed part of the fashionable young gentleman's vocabulary. Donne did well to escape the affected wit and precocity, the sententious, proverbial philosophy, attired in veils of ambiguity—of which Lyly's *Euphues* is the extreme example—which set its mark upon English writing at the close of the sixteenth century. But his taste for obscurity resembles this tendency, while not exactly following it. Shakespeare, in *Love's Labour's Lost* describes his Spanish Courtier as a man 'that hath a mint of phrases in his brain', and much that is gritty and hard to digest in Donne's earlier poetry seems to come from the same type of close-packed mind, speaking in short, compact phrases.

As Donne grew older and tension slackened, the tendency towards ambiguity diminished. The *Holy Sonnets* are smoother in style although equally tortured in thought. But now it is a sacred torment. Whereas before he had written:

> 'Shadow that hell unto me which, alone,
> I am to suffer when my love is gone,'[1]

now, in even stronger accents he pleads with his God not to desert him, lest he be cast into everlasting misery—'privation of the sight of God, banishment from the presence of God, an absolute hopelessness, an utter impossibility. . . .'[2] This spirit of maceration, of self-suppression in order to attain to a perfect union with God, permeates the *Holy Sonnets*. No doubt Donne drew it from the Spanish mystics, for the gentle simplicity of the Italian St. Francis he might never imitate. The conflict in his own soul was too intense, too self-conscious and too permanent.

---

[1] *Elegy* XII. [2] Sermon, St. Paul's, Easter Day, 1622.

The Divine Poems cannot have been written all at once but the impact which urged Donne into their expression was Ann's death, and Walton describes his state perfectly when he says that 'his very soul was elemented of nothing but sadness' and that 'grief took so full possession of his heart as to leave no place for joy'. Donne's longing was also for death. 'As the grave is become her house, so I would hasten to make it mine also: that we two might there make our beds together in the dark.'[1]

Such a yearning for annihilation, such an acute deprivation of balance, and accent on morbidity, cannot co-exist with life for long, and Donne at length issued forth to preach at St. Dunstan's in the West, not far from St. Clement Danes, where his wife lay buried. 'Lo, I am the man that have seen affliction' was the text which the suffering voice gave out from the pulpit and his auditors, as always, were moved by the spectacle of his grief and his intense, dramatic sincerity. But there was nothing self-pitying or mawkish in his words; the Sermon was dignified and restrained.

No longer might he re-create himself in the riverside gardens at Twickenham for his 'orient light-bringer',[2] Lucy, Countess of Bedford, involved in crippling debt,[3] saddened by the loss of her father and only brother and her husband's paralysis after a fall from his horse, had retired to Moor Park in Hertfordshire. Nor were the doors of Drury and York House open to him, for both Sir Robert and the old Lord Chancellor had died, the latter five months before Ann. (Lord Bacon thereupon crept assiduously into the shoes of the office of Lord Keeper which his own father had worn before him, and which he had for so long coveted from Donne's former

[1] Walton, p. 30.   [2] Carlyle's epithet for Jane Welsh.

[3] Nicholas Stone, the Devonshire mason, whom Kings besought to make their effigies, notes that Lucy, Countess of Bedford had agreed to pay him the sum of £1,020 for a monument and to defray all charges for 'carridge and iron' as well, and Gosse speaks of her reckless buying of Holbeins, vol. ii, p. 70. See also Social England, vol. iii.

master.) With his mind revolving upon his years of companionship with Ann, Donne must often have turned to the thought of their 'first, strange and fatal interview', of their courting and headlong rush into clandestine matrimony, under the kind Lord Keeper's eye. Finally, the Benchers at Lincoln's Inn, and the King himself, were forced to take note of Donne's dangerous lethargy and overtaxed energies and, in 1619, the latter decided to send him, together with his old friend Lord Hay, now Lord Doncaster, upon a mission to Germany. Donne's position was entirely unofficial and the journey intended merely as a fillip to recuperation.

4

Trouble had begun to brew in Bohemia over the ever-recurrent question of religious policy and a new heir to the crown. The Bohemians who were strongly Protestant objected to the appointment, by the Emperor Matthias, of a Catholic Archduke as their ruler and an appeal was made to James the Ist, as a champion of Protestantism, to arbitrate between the new King and his baulking subjects.

The embassy from England was to set out in May. In April, Donne circulated copies of *Biathanatos*, with cautionary phrases, to his especial friends, together with some of his poems. His concentration on death and his reduced state of health made him apprehensive for his own physical welfare. The mental distress he had been suffering aggravated his digestive troubles and brought into prominence in his own mind the idea that he was, at root, never well and might at any moment succumb to one or another fatal disease. He feared that he might not return to the land and the friends whom he loved. Despite his early experiences in the nautical expeditions to Cadiz and the Azores Donne did not like or trust the sea. As a young man he had asked:

> . . . 'and dar'st thou lay
> Thee in ship's wooden Sepulchres, a prey
> To leaders' rage, to storms, to shot, to dearth?
> Dar'st thou dive seas, and dungeons of the earth?'[1]

and declared that:

> 'To mew me in a ship, is to enthrall
> Me in a prison, that were like to fall;
> Or in a cloister; save that there men dwell
> In a calm heaven, here in a swaggering hell.
> Long voyages are long consumptions,
> And ships are carts for executions.
> Yea they are deaths—'[2] . . .

Now he preached a farewell sermon to his friends the Benchers,[3] in which he emphasized the tempestuous sea through which we must travel to the Kingdom of God, 'where no soul suffers shipwreck; though we must be blown with strange winds, with sighs and groans for our sins. . . .': and wrote his *Hymn to Christ*, a poem of relinquishment, in which he uses the simile of the fragile soul sailing on her homeward journey, and the waters of Christ washing away mortal sin.

The death of Queen Anne and the grave illness of James the Ist caused a postponement of the journey but at length in May, Lord Doncaster, his retinue, and Donne set out. Upon reaching Antwerp, Donne found the Countess of Bedford returning from the very place to which he was going—the court of the Princess Elizabeth. She had been seriously ill and lay in a darkened room, suffering from an affliction of the eyes. It must have been an affecting meeting,[4] but the Countess returned to London and Donne continued his journey.

In June the embassy reached Heidelberg, where Donne had the pleasure of renewing his acquaintance with King James' daughter, the Princess Elizabeth (wife of the Count Palatine and mother of Prince Rupert) for whose wedding he had written an Epithalamion and before whom he preached

---

[1] *Satyre* III.
[2] *Elegy* XX.
[3] April 18, 1619.
[4] Jessop, p. 48.

twice before continuing his journey. The Princess had the
proverbial charm of the Stuarts and was able to bind admirers
and supporters to her with all the magic inherent in the Stuart
character. She regarded Donne with affectionate favour and
part of her hold over her friends was the warmth and con-
stancy of her regard for them.

Late in the year of Donne's sojourn the Elector Palatine received an invitation from the Bohemian nobles to accept the
throne and after some hesitation he was crowned at Prague.
His reign lasted for a single year which caused the people to
give him and the Princess names like those from a Grimm
fairy-tale—the 'Winter King' and the 'Snow Queen'. During
her transitory reign the Queen Consort entertained many
friends from England, among them the old water-poet, John
Taylor, who had arranged the pageant for her elaborate
wedding celebrations.

Lord Doncaster, however, was unsuccessful in bringing
about a satisfactory solution to the problems of the German
states and his embassy duly retired, making its way homeward through Vienna, the Tyrol, Cologne, Salzburg, Nur-
emberg, Munich, Brussels and The Hague. Here Donne
preached before the States General, who had recently been
invaded by English ecclesiastical representatives to the Synod
of Dort, in the hope of mediating between the extreme followers of Calvin and the less ferocious adherents to his doctrines. The Synod had dispersed but Donne, as a signal
favour of the esteem in which the Dutch held him, was
presented with a gold medal struck as a memorial of the
Synod, which he treasured and eventually willed to Henry
King, Bishop of Chichester, poet and son of Doctor King,
the old friend who had ordained him.[1]

Pleasant as it was for Donne to be attached to an embassy,

[1] Huyghens, the Dutch poet who had been attached to the Dutch embassy in London in 1618 and who became an enthusiastic admirer both of
Donne and his poetry, may have written about him to his Dutch friends,
heralding his advent.

to have no specific work or responsibility and yet to share in the glory, the journey cannot have been entirely pleasurable. There had been long delays, doublings back on the course like beagles in pursuit of a hare, the tedious business of being dragged upstream against the current by heavy horses, and the inevitable breakdowns of conveyances. An uncertainty of the fruitfulness of the whole adventure was added to the suspected insincerity of the various royal parties concerned. The Benchers at Lincoln's Inn were anxious for the return of their valued preacher and Lord Doncaster had to write more than once to beg for their clemency in keeping him beyond the time originally allotted for the embassy.

Links with three of Donne's friends occured upon the journey, for Sir Henry Goodyer's son-in-law, Nethersole, became official secretary to Lord Doncaster at his request, and in an appeal for leniency to the Benchers the latter refers to 'Mr. Brooke, a person I think known to you, who will wait upon you for such a letter'. This was doubtless Christopher, faithful still in service. And at some time during the foreign tour Donne met Sir Henry Wotton who was then returning to London.

Refreshed by his travels abroad, Donne returned to London to take up his duties and the care of his seven motherless children, of whom Constance, well and truly named, was the eldest, a girl of seventeen, shortly to be courted by the most incongruous suitor imaginable.

5

History in retrospect provides us with a confusion of events, kaleidoscopic in nature and ironic in their significance. In 1620 the Pilgrim Fathers set sail in the diminutive *Mayflower*. In 1621 John King, Bishop of London, whom Donne had had as companion to him in his first studies at York House, died, and Archbishop Abbot had the misfortune to

shoot a keeper whilst hunting in Lord Zouche's park. The
first event did not excite one half the interest which the last
did, yet its consequences have been multiplied a thousand-
fold. The Archbishop's action, although condoned by the
sovereign, brought the condemnation of other church dignitaries who maintained that, since he was guilty of culpable
homicide, the Archbishop was not fit to hold office or carry
out the duties attaching it to. William Laud, and others, were
therefore consecrated without his presence and Abbot became a broken man, never recovering from the stigma attached to an accident which might have befallen the meanest
citizen. Donne remarks upon his misfortune in a letter to
Goodyer:

'I have been sometimes with my Lord of Canterbury since his
accident, to give you his own words. I see him retain his former
cheerfulness here and at Croydon, but I do not hear from Court
that he hath any ground for such a confidence, but that his case
may need favour and not have it.'[1]

Donne was at this time engaged in angling for promotion
through the mediation of Buckingham. He terms himself in
his letter to the new favourite 'so poor a worm as I am', 'a
clod of clay', and calls the begging letter a 'rag of paper'. Yet
this miserable creature was at this time, according to his own
account, enjoying pleasant and aristocratic company in a
variety of places—Bedington, Chelsea, Highgate, Hackney
and Peckham,—and performing his work consummately.

Throughout September and October 1621, Donne's hopes
for preferment hung like a pendant in a faint wind, now flying
buoyantly, now drooping dispiritedly, until one day in November the King sent for him, asking him to dine at the royal
table.

'When His Majesty was sat down, before he had ate any meat
he said, after his pleasant manner "Dr. Donne, I have invited you
to dinner; and though you sit not down with me, yet I will carve

to you of a dish that I know you love well; for, knowing you love London, I do therefore make you Dean of St Paul's; and when I have dined, then do you take your beloved dish home to your study, say grace there to yourself, and much good may it do you." '[1]

The spiritual repast was not quite so quick in coming to table as the King had prophesied, for there were various delays consequent upon the raising of new deans to the episcopate, the consecration of new bishops, and the Archbishop's accident which hindered the performance of the consecrations. Nevertheless, the Deanery was in the King's own gift and as soon as the ecclesiastical machinery had been put in order Donne was able to sup in full. He entered upon his new office at the close of November.

With what pride the Dean must have surveyed his new home and garden lying to the south of 'old Powl's' and running in a strip from the cathedral yard through to Carter's Lane! The gatehouse and porters' lodges, the grassplots, vines and borders, even the private chapel, may have reminded him of the gates, gardens, lodges and chapels of his father's Company and seemed strangely like home to him. With a rush of architectural fervour and pride of possession Donne immediately ordered the repair of the chapel and the furnishing of the Deanery. He refused to accept any longer the allowance which Sir George More had granted him since Sir Francis Wooley's intervention, with the gracious words: 'It is enough: you have been kind to me and mine: I know your present condition is such as not to abound, and I hope mine is, or will be such, as not to need it.'[2] He relinquished the position of Reader to the Benchers of Lincoln's Inn, receiving from them the honorary station of fellow Bencher: and gave up the living at Keyston, not without some legal quibbling, believing that his stipend would in future be ample. In less than a year, however, he was excusing himself

[1] Walton, p. 33.   [2] Walton, p. 33.

from assisting Sir Henry Goodyer because of his own indebtedness.

'I have locked myself, sealed and secured myself against all possibilities of falling into new debts, and, in good faith, this year hath thrown me £400 lower than when I entered this house.'[1]

However, his generosity to Goodyer upon another occasion went pleasantly hand in hand with the new expenses of moving upon terms of increased intimacy with the Court and extravagant nobility.

Donne's first appearance as Dean in the pulpit of Saint Paul's was upon Christmas Day. The long apprenticeship which he had undergone, stretching from his first sermon in the little ruinous church at Paddington, had given the orator increasing confidence and trained him well in that art which combines literary, dramatic and oratorical abilities. Preaching was, in fact, for Donne, the solution to many of his quandaries and the resolution of tendencies which before had too often warred against each other rather than marched amicably together.

It was not for nothing that his grandfather had been court player and 'jester', or that he himself, as a young man, had been elected Steward of Christmas at Lincoln's Inn. The training he had from his Jesuit tutors as a child in casuistry and declamation stood him in good stead. His knowledge of Scriptures and the Law; his gifts as a poet, which made him aware of the value of words, even syllables, and of their sound as well as their meaning; his practice in prose writing in which emphasis, proportion and arrangement are all of value; his wide interests, ranging from ancient lore to modern navigation, astronomy, chemistry and medicine, from the arts to science, kept his listeners' minds attentive. Finally, his manner of delivery which combined the gifts of the conversationalist with an obvious charm of voice and bearing, attracted

[1] October 4th, 1622.

even those who were unaware of his deeper contribution—a knowledge of the progress of the human soul through the valleys of temptation and disappointment. Here was a preacher who outdistanced the magnificence of other preachers as the eagle outflies the sparrow, who clothed 'even the dead bones of theology . . . with comeliness and who made metaphysics and morality into an epic poem: while without any clerical unction he yet paid his service to God with something of the considered grace, the gesture and formality of a courtier'.[1] And here was a man who spoke with conviction, proving that 'his own heart was possessed with those very thoughts and joys that he laboured to distil into others; a preacher in earnest; weeping sometimes for his auditory, sometimes with them; always preaching to himself like an angel from a cloud, but in none; carrying some . . . to heaven in holy raptures, and enticing others by a sacred art and courtship to amend their lives; here picturing a vice so as to make it ugly to those that practice it, and a virtue so as to make it beloved even by those that loved it not; and all this with a most particular grace and an inexpressible addition of comeliness'.[2]

Such pronounced ability brought enemies as well as admirers. The Puritans naturally suspected Donne of an inherent tendency towards Popery, the Anglicans were on the watch for him to ally himself with the Puritans. Some distrusted his minute and mediaeval reasoning, and his strict bibliolatry, others his toleration and enthusiasm, too modern for their narrow minds. Mysticism, metaphysical conceit, and allegory with its heavy, rich and indigestible analogy, were spider-webs from which the plain-spoken citizens of the new era shrank, as if Truth was garbed in embroideries too fine, too intricate for their comprehension. Yet, on the whole Donne maintained an even course between the treacherous shoals of extreme parties, trimming his sails neatly with

[1] Fausset, p. 227.   [2] Walton, p. 28.

orthodox theology, keeping his ballast of scholastic authority, and sweeping the decks free from ecclesiastical prejudice.

Of the fact that there was a disapproving Puritan element in his congregations Donne was fully aware. He even had the courage to speak directly to it declaring that he knew that some of his audience were half-assenting, half-dissenting:

'You are here now, hearing me, and yet you are thinking that you have heard a better sermon somewhere else, of this text before; you are here and yet you think you could have heard some other doctrine of down right Predestination, and Reprobation roundly delivered somewhere else with more edification to you.'[1]

Two of his eulogists after his death draw a picture of the 'doctrine men' as they were named, sitting with 'sour faces, humming against him', who:

> 'Called him a strong lin'd man, a Macaroon,
> And no way fit to speak to clouted shoon.
> As fine words, truly, as you would desire,
> But verily, but a bad edifier.
> Thus did these beetles slight in him that good,
> They could not see, and much less understood.'[2]

This use of the scoffing epithet 'Macaroon' is interesting since it was Donne who (when a young man) imported the word into the English language, introducing it in his fourth Satyre.[3]

Another eulogist pays him the compliment of saying that:

> 'Such was thy carriage, and thy gesture such,
> As could divide the heart, and conscience touch.'[4]

But the highest tribute of all to Donne's eloquence came from a foreigner. 'From your golden mouth, whether in the chamber of a friend, or in the pulpit, fell the speech of God

---

[1] 50 Sermons, 14, 116.   [2] Richard Busby. Grierson, vol. i, pp. 386–7.

[3] ' 'To hear this Makeron talk.' This is the earliest instance of the Italian word used in English which the O.E.D. quotes, and is proof of Donne's Italian travels. . . . His use of the word attracted attention.' Grierson, vol. ii, p. 123.

[4] Jaspar Mayne, 'On Dr. Donne's Death', Grierson, vol. i, p. 384.

whose nectar I drank again and again with heartfelt joy.'[1] So spoke Constantine Huyghens, himself a poet, who showed a peculiarly sensitive appreciation of Donne's words, whether written or spoken.

6

The year which brought Donne his Deanery brought good fortune at last to his old friend and intermediator, the Earl of Northumberland, who had for so many years suffered imprisonment in the Tower. Raleigh had been ignominiously done away with in 1618, the year between the death of Ann and Donne's participation in the embassy to Germany, and Northumberland, the head of the English aristocracy, might consider himself fortunate to be alive. He very naturally resented the humiliating stipulation that he must never venture more than thirty miles from his home, Petworth Park, in Sussex.

The lives of Donne's friends entwine and intermingle in a curious manner, like tendrils of clematis in the hedge of a wild garden. Northumberland's daughter, another Lucy, had been courted by Lord Doncaster, who had recently received yet another title, that of Earl of Carlisle from his appreciative Sovereign. Lucy, Countess of Bedford, had fostered the suit, the King had favoured it and the younger Lucy had married Donne's friend without her father's consent, while he was still imprisoned. Upon his release the Earl was therefore faced with the unpleasant business of stomaching a new son-in-law, whom he considered an upstart, a new favourite, Buckingham, whose lineage, morals and extravagance disgusted him, a Monarch for whom he had both contempt and hatred, and a daughter whose high-willed independence and lavish entertainment amazed him. In fact, Northumberland had been imprisoned in a world still Elizabethan in character

---

[1] See Grierson, ii, pp. lxxvii and xv.

and now came out into the Jacobean sunlight, to be, like Rip van Winkle, both astonished and dismayed. His son-in-law proved, however, to be a man of worth and ability to whom the Earl owed his release from prison, who was willing to advise and admonish him concerning the dangerous paths of new court intrigue and who, finally, secured the cancellation of the odious parole upon which his father-in-law had been placed.

Thereupon, Lucy, Countess of Carlisle, and her husband threw open the doors of their palatial home of *Hanworth* inviting members of the nobility to welcome back their titular head, amongst them the all-powerful Marquis of Buckingham, who was ready to extend his hand in an easy and graceful manner which cost him nothing. (It was an ironical setting, for *Hanworth* had been the dower house of Queen Katharine Parr, and a former holder of the title, the 6th Earl of Northumberland had been in love with Anne Boleyn, but such was the fast-changing scene of English life in three generations— the monasteries taken over by merchants, bishops seizing the lands of disgraced favourites and the Sovereigns issuing orders for possession according to individual caprice—that no one had time to reflect on history stale in so short a time.) The one thing considered essential as a crown for the ceremony of welcome was a fine sermon, and who fitter to deliver it than the friend of both father and son-in-law, John Donne? The new Dean obliged fittingly, to the pleasure of the whole company and subsequently dined with Northumberland at Sion House, in Middlesex. Thus, after a long hiatus, Donne renewed his friendship with a man with whom he had much in common mentally and to whom he owed the courageous but unsuccessful intervention at the time of his marriage twenty-one years earlier.

The more practical fruits of his sermon at *Hanworth* were the recognition of the King's favourite, Buckingham, and the King's order that Donne should, in September 1622, butter the unpalatable bread which James was attempting to force down the throat of clergy and people alike, the *Instructions to Preachers*. These were in the nature of a royal poultice to alleviate the heat and soreness rising between antagonistic parties in the Church. Neither the *Instructions* nor Donne's pacificatory Sermon were intelligible to those involved, who suspected that they were being gulled by fair words into a denial of their principles, a restriction of their liberty of speech, and a truce with their opponents. The toleration of James the 1st, Donne, and other ecclesiastics of the reign,—such as the prelates who went to the Synod of Dort,—was too much in advance of its day to be acceptable to men riddled with animosity. Donne made an intelligent attempt at pacification. His talents and services were increasingly in demand.

7

'On Wednesday night, the Virginia Company had a feast, or meeting, at the Merchant Taylor's Hall, whither many of the nobility and Council were invited, but few came. They were between three and four hundred, at three shillings a man. The Dean of Saint Paul's preached according to the custom of all feastings nowadays.'[1]

Thus, towards the close of the same year, Donne delivered what has been called the first missionary sermon. He himself was one of the 'adventurers', or early shareholders, together with the father of the saintly Nicholas Ferrar and the Earl of Southampton, who had just been chosen Treasurer. Board-meetings were called to investigate the accounts and other neglected matters of the Company, and Donne, with all the inner tormoil he had experienced since he and Southampton had sailed away to scour Cadiz, in eyeing him across the table at one of these meetings, might congratulate himself that he was not a peer of the realm and had not been too

[1] Nicholls, 1622, vol. iv, p. 781.

closely associated with the ill-starred Essex. For Southampton, imprisoned, condemned and then released, was suspect, either because of his early association with Essex, his religion, or his volatile disposition, and constantly blocked in attempts to receive court preferment. He had to be content with ornamental offices and sought to occupy and distract himself in forwarding various colonial enterprizes or in patronizing men of letters.

The pious 'adventurers' now gathered together, who counted bishops among their numbers, had come to the conclusion that too much emphasis was being laid upon the commercial side of the enterprise and too little upon the spiritual, and that it was high time that, in spite of the ugly Indian massacre of settlers a few months earlier, some of the company's resources should be used for conversion purposes. Donne's interest in the voyages and colonial attempts of Raleigh so like that of his ancestor Rastell had been evident in many poems, and now, as a noted preacher with a honey-golden tongue, he was persuaded to advertise the good intentions of the company, whose earlier broadsheets, giving the advantages promised to emigrants, the progress of the enterprize and the date for drawing a lottery intended to attract subscribers, had not always succeeded.

Perhaps the most interesting paragraph of his Sermon is that in which he prophecies the future greatness of the colony:

'And you that are young now, may live to see . . . your friends, yea children, as well accommodated in that place as any other. You shall have made this island, which is but as the suburbs of the old world, a bridge, a gallery to the new, to join all to that world that shall never grow old—the kingdom of heaven, and add names to the books of our chronicles, and to the Book of Life.'

Such vague but tantalizing promise of immortality, may, or may not, have tempted subscribers but it added to Donne's increasing popularity and the sermon was published and eagerly sought after.

This insistence upon the Sermon as a necessary part of court, private and commercial ceremonies is in odd contrast to the pathetic condition of old Saint Paul's in the year in which Donne received the Deanery. Practically nothing had been done to repair the cathedral church since it had been struck by lightning more than half a century before. It lacked its steeple and was in bad structural repair. One wide-awake citizen,[1] conscious of the discrepancy between the outward appearance of St. Paul's and the spiritual richness of her preachers, tried, time and again, to have the church repaired, by petitions to the King couched in verse, by drawings and texts, and the promotion of bills before Parliament. He even paid for the execution of an engraving depicting a preaching at the Cross during an anticipated royal visit to St. Paul's. The visit took place in March of 1620 and although Donne was not made Dean until November of 1621, he had already preached at St. Paul's Cross. In this engraving[2] the King and Charles, Prince of Wales, the Court, Mayor and Aldermen, who generally attended on horseback, the beadle, who tapped slumbrous worshippers and removed stray dogs from the churchyard close, the Archbishop, Bishops and Officers of State, and a few choice citizens may all be seen attending the preacher, who was, the print states, Dr. John King, Donne's old friend, the Bishop of London, who died in the following year. The braziers filled with burning coals to dissipate the germs of the dreaded plague, and the jackdaws or pigeons flying symmetrically in and out of the tower enliven the drawing.

Alas, the prevailing taste of the Londoner was, according to the satirist, not for religion, but for vulgar amusement. He cared only:

> 'To see a strange, outlandish fowl,
> A quaint baboon, an ape, an owl,

[1] Henry Farley, who got into Ludgate Prison for his schemes about Paul's. See Rye, p. 188.

[2] In the possession of the Society of Antiquaries, London.

A dancing bear, a giant's bone,
A foolish injin move alone,
A morris dance, a puppit play,
Mad Tom to sing a roundelay,
A woman dancing on a rope,
Bull-baiting also at the Hope;
A rimer's jests, a jugler's cheats,
A tumbler shewing cunning feats,
Or players acting on the stage,
There goes the bounty of our age;
But unto any pious notion,
There's little coin, and lesse devotion.'[1]

8

'Dabbling on foot and bareheaded'[2] the members of a procession from the Serjeant's Feast in the Temple marched in
the cold October rain of 1623 from Lincoln's Inn to St.
Paul's. Here, Donne, sickening for an almost mortal disease,
fulfilled his duty of preaching uncomplainingly. Then he went
home to the Deanery, dejected and feverish, apprehensive of
the unknown illness, since the symptoms were extremely
painful. A modern patient's condition would be eased, and
his mind reassured, by the use of drugs as well as medicines
but the seventeenth century treatment of blood-letting, ap-
plying pigeons to the head to draw off the vapours and other
primitive remedies, only increased Donne's debility and in
no way allayed the ferociously heightened activities of his
brain. As if he were at once both patient and medical observer, suffering, yet at the same time disembodying himself and
analysing his least sensation, thought and emotion, he lay
and anatomized his condition.

The result, the *Devotions upon Emergent Occasions*, is gruesome in the extreme and yet strangely enthralling. It is a

[1] Henry Farley's *St. Paul's Church*, 1621. A similar list is given in lines
prefaced to *Coryate's Crudities*, to which Donne had been a contributor,
in 1611.

[2] Gosse, vol. ii, p. 181, quoting.

singular account, rare in the annals of spiritual and physical combat, resembling the story of Christian's torment in *Pilgrim's Progress*. It resembles the work of a medical and psychological research worker, and is a kind of case-sheet or spiritual temperature-chart from which both the skilled physician and therapist of today might deduce most of Donne's mental and physical states. The abiding darkness of his mind, which underlay the more obvious vivacity, (which he called 'alacrity'), now became profusely apparent, etched in even deeper lines by the heavy disease. Not for a moment did the tautness of his mind relax and, as if observation might assist recovery, he noted with microscopic precision every detail. Humour about himself was never one of Donne's greatest attributes, but it is a quality noticeably lacking in egoists, neurotics and invalids, and the Dean was then compact of all three types.

The bells of the cathedral and the city churches especially disturbed him, for they brought sudden, sharp, painful reminders of the reasons for which they tolled. Perhaps it is some friend of his who is being interred today. Perhaps they will toll for him, John Donne, tomorrow. He remembers the bells of foreign cities, of Antwerp, Rouen and heaven knows what other cathedral town, visited in the reckless days of his youth or upon the more sedate occasions of mature manhood. The bells of all the cities in the world roll into one vast, booming, intolerable noise, in which he swims like a drowning man, only to wake and find the fever slightly abated, the night chill, and the tallow burning low—only himself lying huddled in the vast, uncomfortable bed, over whose fusty hangings and ornate antiquity the shadows wamble grotesquely.

'Who casts not up his eye to the sun when it rises? but who takes off his eye from a comet when that breaks out? Who bends not his ear to any bell, which upon any occasion rings? but who can remove it from that bell, which is passing a piece of himself out of this world? No man is an island, entire of itself; every man is a piece of the continent, a part of the main; if a clod be washed away by the sea, Europe is the less, as well as if a promontory were, as well as if a manor of thy friends or of thine own were; any man's death diminishes me, because I am involved in mankind; and therefore never send to know for whom the bell tolls; it tolls for thee.'[1]

Here, in the *Devotions*, is Donne for us in the round; Donne stretched upon the vivisectionist's board, pinned, flayed and exquisitely dissected. The work of Dürer in anatomy had interested him as a young man and when he died Donne willed to a friend a painting of a skeleton. Such grim reminders of the frailty of life were not unknown to others in that gruesome age when the stone-mason did all that he could to emphasize the contrast between pulsing life and bare-ribbed death, but Donne's interpretation is even more intensely personal. A modern reader, turning the pages of the *Devotions* for the first time, if he were not repelled by the morbidity, or distracted by the idiom, might baulk at the grotesqueness of the imagery, the display of metaphysical conceit, with its far-fetched allusions and delight in paradox, the immense and obsolete learning. Yet he would be held by the quality which still makes Donne alive, the passionate sincerity and the reality of the conflict waged.

For the *Devotions* are not merely the literary effusion of a distempered mind, they are, like the poems and the sermons, the key to Donne's disordered soul and the story of his life's battle—how first the joyful predominates and then how melancholy undermines. Donne is one of the greatest examples of the despairing sinner, that is, one who dares to believe himself very nearly damned—'Murmuring, murmuring in their hearts, secret disobediences, secret repugnances, against His declared will; these are the most deadly, the most pernicious' sinners.[2]

---

[1] *Devotions upon Emergent Occasions*, Meditation XVII.

[2] *Devotions upon Emergent Occasions*, Meditations IX. The following quotations are all taken from the Meditations.

'The child of desperation' is grouped with 'the child of the world', 'of the devil,' 'of perdition' and 'of hell'. The man who excludes himself from the Kingdom of Heaven does so

'in a sinful and rebellious melancholy. But as melancholy is the hardest humour to be purged, so is the melancholy in the soul, the distrust of thy salvation, too. Flashes of presumption a calamity will quench, but clouds of desperation calamities thicken upon us; But even in this inordinate dejection thou exaltest thyself above God, and makedst thy worst better than his best, thy sins larger than His mercy.'[1]

Here we see Donne openly discoursing upon the two great sins against the Holy Ghost, Presumption and Despair, in a manner reminiscent of the Catholic priest and indeed, many of his allusions, such as that to the guardian angel watching over each man's destiny, have a pronounced Catholic flavour which cannot have been offensive in his day and, surviving in the Anglican church, escaped the Puritan critics.[2]

The subjects of the *Devotions* are the Power of Sin, the Miseries of Human Life, the Universality of Death, the Everlasting Mercy, the Judgment of God, the Hope of Forgiveness and Resurrection. But as the beginner in painting or writing draws self-portraits, the God upon whom Donne leans is an image of himself. All the hatred he bears for himself, and all his wretched impulses he attributes to his Divine Maker: he queries ingenuously whether God may, like man, not sometimes be ill, and then denies it, but behind the ingenuousness lies an awful doubting.

'What, a God, and need a Physician? A Jupiter and need an Aesculapius? ... God is presented to us under many human

[1] Sermons, Lincoln's Inn, Sunday after Trinity, 1621 and St. Paul's, Whitsunday, 1625.

[2] In 1621, Burton, had published his famous *Anatomy of Melancholy*, and although Donne was acquainted with Galen's summary of the humours before Burton, his constant references to melancholy in his letters and writings would make an interesting comparative study with Burton's work. Both men were ardent cosmographers.

affections, as far as infirmities: but never a sick God: for then he might die like men, as our Gods do.'[1]

He cannot for a moment decide if his sickness be from God or Lucifer.

'My God, my God, thou wast not wont to come in whirlwinds, but in soft and gentle air. Thy first breath breathed a soul into me, and shall thy breath blow it out? . . . Surely it is not thou; it is not thy hand. The devouring sword, the consuming fire, the winds from the wilderness, the diseases of the body, all that afflicted Job, were from the hand of Satan; it is not Thou. It is Thou; Thou, my God, who hast led me so continually with thy hand. . . .'[2]

Then the nature, resilient even in sickness, springs up, declaring:

'As a man cannot flatter God, nor overpraise Him, so a man cannot injure Man, nor undervalue him.'[3]

or:

'No man is well that understands not, that values not his being well; that hath not a cheerfulness, and a joy in it and whosoever hath this joy, hath a desire to communicate joy, to others; for every man loves witnesses of his happiness; and the best witnesses are experimental witnesses; they who have tasted of that in themselves, which makes us happy.'[4]

Then the pendulum swings back again, vengefully, and with Job-like despair he cries out;

'How little of a man is the heart, and yet it is all, by which he is; and this continually subject, not only to foreign poisons, conveyed by others, but to intestine poisons, bred in ourselves by pestilential sickness. O who, if before he had a being, he could have sense of this misery, would buy a being here upon these conditions?'[5]

This is a complaint against life itself. Again he declares:

'Man hath no centre but misery; there and only there he is 'fixt, and sure to find himself.'[6]

---

[1] *Devotions*, VIII.   [2] *Devotions*, pp. 29–30.   [3] *Devotions*, XIV.
[4] *Devotions*, VIII.   [5] *Devotions*, XI.   [6] *Devotions*, XXI.

The theme of *Pseudomartyr* occupies his mind again:

'Madness, upon misplacing, or overbending our natural faculties, proceeds from ourselves, and so, as that ourselves are in
the plot, and we are not only passive, but active too, to our own
destruction. . . . There are too many examples of men that have
been their own executioners, and that have made hard shift to be
so. . . .'[1]

How stupid in misery he is:

'We say the elements of man are misery and happiness, as
though he had an equal proportion of both, and the days of man
vicissitudinary, as though he had as many good days as ill, and that
he lived under a perpetual equinoctial night and day, equal good
and ill fortune in the same measure. But it is far from that; he
drinks misery, and he tastes happiness; he mows misery, and he
gleans happiness: he journeys in misery, he does but walk in happiness; and which is worst, his misery is positive, and dogmatical,
his happiness is but disputable, and problematical; All men call
misery, Misery, but Happiness changes the name by the taste of
man.'[2]

There are various indirect personal references valuable for
their rarity: 'My parents would not give me over to a servant's correction. . . .' or: 'the eldest is oftentimes not the
strongest of the family. . . .' which implies Donne's hesitancy
over his own health. In the passage:

'A woman is comforted with the birth of her son, her body is
eased of a burthen; but if she could prophetically read his history,
how ill a man, perchance how ill a son, he would prove, she should
receive a greater burden into her mind. . . .'

is perhaps a picture of Donne's regret for the neglect of his
own mother, or possibly prophetic of the worthlessness of
his elder son, John, who had some of his father's abilities but
was 'clogged with the secret encumbrances' of his failings.
He speaks of childbirth, and of how a woman cannot hasten
or forward her pregnancy. Ann's sufferings must often have
haunted him in his sickness, and when he writes,

[1] *Devotions*, XII.   [2] *Devotions*, XIII.

'Some men lock up, not only their liberality, but their justice and compassion, till the solicitation of a wife, or a son, or a friend, or a servant turn the key',

doubtless he thought of her choleric father, old Sir George More, and of young Francis Wooley, dead so long, and his generous intervention upon his and Ann's behalf.

The King sent his own physician and at length the doctors with their curious practices, still half savouring of necromancy, pulled round the feeble Donne. 'Not death, not disease, not piercing agony, is capable of cowing, of shaming into quiescence, that incorrigible heathen force that we call life, and which is as quick to jump, and as inimical to cessation, as a little red flea on a nipping frosty morning.'[1]

He sat up in bed and looked forward to having his *Hymn to God the Father* set to music. Possibly Mr. John Hilton, organist to Saint Margaret's church, would oblige him in the composition and rendering.[2]

9

In the same year in which Donne struggled with his disease of mind and body two cheerful matters, more closely related to life, were afoot at the Palace of Saint James and in the Deanery.

Prince Charles, to whom Donne had dedicated the restless *Devotions*, had been to Spain to court the Infanta, and Constance Donne was betrothed to, and shortly to marry, Edward Alleyn, the famous actor. The Infanta was a beautiful girl, tall, fair-skinned, and with full lips which met with the approval of connoisseurs. The impetuous young Prince of Wales got himself into trouble by following her across the river to watch her gather May dew in the gardens of her father's palace. 'He rose betimes and went thither' where he was 'let into . . . the garden, but the Infanta was in the

[1] Llewellyn Powys, *The Verdict of Bridlegoose.*
[2] See Grierson, vol. ii, p. 252.

orchard, and there being a high partition wall between and the door doubly bolted, the Prince got on the top of the wall and sprung down a great height and so made towards her. But she, spying him first of all the rest, gave a shriek and ran back. The old Marquis, her guardian, came towards the Prince and fell on his knees, conjuring his Highness to retire, for he forfeited his head if he admitted any to her company. So the door was opened and he came out *under* that wall, *over* which he had got in.'[1]

We have no such portrait of the courting of Constance Donne, nor of her appearance. Whether she had her father's large eyes and outrageous charm, softened by some sweet simplicity of her mother's character, we do not know. Unknown to her, her hand had already been sought in marriage by the parents of a young man of position, who, knowing as little as she of their superior machinations, changed his plans, refused to go into the church, begged to travel, and threw the careful paternal concoctions into ferment. Now she was to marry a man even older than her father, thirty-eight years her senior!

Edward Alleyn was first and foremost an actor, secondly a manager, and thirdly the founder of Dulwich College. He had been for years in the very front rank of Shakespearian actors. He and his father-in-law, Phillip Henslowe, (for Alleyn had been married before), had built the Fortune Theatre which, having been burnt to the ground, was rebuilt of stouter brick in the very year that Alleyn married Constance Donne. Nash and Ben Jonson both openly referred to him as 'famous Ned Allen' and his papers, preserved at Dulwich College, including a playhouse MS, written on small sheets, pasted together to form a roll which may slip through the fingers of a busy actor as he learns his part, are amongst some of the most interesting fragments of Eliza-

---

[1] Captain Porter to his brother Endymion. Nicholls, *Progresses and Processions of James 1st*, 1623, vol. iv, p. 877.

bethan drama left to us.[1] Like other actor-managers Alleyn was also a promoter of public amusements, such as bull and bear baiting. He and Henslowe between them had purchased the office of 'Mastership of the royal bears, bulls and mastiff dogs' in 1604 and controlled the sport without rivals for seven years in Paris Gardens, on the southern banks of the Thames. It was to Alleyn, 'King of the Bears,' that James applied when he wished to test the courage of English mastiffs against the Tower lions.

In one of Donne's *Holy Sonnets* he reflects the current interest in these animals. Why, he asks, should the simple, uncorrupted creatures wait upon humankind of doubtful superiority.

> 'Why brook'st thou, ignorant horse, subjection?
> Why dost, thou, bull, and bore[2] so seelily
> Dissemble weakness, and by one man's stroke die,
> Whose whole kind, you might swallow and feed upon?
> Weaker I am, woe is me, and worse than you,
> You have not sinn'd, nor need be timorous.'[3]

There is nothing to show that Alleyn treated Constance with anything other than dignity and kindness, although subsequent bickerings between Donne and his son-in-law prove that their relations were strained. What is extraordinary is that Donne, who had been such an ardent example of the man who throws away all for love, should marry his daughter off in so worldly a fashion. Constance had met Alleyn at the home of her aunt, Lady Grymes of Peckham, who had always been hospitable to Donne, who had a daughter of her own also called Constance to whom Donne was godfather, and who, it is thought, took in the motherless children during the Dean's long illness. The matter was discussed by Alleyn and Donne in the parlour of the Deanery and it was agreed that

---

[1] See *Shakespeare's England*, vol. ii. and The Alleyn Papers at Dulwich College, calendered by G. F .Warner, 1881.

[2] bear.   [3] Sonnet XII.

the marriage settlement was to be adjusted between Sir Thomas Grymes and the suitor who evidently had a poor opinion of the Dean's business capacities. Constance was married from her aunt's home and was fortunately tied only three years to this incongruous mate. The gossiping chron-icler-letterwriters of the day remarked that no doubt this marriage of the old player 'would diminish his charity and devotion to his two hospitals',[1] and apparently they were right.

Prince Charles' courting came to nothing, for the country took fright at an alliance with Popish Spain, so long the dragon threatening St. George, and four days before the ceremony was to have taken place the whole affair was can-celled with national rejoicings. Donne reflects the proceed-ings in his letter of May 1623 addressed to the Marquis of Buckingham in Spain, which is chiefly interesting because of his reference to his knowledge of Spanish literature. The King's concern for 'his bonny boys' while they were abroad is well known and he was glad to see them safe home again.

In 1624 Donne was made Rector of St. Dunstan's in the West. He had long had the reversion of this living from Richard, Earl of Dorset, and upon his death and the living falling vacant, his friend Edward, the new Earl, sealed and secured the matter.

Donne's tenacity was extreme. When he resigned his position as Reader to the Benchers of Lincoln's Inn he went to law over his right to the living of Keyston in Huntingdon, and now upon receiving that of St. Dunstan's in the West, he was loth to forfeit his right to the valuable living of Blunham, in Bedfordshire, which he had held since 1622 through the offices of Charles Grey, Earl of Kent. With his usual charm and determination he got round the difficulty—('his winning behaviour, which, when it would entice, had a strange kind of elegant irresistible art')[2]—by obtaining a special dispen-

---

[1] Chamberlain, Nichol's *Progresses and Processions of James the*
[2] Walton, p. 9.

sation from the King which was so cleverly worded that it
enabled him to 'continue to hold Blunham and Sevenoaks
whatever ecclesiastical or other spiritual promotions it might
afterwards please the King to grant him'.[1] In this pleasant pie
the miraculous finger of Buckingham must have had a profit-
able stir.

Amongst Donne's parishioners at St. Dunstan's in the
West, was gentle Isaac Walton, who lived to be his tender
biographer and who, like Donne's father, became a Member
of the Ironmongers' Company. Walton admired Donne for
all manner of earthly graces and spiritual qualities, but no
doubt he was also drawn to him because of Donne's humani-
tarian nature. There are lines of irresistible appeal for Walton in *The Progress of the Soul*:

> 'Is any kind, subject to rape like fish?
> Ill unto man, they neither do, nor wish?
> Fishers they kill not, nor with noise awake,
> They do not hunt, nor strive to make a prey
> Of beasts, nor their young sons to bear away;
> Fowls they pursue not, nor do undertake
> To spoil the nests industrious birds do make;
> Yet them all these unkind kinds feed upon,
> To kill them is an occupation,
> And laws make fasts, and Lents for their destruction.'

His description of the swan, the snail, and of the greedy
sparrow fledgling:

> 'Out crept a sparrow . . .
> On whose raw arms stiff feathers now begin,
> As children's teeth through gums, to break with pain,
> His flesh is jelly yet, and his bones threads,
> All a new downy mantle overspreads,
> A mouth he opes, which would as much contain
> As his late house, and the first hour speaks plain,
> And chirps aloud for meat. Meat fit for men
> His father steals for him, and so feeds then
> One that, within a month, will beat him from his hen.'

[1] Gosse, vol. ii, p. 204.

are all delightful thumbnail sketches which would appeal to an observant lover of nature like Walton.

Donne's larger humanity is visible in a passage from one of his letters in which he says:

'As the Indian priests expressed an excellent character by building hospitals and providing surgery for birds and beasts lamed by mischance, or age, or labour, so must we not cut off, but cure, these afflictions.'[1]

He has been referring to his own melancholic temperament and is now speaking of afflictions of the mind, and thus we see his extraordinary streak of modernity peeping out from the tangled mat of mediaeval thought which he inherited. For in this suggestion he startlingly anticipates his successors of today in his concern for mental as well as bodily health, and in his apparent advocacy of analysis and synthesis, rather than stern repressive measures, as the method.

10

The month of March, 1625, was inauspicious. The malignant fever was much about and on the second day one of the most promising courtiers died, the young Marquis of Hamilton, the 'flower of the nation and the gallantest gentleman of both Scotland and England'. Donne, at the request of Sir Robert Ker, unwillingly obliged with an Elegy. It was considered beneath the powers and merits of a great divine that he should write even commemorative verses and for doing so Donne was much censured. The accompanying letter to Sir Robert is illuminating for in it Donne says that, as regards these funeral offerings, 'I did best when I had least truth for my subjects'. His emotions evidently crippled rather than strengthened his ability, and Wordsworth's summary of poetry as 'emotion recollected in tranquillity', does

[1] Gosse, ii, p. 10. Letter to Sir Henry Goodyer.

not seem to apply to one of such a tempestuous nature as Donne.

At the end of the month the old King likewise succumbed, and although it is unlikely that Donne had been drawn to him personally, for with all his pedantry and religious toleration James was not a lovable man, the Dean was grateful to him for insisting that he enter the Church.

'I date my life from my Ministry, for I received mercy, as I received the Ministry, as the Apostle speaks'[1]:

he declared in a sermon, and to the succeeding monarch:

'In my second birth, your Royal Father vouchsafed me his hand, not only to sustain me in it, but to lead me to it':[2]

and to a friend, long afterwards:

'When I sit still and reckon all my old Master's Royal favours to me, I return evermore to that, that he first inclined me to be a Minister.'[3]

Upon his father's death, the young Prince of Wales who was only twenty-five and of a serious but beautiful caste of countenance, shut himself away in his room, where he remained for the space of a week. Upon Saturday, the sixth day, Donne received a startling command to preach in the afternoon of the Sabbath. Deeply agitated he appealed to his old friend at Court, Sir Robert Ker, to provide him with an escape after the service, for it was the Dean's custom to preach fasting and he did not feel strong enough to face the court, or possibly the new King, after the ordeal. Sir Robert obliged and urged Donne to stay in his chambers to dinner. To this kind suggestion Donne returned a refusal, explaining that '. . . so much hath my this year's debility disabled me, even for receiving favours. After the sermon, I will steal into my coach home, and pray that my good purpose may well be accepted, and my defects graciously pardoned'.

[1] *Sermons 27*, p. 234.   [2] Dedicatory Epistle to *Devotions*.
[3] Letters. Tobie Mathew Collection, p. 308.

The young King remained pale and inscrutable throughout the delivery and Donne may well have been in a state of anguish as to the reception of his sermon. The Sovereign was still the omnipotent head of both State and Church and as always, upon the accession of a new ruler, there were wild speculations as to his preference for one form of religion or another. But Donne was not left long in suspense. Charles, who showed the highest appreciation for Donne as a poet as well as divine, intimated his pleasure and ordered the Sermon to be published. He preached again to the nobility before the old King's burial.

In the same year (1625) the raging fever called the plague came, for the third time in Donne's life, to terrify and decimate the people. Astrologers pointed out that an unfortunate conjunction of the planets caused it: others, that the disease was a curse brought back from the ill-fated Virginian expeditions: others, that it was carried about by the wretched dog, so that no less than five hundred animals were killed in Westminster alone. The primitive measures adopted to prevent the spreading of the disease only increased its virulence. When an inmate was taken ill the door and windows of his house were locked up, the cross of death splashed in red upon the walls, a guard stationed without, and the sufferers within were left to contemplate each other in dumb despair. The besieged city resembled a vast charnel house from which the strongest-hearted might shrink in horror.

'. . . For he that durst, in the dead hour of gloomy midnight, have been so valiant as to have walked through the still and melancholy streets, what think you should have been his music? Surely the loud groans of raving sick men: the struggling pangs of souls departing; in every house grief striking up an alarum; servants crying out for masters; wives for husbands, parents for children, children for their mothers. Here he should have met some, franticly running to knock up sextons; there, others fearfully sweating with coffins to steal forth dead bodies, lest the fatal handwriting should seal up their doors. And to make this dismal consort more full, round about him bells heavily tolling in one place, and ringing out in another. The dreadfulness of such an hour is unutterable.'[1]

Donne, caught up in the universal misery, fled to the fields of Chelsea, finding in the house of his old friend Magdalen Herbert, now Lady Danvers, a serene oasis in the deserts of death. Here, shut away from outside contagion, he worked quietly at his sermons, revising and rewriting, and here in pleasant relaxation he spoke with George Herbert, intent upon entering the Church against the best persuasions of his courtier friends, who declared that it was 'too mean an employment, and too much below his birth, and the excellent abilities and endowments of his mind'. George Herbert, cousin to the Earls of Pembroke, knew this emphasis upon an earthly inheritance to be of less value to him than that upon a spiritual and he replied with dignity that 'though the iniquity of the late times have made clergymen meanly valued and the sacred name of priest contemptible, yet will I labour to make it honourable . . . and to make humility lovely in the eyes of all men'.

Herbert's hesitancy to join the Church, although coming ten years after Donne's entry, reflects much of the latter's quandary. A proud man, set upon making his mark in the world, would not easily accept the scoffings and criticisms of his courtier friends, until convinced of the justness of his action. An echo of Herbert's experience lies in Donne's lines:

> 'Why doth the foolish world scorn that profession,
> Whose joys pass speech? Why do they think unfit
> That gentry should join families with it?'[2]

At this critical turning point in Herbert's life the influence of Donne, who had been through a similar period of indecision and 'long journeying to God', was incalculable.

But even with the windows shuttered and curtains drawn,

---

[1] Dekker's *Wonderful Year*.
[2] *To Mr. Tilman after he had taken Orders.*

the noise of the great bells, tolling for some new victim borne forth suddenly from his home to his last resting place, poured down the chimneys, hung about the silent room, and bade the hearer pray and ponder in a sharp attack of fearful premonition and penitence. The dreadful months of his sickness two years before were still painfully clear in Donne's mind.

'To him for whom the passing bell next tolls . . .'

had been the opening line of a stanza in one of his most curious poems, 'The Will,' written as a younger man. The spectacle of life under the shadow of mortality never ceased to fascinate him like the inscrutable eye of the basilisk.

With his vivid, dramatic sense Donne was not slow to make use of the horrors resulting from the plague in a sermon preached soon after normal life had been resumed by the citizens of London, early in the following year. He tells how some, driven mad with all they had seen, abandoned themselves to a painful death of debauchery, extinguishing themselves like guttering candles in rioting and drunkenness: others, pillaging the houses of the dead, 'stole their own death,' since they took infection as they worked.

As a preacher Donne now stood singularly and resplendently alone, like a planet in the evening sky before the lesser stars appear. Richard Hooker, his great predecessor, whose mind, like Donne's had been judicial and dispassionate, was dead: Jeremy Taylor, chief of English ecclesiastical orators, whose life bridges the two periods—before the Civil War and after—was still but a lad: Lancelot Andrews, Bishop of Winchester, the finest of Donne's contemporaries, who had laid the foundation of the Anglican position for succeeding men to express and defend, who, like Donne, referred to primitive antiquity and to Scripture in his appeal for an undivided Church, and who, like him, spoke to men's hearts as well as their heads, was to die in the following year. The only other serious rival whom Donne might encounter was his old rival in satire, Joseph Hall, Bishop of Norwich, who rarely took a London pulpit. There were many who poured forth floods of ponderous learning, or who were equally skilled performers in the art of rhetoric, who might be eloquent without being sound, verbose without being effective, but none combined his rich variety of gifts. Thus Donne's popularity increased until he preached to thousands at a time, for the pulpit was the sole vehicle for political and emotional expression, rigidly censored by the State and resorted to for general catharsis. Thus we hear of courtiers standing in the press, fainting from emotion, being 'taken up as dead' and carried from the gathering. Modern hygiene suggests that either clothing or atmosphere had something to do with such a collapse. But Donne's learning, his sincerity, the conscientious fulfilment of what was expected from him, despite ill-health or the distractions of personal grief and petty discouragements, endeared him to friends and strangers alike. His increasing ability as a preacher surprised even those who had, from the beginning, expected greatness from him. He was, in fact, 'the most stimulating and persuasive divine of the age,'[1] and his friend, Henry King, bishop and poet, summed up his skill when he wrote of him that 'as he exceeded others at first, so at last he exceeded himself'.[2]

But the great bells which had boomed out and tolled so remorselessly when Donne himself had lain ill, and which harassed his thoughts at Chelsea, now gave him little peace, for one by one, like leaves slowly detaching themselves from the parent tree when the sap sinks backward to the root, his friends began to die around him. First, his daughter Lucy died. Like Goodyer's child, she had been named after the Countess of Bedford, and had barely reached the age of eighteen. In the following May, the gracious Countess herself died, and close upon her, Magdalen Herbert. She was in turn followed by Goodyer and Christopher Brooke. Well

[1] Gosse, vol. ii, p. 231.   [2] Preface to Donne's *Death's Duell*.

might Donne contemplate the lines he had written earlier, upon going into Germany:

> 'As the tree's sap doth seek the root below
> In winter, in my winter now I go,
> Where none but Thee, th'Eternall root
> Of true Love I may know.'[1]

Slowly being weaned from earthly affections he struggled to be content with Divine sustenance only. The night was fast drawing in and he had much to do to prepare himself for the last surrender from which his whole egotistical and animal nature recoiled.

II

Once, whilst on a continental tour, Sir Joshua Reynolds halted before Brueghel's 'Slaughter of the Innocents' and compared the painting of the Dutch master to the poetry of Donne, remarking that although it lacked the graces of composition it provided enough food for twenty pictures. The painter discerned not only the crowded canvas of the mind but the tormented thought and the predisposition for self-torture which the poet showed in his life and writing. It may be, too, that Brueghel's quaint contortion of the human figure unconsciously reminded Sir Joshua of Donne's wit, of his

> 'Quips and cranks and wanton wiles'[2],—

the shining or prickly armour with which, like the knight errant or the humble hedgehog, he sought to shield his vulnerability and divert his assailant's attention. But wit diminished as the poet grew into the prelate, and the close-packed directness of the early verse spread into intricate and labyrinthine channels of thought and concurrent emotion.

'To contemplate an idea, because it is present for the moment in my own mind, to observe my emotion colour it, and to observe it colour my emotions, to play with it, instead of using it as a plain and simple meaning, brings often odd or beautiful objects to

[1] *A Hymn to Christ.*   [2] Milton's *l'Allegro.*

light . . . though it may lend itself, this petting and teasing of one's mental objects, to extremities of torturing language. With Donne it is not, as it is with the Elizabethans in their worst excesses, the vocabulary that is tormented—it is the thought itself. . . . The idea is thoroughly teased and tousled. . . . The usual course for Donne is not to pursue the meaning of the idea, but to arrest it, to play catlike with it, to develop it dialectically, to extract every minim of the emotion suspended in it.'[1]

No one now is interested in the framework of the great Jacobean sermons, how they pile thought upon thought in a whirling drift of words, beneath whose apparent careless profusion lies an almost architectural structure. 'As the shrines and chapels which wind out of the aisle of a cathedral belong to the same edifice, because they are under the same roof, so these digressions of the preacher, like little shrines of imagination attached to the sermon, are members of the same structure—overhung by the grandeur of one sacred and predominant conception.'[2]

It is more interesting to follow the crystallization of Donne's thought, as it hardened in the mould prescribed by the church which he had adopted. In one sense, to have entered the church was the worst thing which Donne could have done, for it set his mind, which was ardently longing for new modes of thought and new forms of expression, and made him literal and text-ridden. It fastened him down more and more to an intensive study of the scriptures and, such was the trend of Anglicanism as determined by Bishop Andrews, to a literal adoption of many of the phrases and thoughts now considered obsolete and preposterous. It is this tendency which made Coleridge declare, in speaking of Donne's use of some holy fable:

'That Donne should have imposed upon himself a set of idle tales for facts of history, is scarcely credible, but that he should have attempted to impose them on others is most melancholy:'[3]

---

[1] 'Donne in our Time', T. S. Eliot, pp. 12–13, in *A Garland for Donne*.

[2] Wilmott, *Jeremy Taylor*, p. 77.

[3] *Notes on English Divines*, vol. i, 1853, Edward Moxon.

and Lytton Strachey:

'By what perverse magic were intellectual ingenuity and theological ingenuousness intertwined in John Donne!'[1]

Coleridge hits the nail even more squarely on the head when he says:

'It is affecting to observe how this great man's mind sways and oscillates between his reason . . . and the habitual law for the letter. . . . It is most affecting to see the struggle of so great a mind to preserve its inborn fealty to the reason, under the servitude to an accepted article of belief.'

He then shows how Donne, in speaking of the wounds of Christ, vacillates from the symbolic to the spiritual interpretation, 'so that he seems uncertain whether he means the physical lymph . . . that trickled from the wounds . . . of Jesus, or the blood of the Son of Man, without which he who drinketh not cannot live.'

This was always Donne's method, in part the method of a poet, to take a text and its inherent thought, and then, holding it to the light of his mind, regard its facets, twist it and turn it, until every refraction was visible: to say the same thing in different manners, to employ metaphor to illustrate his meaning, just as an artist may paint in different mediums, or a musician weave his variations on another's theme. His macerating tendency is to seek out the painful in order to force home his antithesis. Even in one of his Christmas sermons he introduces a note of physical suffering:

'He found a Golgotha . . . even in Bethlehem, where He was born. For, to His tenderness then, the straws were almost as sharp as the thorns after; and the manger as uneasy at first, as His Cross at the last.'

The result is sometimes wearisome, especially to those uninterested in structure, or rhetoric, but it is often imposing and at best sombrely magnificent.

[1] *Elizabeth and Essex*, p. 9.

12

The remaining years of Donne's life were ones of constant effort and strain. The engine which drove and provided the power was worn and perpetually in need of repair. Recurrent illnesses discouraged him, for his eagerness in harness had always exceeded his physical strength, until he declared that he was forced 'to pay a fever every half year as a rent for his life'.

In 1627 his horizon was once again clouded by royal displeasure. He was reminded of the first occasion upon which this had happened. In 1624, when the old King had involved himself in difficulties over the Spanish marriage of his son, the recusants, abounding in hope that their cause might be heard at last, had grown overbearing. Malicious whisperers implied that James was going to wed the country to Rome at last, and James regarded his court with sudden suspicion. He imprisoned and expelled two peers and presently the serpent spoke softly in his ear and bade him beware his Chaplain, Donne.

'His Majesty was the more inclinable to believe this, for that a person of nobility and great note, betwixt whom and Dr. Donne there had been a great friendship, was at this very time discarded the court[1] . . . and justly committed to prison. . . .

The King received this news with so much discontent and restlessness, that he would not suffer the sun to set and leave him under this doubt; but sent for Dr. Donne, and required his answer to the accusation; which was so clear and satisfactory, that the King said, "he was right glad he rested no longer under the suspicion."

When the King had said this, Dr. Donne kneeled down and thanked his Majesty, and protested his answer was faithful, and free from all collusion, and there "desired that he might not rise till, as in like cases he always had from God, so he might from his Majesty, some assurance that he stood clear and fair in his opinion". At which the King raised him from his knees with his

[1] Probably John Digby, Earl of Bristol, who took orders about the same time that Donne did. He was made Earl of Bristol in 1622 and at this time imprisoned in his house at Sherborne.

own hands, and "protested he believed him; and that he knew he was an honest man, and doubted not but that he loved him truly".

And having thus dismissed him, he called some lords of his council into his chamber, and said with much earnestness, "My Doctor is an honest man; and, my Lords, I was never better satisfied with an answer than he hath now made me; and I always rejoice when I think that by my means he became a divine.' "[1]

Now, through the antipathy and jealousy of William Laud, Bishop of Bath and Wells, Donne was once more suspected of dabbling in doctrines dangerous to the State. The presumptive Bishop of Chichester had written a work which Archbishop Abbot refused to license for publication. Laud, Andrews, and Charles I. were in favour of it but Donne, in a Sermon which he preached upon the 1st of April before the King at Whitehall, was suspected of supporting the old Archbishop, who despite his rectitude and his constant espousal of royal policy in the church, never had the good fortune to be popular with either King or country. As a matter of fact, Donne's sermon had been prepared by him two months before the incident; he had not been present at the delivery of an offensive one by Archbishop Abbot; and the views set forth in the controversial book were very much those of Donne himself. Probably Donne had not even had time to read the work since it had only recently been pushed through the press despite the Archbishop's veto, but he would have been in full agreement with the author's beliefs that the Church of England should eschew both the doctrines of Rome and Geneva and maintain an even course of her own. Laud, in short terms, demanded a copy of Donne's Whitehall sermon for the King, and Donne with trembling hands wrote off twice to his friend Sir Robert Ker to ask what it was all about, to justify himself and to beg Sir Robert 'to hearken farther after' the fate of the offending sermon. He tactfully offered to absent himself from the Court until he should hear the King's decision, excepting for the saying of prayers.

[1] Walton, pp. 34-35.

In his second letter to Ker, Donne remarks that 'the King hath let his eye fall upon some of my poems'. The Dutch poet, Huyghens, testifies to Charles Ist's appreciation of Donne as a poet. The King doubted if Huyghens in translating the poems could render Donne's ingenuity and beauty into his own language. A copy of the first edition of Donne's poems, marked by the royal hand, exists as testimony of Charles' appreciation.[1]

At last, upon the intervention of Carlisle and Buckingham, Donne's name was cleared, his innocence established and his subserviency to the Royal wishes in all matters of Church policy, which would have filled his proud recusant ancestors with horror, renewed. But the event was a strain upon nerves and health already shattered, and dangerously in need of support rather than condemnatory criticism.

Bishop Andrews, against whom Donne was so unexpectedly ranged in this ecclesiastical battle, was an old and honoured friend. Once, in the Mitcham days, Donne borrowed a book from Andrews, which his children tore up in play. Donne, who was thus put to the trouble of piecing together and copying out the pages by hand, evidently felt that some additional apology was due to the owner, for he returned the damaged book with some Latin verses. But the 'gamesome children' were now grown-up and Ann was not there to comfort him in this time of royal disgrace.

13

'It hath been my desire, and God may be pleased to grant it, that I might die in the pulpit.'[2] These were the words of Donne very nearly fulfilled by him. Thus, like Elijah, he might have been carried up to heaven in a fiery chariot of his own eloquence, transported above pain and fearful anticipation, snatched away in an instant by the snapping of too taut-

[1] In the British Museum.   [2] Walton, p. 50.

stretched nerves, or the cracking of a heart too compassionate for the callousness of the age into which it had been born. But this was not to be. The battle was to be fought out in public, as on the rostrum of some ancient war-galley, and Donne was to essay to cheat the triteness of death in a pantomime original even in those dramatic days, but still he must die in seclusion.

For five days of the week the earnest preacher worked at his sermons, issuing out from his cave of darkness to visit the London prisons, or to preach on the Sabbath; distracting himself on Saturdays by calling upon his friends and relations, or by receiving them round the Deanery fire. Various domestic events raised or lowered his fluctuating vitality: Margaret, a younger daughter had the small-pox and Donne had to withdraw into the country: Constance's old husband died and she married an Alderman of the city of London, to whose home at Aldborough Hatch, in Essex, Donne and his aged mother were able to retire: John, the talented elder son, made a questionable marriage, and since his name comes seldom in his father's correspondence, cannot have brought much comfort to his failing heart: George, the favourite, who was a soldier and away campaigning in Spain, was shortly to be taken a prisoner of war and to be held for five years. Eventually he escaped by bribing his gaoler, but Donne never saw him again. A late friendship with Mrs. Cockayne, whose father, like Donne's, had been Master of the Ironmongers' Company, and with whom Donne may have played in Bread Street as a child, brightened the gathering darkness.

In 1630, the question of a Bishopric for Donne was mooted but his health did not permit him to accept the honour with its incumbent labours and responsibilities.[1] The illness, to which he was to succumb, had laid hold upon him and in his daughter's house, near the wild expanse of Epping Forest, he strove to shake it off. For the first time in twenty years he

[1] Gosse, vol. ii, p. 264.

was unable to preach his customary sermon upon the feast of Christmas. The fertility and incessant activity of his mind remained till the last. In this, as in other illnesses, he wrote unceasingly, revising old sermons, devising new, composing holy verses, making out his will in his own hand, ordering the cutting and engraving of some stones, or seals, for his especial friends.

False rumours sprang up that he had died, or that he abstained from preaching because of inordinate melancholy. These could not be entirely ignored and must have been hurtful to him. The future of his children weighed upon his mind. He commended George to the care of the Earl of Carlisle. He was under an obligation to preach at St. Paul's on Candlemas Day and doubted if he had the strength. His good physician, Doctor Foxe, recommended the drinking of milk in quantity but the stomach rebelled against it and Donne forlornly says that he would 'as soon look for roses at this time of the year as for increase of strength'. He had a horror of lingering on uselessly, unable to employ the powers of that mind which, through its very activity, had been his friend and worst foe.

'I am afraid that death will play with me so long, as he will forget to kill me, and suffer me to live in a languishing and useless age, a life, that is rather a forgetting that I am dead, than of living.'[1]

When the weather was not 'spitefully foul' he was able to get out a little in the garden and finally, in January of the new year, he went up to London. He was anxious to see to certain matters of business, amongst them the finishing and distribution of the curious little seals, which he called Heliotropes, like the purple clustered flowers which turn towards the sun, and which we now call, less poetically, bloodstones. Upon these stones, set in fine gold, he caused a crest to be cut,—Christ crucified upon an anchor, the emblem of hope and sustained life. The act, like Donne's own use of similes,

[1] Letter to Mrs. Cockayne, Jan. 1630/1. Hayward, p. 500.

was a symbolical one, and it signified more than the giving of tokens of affection to his friends. The crest of the Donnes, which may be seen in the corner of the Marshall engraving, was a bundle of snakes bound like a sheaf of corn. Now these snakes, which have been regarded as symbols of health, medicine, wisdom or good genius all down the ages, stood to Donne for something loathsome. The serpent had corrupted Eve; the serpent bore deadly poison in its fangs, stole silently upon its belly, writhed, extended itself mysteriously, penetrated without warning and discharged corrupting venom. The worm, which he dreaded, and which made his ageing flesh creep as he peered into the approaching abyss of the fathomless tomb, was akin to it, and thus, just as he had striven to blot out his religious ancestry by changing and conforming to an altered church, he strove to obliterate his own fear of corruption by the substitution of a new crest.

Hand in hand with this righteous business went his settlement of a more worldly affair—some transaction over jewellery. A lady of title had evidently deposited with him, for safe keeping, or as settlement of a debt, a valuable diamond ornament. In a letter from Aldborough Hatch he had begged George Gerrard, now Master of Charterhouse, to interview her with regard to her wishes in the disposal of this property:

'for I would be loth to leave anything in my house, when I die, that were not absolutely mine own. I have a servant, Roper, at Paul's House, who will receive your commandments at all times.'[1]

And in another letter 'For the Diamond Lady'—(he had previously called her 'the Lady of the Jewel')—he writes:

'You may safely deliver Roper whatsoever belongs to me, and he will give you a discharge for the money.'[2]

What stranger mating of sacred and secular might there be than this conjunction in jeweller's affairs—the setting of the heliotropes with their holy symbol, and the disposal of a lady's

[1,2] Letters dated Dec. 1630 and Jan. 1630/1. Gosse ii, pp. 267 and 269.

diamonds? But it is all of a piece with this fantastic man in whom opposites ran so strongly, who threw away his career for love, and yet haggled over his daughter's dowry, who angled for ambassadorial posts hardly relinquished by his friends, while at the same time begging entrance to the Church.

At Candlemas the delivery of his customary sermon was out of the question and, as at Christmas, Donne had to find a substitute. About this time, too, upon 'his old constant day' fell the Lenten Sermon, which he was determined to preach as usual. His friends, seeing his emaciated condition and fearing the strain would be too great for him, tried to dissuade him from performing his work, but all to no purpose. The Sermon, which he called *Death's Duell*[1] was preached before the King and the Court at Whitehall.

The courtiers and those gathered together to hear him, now a mere shadow of vitality, feared for him and, as Walton puts it, 'doubtless, many secretly did ask that question in Ezekiel: "Do these bones Live?".' Yet the indomitable will and the tenacious mind never for an instant failed their possessor. Despite the pauses necessary for collecting himself, both physically and mentally, despite the surges of painful emotion, despite the caitiff voice which nearly failed him—so faint and hollow came the words—the long sermon was delivered. Then, the tremendous ordeal over, Donne hastened home to the Deanery, from which he never reappeared.

The next day, too feeble to rise or to go out, he talked with a friend, probably Walton himself, who asked him, 'Why are you sad?' To this simple question Donne replied that he was not sad, and that he had been meditating upon his friends most of the night, upon the goodness of God's providence to him, and upon his preparations for a new life.

'Looking back upon my past life, I now plainly see it was His hand that prevented me from all temporal employment; and that

---

[1] *Death's Duell, or A Consolation to the Soul, against the Dying Life, and Living Death of the Body*. Preached on Feb. 12, 1630/1.

it was His will I should never settle or thrive till I entered into the Ministry; in which I have now lived nearly twenty years—I hope to His glory.'[1]

Seven weeks lay between the delivery of *Death's Duell*, which his auditors were convinced was his own funeral sermon, and Donne's death. During this time the poetic ability which had been so vigorous in his youth, revived once more. The *Hymn to God, My God, in my Sickness* belongs to these days and as in some of his earliest poems, so in his last, the mind took up the image of the voyagers. Maps, currents, straits, the eastern riches and parts of the globe, remained for him symbols of spiritual discoveries.

The preparations for his extraordinary monument and, almost as an afterthought, the bequeathing of his manuscripts, representing the vast bulk of his mind's endeavours, occupied much of the fast-ebbing time. He had neglected to mention these in his will, and so by word of mouth and before three witnesses he arranged that they should go to Henry King, one of his executors. Unfortunately, John the reprobate son, as heir male, while the estate was still in the hands of the executors, forced them to surrender his father's papers. His piracy and his careless, almost frivolous method of handling them, is a story belonging to another generation.

As for the monument, when Donne had settled upon a design, he:

'sent for a carver to make for him in wood the figure of an urn, giving him directions for the compass and height of it; and to bring with it a board, of the just height of his body. These being got, then without delay a choice painter was got to be in readiness to draw his picture, which was taken as followeth: Several charcoal fires being first made in his large study, he brought with him into that place his winding-sheet in his hand, and having put on all his clothes, had this sheet put on him, and so tied with knots at his head and feet, and his hands so placed as dead bodies are usually fitted, to be shrouded or put into their coffin or grave.

[1] Walton, p. 52.

P

Upon this urn he thus stood, with his eyes shut, and with so much of the sheet turned aside as might show his lean, pale, and death-like face, which was purposely turned toward the east, from whence he expected the second coming of his and our Saviour Jesus. In this posture he was drawn at the just height; and when the picture was fully finished, he caused it to be set by his bed side, where it continued and became his hourly object till his death, and was then given to his dearest friend and executor, Dr. Henry King, then chief Residentiary of St. Paul's, who caused him to be thus carved in one entire piece of white marble, as it now stands in that church. . . .'[1]

It seems incredible that a dying man could have gone through the ordeal of standing for his portrait, even in a heated room, and a modern artist questions this, pointing out 'that although the statue is erect, as we know it was intended to be, yet the drapery is studied, as the direction of the fall of the folds shows, from a recumbent model'.[2] Yet such was Donne's determination to die actively, rather than passively, that it carried him through the final test.

'I would not that death should take me asleep. I would not have him merely seize me, and only declare me to be dead, but win me and overcome me,'[3]

he had written, twenty-one years before, when melancholy had its greatest hold on him, and now, when the hour struck he did not deviate from that course. Life for Donne was to struggle, to throw his powers of mind about in a violent effort to shake himself free, to strive, to contend—above all, to escape, only to bind himself anew. He died on the last day of March, 1631, aged fifty-nine.

His soul, like a ship, had beat out its storm at sea—had 'hulled it out'. Now at last she might find peace in an absorption of that infinite wisdom which Donne in his moments of serenity surely apprehended.

[1] Walton, p. 55.
[2] Gosse, vol. ii, p. 288, quoting Hamo Thornycroft, R.A.
[3] Letter to Goodyer, 1608. Gosse, vol. i, p. 191.

'In her Resurrection, her measure is enlarged, and filled at once; There she reads without spelling, and knows without thinking, and concludes without arguing. She is at the end of her race, without running; In her triumph without fighting; In her Haven, without sailing. . . . She knows truly, and easily, and immediately, and entirely, and everlastingly; Nothing left out at first, nothing worn out at last, that conduces to her happiness. What a death is this life! what a resurrection is this death!'[1]

The monument, made by Nicholas Stone,[2] was duly set up in old St. Paul's under whose shadow Donne had been born, whose nave had echoed so tellingly his pleading or exhorting tones. Like some fantastic chrysalis of a creature neither human nor animal, miraculous even in its powers of survival, it remained unharmed by the Great Fire, which sent the beams and rafters of the cathedral crashing over it in a searing sea of flame. The fire brushed the front of the urn, the toe of one foot was slightly damaged, but the figure, whose face delicately featured is surmounted by the strange, petunia-like knot of shroud, rises still to confound us. Had the closed and stony eyes been able to look out upon the mounting flames of destruction in 1666 and once again in 1940, would they have gazed with sorrow at the scene or would they, with faintly mocking, triumphant gleam have smiled sardonically, as much as to say: *I am like the Phoenix and the famed Salamander. The flames which lapped the Holy Martyrs, the fiery torments of Hell itself, have been powerless to consume or destroy me.*

For Donne meant the world to remember him. The poet, the artist, and the egoist in him insisted upon immortality, while the Renaissance character of his nature cried out for

[1] Sermon at St. Paul's, Easter Day in the Evening, March 28th, 1624.

[2] Humphrey Mayer was entrusted with the completion of the effigy, Robert Flower worked the niche and Mr. Babbe blocked the inscription. For details of the payment to Stone by Donne's executors see *The Notebook and Account books of Nicholas Stone* by W. L. Spiers, edited by A. J. Finbery, 7th vol. of *The Walpole Society*, 1918–1919, University Press, Oxford (pp. 33, 63–4, 85 and 90).

perpetuation, in a form more original than that of his contemporaries and less peaceful than that of his mediaeval predecessors. Sir Philip Sidney had died with musicians playing and singing a poem of his making round his bedside, and George Herbert, who, although twenty years Donne's junior was to outlive him by only two years, attempted on his deathbed to sing to his favourite lute—'holy hymns and sacred anthems.' What appears to us to be mere attitudinizing and humourless effrontery of an almost indecent nature was to these men, of a world fast dying, an essential gesture—a gauntlet thrown down to an enemy whose invincibility they acknowledged but whose challenge they took up with the last frail breath.

There is, in Tewkesbury Abbey, a monument to one of Donne's ecclesiastical predecessors. The corpse, lying upon a plaited mattress and covered with a knotted shroud, turned back to disclose the body, lies naked and defenceless against every loathsome symbol of corruption. It is only surprising that Donne, irresistibly attracted to the work did not adopt a similar style. Instead, as if folding the secret of his peculiar fascination within him, he remains shrunken away into a world of his own divining, neither standing firmly as the living stand, nor lying resignedly like the dead, but rather suspended in a quiescent state, as if he wished to breathe but dared not.[1]

---

[1] Sir Henry Wotton's impression of the monument, quoted by Walton, agrees. 'It seems to breathe faintly, and posterity shall look upon it as a kind of artificial miracle.'

TOMB OF JOHN DONNE

CHAPTER V

INTERPRETATION

'Like John-a-dreams, unpregnant of my cause...'
Hamlet, Act II, Scene 2.

'And we sleep all the way; from the womb to the grave we are never thoroughly awake; but pass on with such dreams, and imaginations as these....'

Donne's Sermon to The Lords upon Easter Day, 1619.

I

What, then, is the mystery and meaning of Donne? In ranging over his writings, from the highly passionate verse of his youth, through the wan, disconsolate stuff of middle age, to the measured grandeur of the Sermons, and in considering the life of the man, one is faced with a conundrum —where did he stray from his rightful course and what would have satisfied his essential nature?

For despite his greatness, in spite of the moments when faith, like the sun drawing water from summer-bright fields, draws him skyward in a shaft of trembling light, in spite of the passages in which joy and certainty expand, one is never convinced of the soundness of his faith or of his true happiness. He gives the impression of a man who has lost his way, who has wandered into a baffling world of theory and linguistics, who is never at heart contented.

Is it simply that, like men of true genius, he was born too soon, so that no matter what he did or said, the times were inevitably 'out of joint'? Was it the character of the age which hampered him, forcing him to conform to paths too cramped, too mean for his powers and rich endowments? Would some profession other than the ecclesiastical have suited him better? Imagine him a Judge, a Discoverer, a Scientist, a

Physician, an Actor, a Novelist like Daniel Defoe or Swift, a
Philosopher like Montaigne or Descartes, a Cartographer, an
Experimenter in lonely uncharted fields, in which those around
him dare not believe. Or is the problem an inward one, implying a discord which prevents him from ever attaining
serenity and from ranking amongst those felicitous souls who
'beat out their music' harmoniously?

He was of the stuff of which patriots and rebels are made,
and for all his aristocratic leanings had the makings of a
democrat. Above all he had the fervour of a reformer, narrowly separated from the fanaticism of the martyr. Yet the
patriot must forever be at war with the martyr, the saint with
the exulting sinner. Such was the inner conflict, and his
attempts to stifle it, that his spirit must forever tread a path
of pain, constantly striving 'ere age, death's twilight', might
bring it even a measure of peace.

It is no use saying 'had Donne been drawn from different
stock, had he been born in a different century,—the seventeenth, when rationalism was finally awake, or the twentieth,
when science rules supreme,—had his training been less
exigent, his profuse gifts garnered less closely, born into
contentment he might have been'. For this is cutting away
both the age and the individual and does not solve the riddle.
A man cannot be separated from his era nor from those forces
of development, heredity and environment, which give the
pattern to his life, and shape his ends unwittingly.

There are, on the continent, temples to pagan gods diverted
to Christian use, around whose classic walls run painted
processions of the saints, representations of the life of the
Virgin, or other holy legends, upon whose floor of rich tessell-
ation, patterned with vine and flower, stands an altar slab of a
later faith, austere in its simplicity: and from the Cornish
hedgerows, from the undulating, monotonous moors, rise
ancient crosses of dim uncertain origin, covered now with
oary lichen and small, downy tufts of moss. Such a stone,

raised for who knows what barbarous symbol or ceremony, became a signpost for the pilgrim, yet long before the Christian worshipped it it had a pagan meaning, and the cross cut deep into the unyielding granite, marks a face once stark and plain. 'You seldom see a coin', writes Donne, 'from which the stamp were removed, though to imprint it better, but it looks awry and squints.'[1] This metaphor is true of himself. The arguments which he employed, the doctrines which he assimilated, were never wholly digested by him, and Donne appears unconvinced. His nature, like temple, cross, and metal coin, took on a guise ill-adapted to its originality.

The qualities which as a young man he possessed and which never entirely deserted him, resented their mishandling and altered his conscious, but not his unconscious, attitudes. For he was gentle and sensitive, proud to the point of aggressiveness, disdainful, ambitious, self-confident, eager to assert his rights, especially that of thinking and choosing for himself, tolerant of thought, intolerant of evil. But his early training confused him by submission, gave him a certain hang-dog air as of one who looks down habitually, who grasps at the support of authority while yet he suspects it, who distrusts himself profoundly, who seeks with passionate earnestness for some system of dogma, some way of life, beneath which to hide the nakedness in which, in earliest days, he had delighted. Slowly, and with burning resentment, he was bent towards depreciation, humiliation, mortification and sacrifice.

'We are mad for love of this soul, and ready to do any act of danger, in the ways of persecution, any act of diminution in our selves in the way of humiliation, to stand at her door, and pray, and beg, that she should be reconciled to God.'[2]

---

[1] Letter to Goodyer, April 1615. Hayward, p. 467.

[2] Sermon LXXV, Preached to the King at Whitehall, April 15, 1628, Easter Sunday.

And in the Litany he says:

> '. . . for Oh, to some,
> Not to be martyrs is a martyrdom.'

Now in the words of a nineteenth-century historian:

'To impose an elaborate system of prejudices on the yet un-developed mind and to entwine those prejudices with all the most hallowed associations of childhood, is most certainly contrary to the spirit of the doctrine of private judgment. . . . Those who appreciate this spirit . . . will desire that opinions should be few, that they should rest as lightly as possible upon the mind, and should be separated as far as possible from the eternal principles of morality. . . .

The vast majority of the human race necessarily accept their opinions from authority. Whether they do so avowedly, like the Catholics, or unconsciously like the Protestants, is immaterial. They have neither time nor opportunity to examine for them-selves. They are taught certain doctrines on disputed questions as if they were unquestionable truths, when they are incapable of judging, and every influence is employed to deepen the impression. This is the true origin of their belief. Not until long years of mental conflict have passed can they obtain the inestimable boon of an assured and untrammelled mind.

Judgment may pierce the clouds of prejudice, and in the moment of her strength she may even rejoice and riumph in her liberty, yet the conceptions of childhood will long remain latent in the mind, to reappear in every hour of weakness, when the tension is relaxed, and when the power of old associations is supreme. . . . Few possess the courage and the perseverance to encounter the mental struggle. The immense majority either never examine the opinions they have inherited, or examine them so completely under the dominating influence of the prejudice of education, that whatever may have been the doctrines they have been taught, they conclude they are unquestionably true. . . . A large proportion cannot endure a conflict to which old associa-tions and, above all, the old doctrine of guilt, and of error, lend such a peculiar bitterness: they stifle the voice of reason, they turn away from the path of knowledge, they purchase peace at the expense of truth.

There is a period in the history of the enquirer when old opin-ions have been shaken or destroyed, and new opinions have not been formed, a period of doubt, of terror, and of darkness, when the voice of the dogmatist has not lost its power, and the phantoms of the past still hover over the mind, a period when every land-mark is lost to sight, every star veiled, and the soul seems drifting rudderless before the destroying blast. It is in this season of transition that the temptations to stifle reason possess a fearful power. For it is when contrasting the tranquillity of past assurance with the feverish paroxysms that accompany enquiry, that the mind is most likely to abandon the path of truth.

It is so much easier to assume than to prove; it is so much less painful to believe than to doubt. . . . Oscillation and timidity characterize the research of most . . . but he who believes that the search for truth can never be offensive to the God of Truth pursues his way with unswerving energy.'[1]

The spirit of enquiry and of dogged pursuit is Donne's. Hear him saying the very same thing:

'Sometimes we had rather believe a traveller's lie than go to dis-prove him, so men rather cleave to these ways than seek new. . . .

When I walk after my slow and imperfect pace, I begin to think that so litigious men, tired with suits, admit any arbitra-ment, and princes, travailed with long and wasteful war, descend to such conditions of peace as they are soon ashamed to have embraced,—so philosophers and so all sects of Christians, after long disputations and controversies, have allowed many things for positive and dogmatical truths which are not worthy of that dig-nity: and so many doctrines have grown to be the ordinary food and diet of our spirits . . . or accepted in a lazy weariness when men, as they might have something to rely on, and to excuse themselves from more painful inquisition, never examined what that was.'[2]

The struggle is Donne's and, in lesser measure, that of every thinking human being. Here is his youth, the torment of early manhood, culminating in the waste-land of spirit in the 'thin little house at Mitcham'. Here is the secret of his despair and feverish excitement of the brain in illness, by which he hoped to evade the horrors of the dark pool of the

[1] Lecky, vol. ii, pp. 93–97.

[2] Donne to Sir Thomas Lucy, 9th October, 1607. Gosse, vol. i, pp. 174 and 176.

unconscious, of his remorse at the death of Ann, of his stagnation, vacillation and deliberation before entering the Church, the explanation of that revolting sermon *Death's Duell*, and of his masquerading before death.

That Donne resented his intense, early mental constraint although he was too loyal to his tutors or too imperceptive of its results to state this in rounder terms, is obvious from the preface to *Pseudo-Martyr* in which he says that those who first instructed him were 'persons who by nature had a power and superiority over my will ... others ... by their learning and good life, seemed to me justly to claim an interest for the guiding and rectifying of mine understanding'. Some of his tutors were men of reason and sanctity who appealed to his sense of fitness, whom he respected, and who could lead him docilely, but the first clause, although uttered without complaint and as a simple recitation of fact, has about it an air of rebellion, as if the man of thirty-seven still resented early intrusion upon the native originality with which he was so remarkably endowed. He gives abundant evidence of having been stretched and made taut to an almost unendurable degree. 'The elements of spirituality to which the progress of his entire life give testimony, of a love of experience of the senses, and of an ardent attachment to things of the mind, were at the beginning poured into a mould whose shape they were ill-constituted to assume.... His first approach to an understanding of the truth was made under conditions that did not permit him to work out matters entirely for himself, nor allow the function of his favourite habit of doubting "wisely".... If his Jesuit instruction stimulated his interest in many kinds of learning it likewise hemmed in the free spirit. If Donne was to discover the truth it must be largely through an examination of himself in a free association with rich and varied experience, not through the exploration of other men's thoughts. . . .'[1]

[1] *John Donne and the New Philosophy*, Coffin, pp. 26–29.

2

One can go a long way in understanding a complex nature like Donne's if one appreciates his emotional instability, and sees that he himself appreciated his unsteadiness but was unable to put his finger on the troublesome source.

In speaking of the mature man Walton says: '. . . he had a soft heart full of noble compassion' and that he was 'too brave a soul to offer injuries and too much a Christian not to pardon them in others'; that he was 'a great lover of the offices of humility, and of so merciful a spirit that he never beheld the miseries of mankind without pity and relief'.[1] As proof of these characteristics we have Donne's generosity to the poor and needy. 'He was inquisitive after the wants of prisoners, and redeemed many from prison, that lay for their fees or small debts; he was a continual giver to poor scholars, both of this and foreign nations. Besides what he gave with his own hand, he usually sent a servant, or a discreet and trusty friend, to distribute his charity to all the prisons in London, at all the festival times of the year, especially at the birth and resurrection of our Saviour.'[2]

It may be as well to go back for a moment and review the childhood influences which moulded such a character. The boy loses his father. His mother, possibly of that masterful and authoritative type apt to provoke rebellion, either overt or covert, marries again and it is possible that the child, thwarted in the gratification of his vital and imperative desires, developed a pronounced hostility to her and all that she stood for. Such hostility may have sprung from Elizabeth Donne's second marriage, occurring, for the child, so cruelly soon after the father's loss, or from the advent of a younger brother, even before Donne senior's death.

At any rate the boy already feels insecure. Then the step-father-physician with his books, lectures, conversation and

---

[1] Walton, pp. 59 and 60.   [2] Ibid., p. 47.

work, over which hung the rude, half-barbarous customs of that yet medically unenlightened age, intervenes as an influence and Donne's worst physical fears are confirmed; the mind, perilously balanced, already inclines towards melancholy, insecurity and a belief in the instability of the human frame as a dependable agent for living. Some misinforming about the processes of birth, or some minute ill-timed informing of an unfortunate birth seems to have scalded his mind with lasting horror so that the grave is never disentangled from thoughts of birth, and until the day of his death the womb remains for him a symbol of pathetic, outlaw territory, dark and strange, immune even to the cleansing spirit of God the Father and His mercy.

Meanwhile the intensive scholastic and religious instruction is initiated and begins to take hold of the pliant and growing mind: it trains the tendrils cautiously but binds them, like the boughs of a young tree plashed against a garden wall, firmly, almost inflexibly. The cast of thought is early determined.

Any unsatisfied questioning of maternal affection, which may lead to difficulties in sexual thought, to misogyny and torment where woman is concerned, is further enraged and then stifled by the old teachings of the Fathers. The tendency towards martyrdom, torture and sacrifice, exemplified by his own living relations in exile or prison and his dead forbears, and by the horrible custom of the day which encouraged the public to witness an abrupt termination of life, or a slow, infinitely painful prolongation of it while death was actually being promoted, cut deep into the receptive mind and urged a nature, already inclined to self-torment and fractious speculation, further along its perplexing path.

Thus, what appears in Donne to be an extraordinary interest, in advance of his day, in the field of science may be regarded as an intense longing for security, either in the heavens above the earth, in the uncertain quarters allotted beneath, in the earth as we know it, or in man himself. What seems to be an honest search for truth and religious serenity becomes a longing for amelioration, an escape into the confines of doctrine or faith to straiten and bind the latent scepticism, which, when plumbed to its lowest depths, developes into an unbearable despair akin to Hamlet's dejection, when even to adhere to doubt and disbelief is scarcely worth the trouble.

Such was Donne's early nature, preyed upon by violent forces, until it could not rest secure in anything. Either the nadir of disbelief or the zenith of exaltation and, in between, fluctuating like moving sea-waters, periods of boastful bragging about the excellence of change and variety, and counter-periods of despair at such inconstancy.

He champions the fickleness, the variableness of women, nature, and his own character:

> 'The heavens rejoice in motion. Why should I
> Abjure my so much lov'd variety. . . .'

Perversely he mocks the very thing he has set on a pedestal and worshipped.

> 'Though I be such a planetary and erratic fortune that I can do nothing constantly, yet you may find some constancy in my constant advising you to it.'[1]

Then the thought-channels deepen. Ethical problems become increasingly important; the question of 'is it life or is it death which is valuable' invades the mind and temporarily swamps it with its urgency.

> 'Beloved, weigh life and death one against another and the balance will be even. Saint Paul could not tell which to wish, Life or Death; There the balance was even. . . .'[2]

or:

> '. . . beg for us, a discreet patience
> Of death, or of worse life:'[3]

---

[1] Letter to Goodyer, Gosse, vol. i, p. 192.
[2] Preached upon the Penetential Psalms. 1627–8.   [3] *The Litany*, X.

The result is emotional instability of which he himself is perfectly aware. Walton says that in Donne:

'The melancholy and pleasant humour were . . . so contempered that each gave advantage to the other, and made his company one of the delights of mankind. . . .'

and that he was 'by nature highly passionate but more apt to reluct at the excess of it'.[1] Another author calls him:

'the most undulating, the most diverse of human beings. . . . His natural temperament . . . was melancholy. He was subject to sudden fits of dejection and to a general depression and emptiness of spirit when alone, or after wearying excitement. But he was equally prompt in recovery and, after one of these down moods, he would radiate life and light about a dazzled and bewitched society. . . . Sadness and joy were balanced in him, both to excess, and so lightly hung that he passed in a few moments from one to the other.'[2]

Donne himself describes his alternations of mood as an almost conscious manipulation.

'Sometimes when I find myself transported with jollity and love of company, I hang leads at my heels, and reduce to my thought my fortunes, my years, the duties of a man, of a friend, of a husband, of a father, and all the incumbencies of a family. When sadness dejects me, either I countermine it with another sadness, or I kindle squibs about me again, and fly into sportfulness and company. . . .'[3]

That there was a conflict which caused the expansion and contraction of the chords of the heart, a dilation and a retraction, he was also perfectly aware. His letters to Goodyer reveal it expressly:

'But of the diseases of the mind there is no criterion, no canon, no rule, for our own taste and apprehension and interpretation should be the judge, and that is the disease itself. . . . I find ever after all, that I am like an exorcist . . . that I still mistake my disease.

[1] Walton, p. 60.   [2] Gosse, vol. ii, p. 289.
[3] To Sir Henry Goodyer. Gosse, vol. i, p. 185.

And I still vex myself with this, because if I know it not, nobody can know it. And I comfort myself because I see dispassioned men are subject to the like ignorances.'[1]

'I am so far from digging to it that I know not where it is.'[2]

And he complains of those smug people, the moralists, who urge one to ignore the imaginary difficulty and state that the way is easy for them because they are virtuous.

'Therefore, this alacrity', (cheerfulness) 'which dignifies even our service to God, this gallant enemy of dejection and sadness . . . must be sought and preserved diligently. . . .
They which place this alacrity in a good conscience deal somewhat too roundly with us, for when we ask the way they show us the town afar off. Will a physician consulted for health and strength bid you have good sinews and equal temper?'[3]

In another letter Donne declares that what 'is physic to one infirmity, nourishes the other',[4] thereby perfectly expressing the nature of his own trouble—the mind enraged by the emotions, and the emotions chafed by the harsh mental discipline or riddling scrutiny of the intellect.

Yet all the while the *cause* of the conflict was unknown to him.[5] Dramatic irony implies the presence of malign or favourable intervention hanging over a protagonist unaware of its coming intervention, but we, like blind actors on the stage of life, are most of us unaware of our prime causes of thought and action and still, despite the aid of recent investigation into the life of the mind, unable to help ourselves.

Donne was an extremely self-aware, self-conscious person, never able to put into words the major discord troubling him, and this realization of a lack of unity gave him a feeling of

[1] Gosse, vol. i, p. 184. Date and to whom written conjectural.

[2] To Sir Henry Goodyer. Gosse, vol. i, p. 186.

[3] To Sir Henry Goodyer. Gosse, vol. ii, p. 9.

[4] Letter to Goodyer. Gosse, vol. ii, p. 7.

[5] 'He was like Bunyan's Christian in the Valley of the Shadow of Death, tormented by evil suggestions of which he could not discern the origin.' Evelyn Simpson, p. 10.

guilt and unfulfilment. He lived apart from the harmonious laws of being, and the current attitude to sin, which he and his congregations recognized and accepted, was in part accountable for his maladjustment. He might try to batter himself into reconciliation:

'As a cabinet whose key were lost, must be broken up, and torn in pieces . . . shaked and shivered before that Jewel that was laid up in it, can be taken out:'[1]

or he might try to browbeat the unreasoning unconscious into submission by means of conscious argument, but his nature did not respond to either method. Violence was not the means and reason was not the key.

'Reason, your viceroy in me, me should defend,
But is captiv'd, and proves weak or untrue.'[2]

Donne might plumb below to the most open sensuality to distract himself from the conflict, he might mount above in mystic ecstasies to assuage it, he might even consider suicide as the way out—'Methinks I have the keys of my prison in mine own hand'[3]—but the prison remained unyielding and the cabinet refused to be so uncharitably handled. The only key which would have opened either, and released the tormented spirit, was a new conception of Divine Love.

3

The rigorous absolutes of theology were essential to Donne, but having discarded the religion of his ancestors, what then? A period of dreadful night and doubt before he should be able to adopt the tenets of another, scarcely different and hardly disguised. Denied the avenue of escape which a healthy attitude to life and sex would have permitted him,

[1] Sermon—The 4th of my Prebend Sermons, upon my five Psalms, Jan. 1626/7. The Jewel is the Soul.

[2] *Biathanatos*.   [3] *Holy Sonnets*, XIV.

he took refuge in another harbour in order to support the insupportable and vexatious burden of life.

Although Donne's long delayed entry into the Church and Hamlet's projected murder of his uncle-stepfather, at first sight, do not appear to have much in common, there is a similarity in the temperament of the two men, of the modes of thought and of the indecision which paralyzed them, which makes it interesting to examine. Both were playing for safety, for escape from the intolerable position in which they found themselves, and they were both hoping against hope that something natural, or even supernatural, some god from the clouds, would descend to decide the matter for them. With hands tied by their own repugnance, both would risk nothing to gain something. If they waited, fate bitterly decreed that it was too late. If they underwent agonies of despair over life, yet, being unhappy egoists, they did the same when facing death. Perhaps, after all, the gods or God, would be merciful, and give the sufferer a second chance.

Both were profound sceptics about life, and if Hamlet speaks for Shakespeare, both he and Donne were undergoing painful sea-changes of thought—attitudes to reality—at about the same time. But such scepticism neither narrowed down the field of motives for action nor fostered its springs. Both were capable of the most decisive action apart from the task in question. Donne found no difficulty in carrying out his travels, his military expeditions, his duties as a confidential secretary, his pamphleteering, or, once he had taken the plunge, his arduous new work as King's Chaplain and Dean of St. Paul's. At no time, either upon Morton or the King urging him to enter the Church, did he suggest to them that he was not *equal* to the task suggested although he might be *unworthy*. He was simply a man who could not bring himself, for a long number of years, to perform what every practical consideration told him was advisable. It is not enough to say that, in the case of either Hamlet or Donne, each suffered

Q

from an excess of toleration and an appreciation of too many courses of action open to them, or that each had grave doubts of the moral legitimacy of the main course. There is some struggle which propels them forward, like fascinated creatures, towards the very thing from which they recoil, until they become almost static. They do not *want* to do the very thing they know they must, if ever they wish to attain peace. They are both 'strong men tortured by some mysterious inhibition' and the struggle lies 'between the natural tendency . . . and the highly developed ethical . . . view which forbids the indulging of this instinctive desire'.[1]

Neither gives an indication of the cause of the conflict distracting them and preventing them from prompt action because neither is aware of the buried cause. They make excuses a-plenty: Donne says that he realizes that the useful, contributing member of society must be fruitfully and contentedly employed. 'I would fain do something, but that I cannot tell *what* is no wonder. For to choose is to do . . .'[2] and the more specious, the more varied the excuses, the more certain we are that none of them is genuine. They are processes of evasion and rationalization, and the order of events is to see and appreciate the duty, to shirk it, and then to suffer excruciating remorse. 'I have a riddling disposition to be ashamed of fear and afraid of shame,' writes Donne to Wotton.[3]

Hamlet's depression and the hopelessness in his attitude toward life are all echoed by Donne, first in *The Progress of the Soul*, then in *Biathanatos* and the *First Anniversary*. His sleeplessness, which seems to have been a life-long symptom of some mental upheaval and which he specifically mentions—

'It is no strange thing, that I do not sleep well; for in my best health, I am not much used to do so. . . .'[4]

[1] Ernest Jones, *The Oedipus Complex, as an Explanation of Hamlet's Mystery*, to whom I owe these thoughts on Donne.

[2] Letter to Goodyer. Gosse, vol. i, p. 191.

[3] Letter, 1600. Hayward, p. 441.

[4] Letter to Mrs. Cockayne, January, 1630/1. Gosse ii, p. 271.

may have been due, like Hamlet's insomnia and dread of sleep, to nightmare visitations.

In Hamlet's case the will to live succumbed to the will to die: he was mercilessly propelled along the only path which he could travel. 'The conflict in his soul was to him insoluble and the only steps he could make were those which drew him inexorably nearer and nearer to his doom.'[1] In Donne's case his native religious inclinations, thwarted and terribly repressed, infected with doctrines too strong for them and examples of sacrifice too terrifying, but inverted at last for his salvation, rose to draw him back into life, but not without ensuring that he bore the scars of the contest for all who had discerning eyes to read. He was destined for life and not for death, but always to walk, to breathe, to draw his halting faith in pain.

What was the buried poison which, when stirred by Morton's, or the King's, insistence caused Donne to be flung into such torment and inordinate despair? What was the memory which was too painful, too agonizing to drag into consciousness? Why this dreadful reluctance 'to dare the exploration of the inner mind'? Was it that the moral conscience, forcefully instilled into him against every inclination of his nature, called him coward and renegade for not following in the footsteps of his martyr ancestors? and that thus he whipped himself for a haunting sense of guilt? Was it that he considered himself damned, as they would have done, for abandoning the Church of Rome? Or was it simply that his early training had given him such a repugnance for all religious authority that he did not believe that he could, in honesty, adhere to any faction? No one can answer the question, for the secret died with its keeper.

[1] Ernest Jones.

4

The tremendous struggle in the unconscious causes Donne constantly to speak on two levels and gives to his speech and imagery a bi-focal view. Women are devils, yet they are angels. Love is a curse, and yet a blessing. God is a tyrant and yet merciful. Thus, almost in the same breath in which he asks:

'Whom do I tremble at, and sweat under, at midnight, and whom do I curse by, next morning, if there be no God?[1]

he can declare with touching simplicity that God:

'was favourable to all our peregrinations, and though he shew himself late, he was our friend early.'[2]

Or he will denounce man as a paradox:

'Nothing but men, of all unvenomed things,
Doth work upon itself, with inborn stings.'[3]

and then praise him as an image of Divinity:

'That Man who dwells upon himself, who is always conversant within himself, rests in his true centre. Man is a celestial creature, a heavenly creature: and that Man that dwells upon himself, that hath his conversation in himself, hath his conversation in heaven.'[4]

His need for security and for the comforting bonds of support, whether the love of women or the love of God, speaks out in his graphic metaphors, mostly of a mathematical kind, of which the most famous is the one of the compass. Speaking of his and his true love's (probably Ann's) soul, he writes:

'If they be two, they are two so
    As stiff twin compasses are two,
Thy soul the fixt foot, makes no show
    To move, but doth, if th'other do.

[1] Sermon, St. Paul's, Easter Day, April 1628.
[2] Sermon, St. Paul's, 1620–22.
[3] Elegy on Lady Markham.
[4] Sermon, St. Paul's, Christmas Day, 1627.

And though it in the corner sit,
   Yet when the other far doth roam,
It leans, and hearkens after it,
   And grows erect, as that comes home.

Such wilt thou be to me, who must
   Like th'other foot, obliquely run;
Thy firmness draws my circle just,
   And makes me end, where I begun.'[1]

Donne paraphrases this in a Sermon:

'But though we cannot make up our circle of a straight line, (it is impossible to human frailty), yet we may pass on, without angles, without corners, that is, without disguises in our religion, and without the love of craft, and falsehood, and circumvention in our civil actions.

A compass is a necessary thing in a ship, and the help of that compass brings the ship home safe, and yet that compass hath some variations, it doth not look directly north; neither is that star which we call the north-pole, or by which we know the north-pole, the very pole itself; but we call it so, and we make our uses of it, and our conclusions by it, as if it were so, because it is the nearest star to that Pole.

He that comes as near uprightness as infirmities admit, is an upright man, though he have some obliquities. To God himself we may always go in a direct line, a straight, a perpendicular line; for God is vertical to me, over my head now, and vertical now to them, that are in the East and West Indies; to our Antipodes, to them that are under our feet, God is vertical, over their heads, when he is over ours.'[2]

The collapse of the recognized universe as revealed in the Copernican discoveries was a shattering revelation for Donne. It mirrored his own tremulous mental and emotional state, and the instability which had always threatened him now appeared, like a contagious disease, to have infected the very Universe. There was nothing at all to cling to until he found his quivering faith.

In the 'Mathematic Point', which he called 'the most in-

---

[1] 'A Valediction: Forbidding Mourning.'
[2] 3rd Prebend. Sermon. November 5th, 1626.

divisible and unique thing which art can present',[1] he found
not only the symbolic, with which he always had an affinity,
and the mystic, but a comforting sense of security. For higher
mathematicians declare that the excitement of using words
in a new sense, and of employing a set of symbols governed
by a grammar of their own, is as intense as that experienced
on discovering a great philosophical truth, or in learning a new
language. But if the sense of liberation, of exploration is
infinite, the mathematical symbol has a fixed meaning and
does not cheat one with its variability.

This bi-focal, or ambivalent view, is akin to another quality
of Donne's, his quicksilver elusiveness. 'Physical of the physical, he can be ethereally ideal: at his touch, abstract becomes
concrete . . . or concrete abstract. . . .'[2] This faculty for
baffling and adroit escape from one mental and emotional
plane to another is observable in a primary sphere in his life,
the sexual. It was strong in youth and did not diminish in
maturity, although it cloaked itself in a different guise.

For Donne was profoundly ashamed of his bodily powers,
and the whole question of sex tormented him to such an
extent that he longed for escape from its responsibilities.
Sometimes it seems as if he wished to escape from life itself
by sloughing off mortality, or by slipping from one form of
life into another, male into female, animal into elemental. A
mysterious parthenogenesis, followed by a bloodless rebirth,
would have allowed him to be free from the horrible stigma
of being human, from the sinful business of lust and repro-
duction.

Thus, as a young man he is attracted to the alchemistic:
(he is charmed by the crystal which hardens in a night, by the
philosopher's stone which miraculously turns all to gold, the
'compassionate' turquoise which alters its colour to mirror
the mood of its wearer) or to the elfin, and this fey quality

[1] Letter to Goodyer. Gosse, vol. i, p. 223.
[2] F. L. Lucas in his review in the *New Statesman*, Nov. 1, 1924.

appears most strongly in the poem called *Song*. The mandrake, cleft devil's foot and the mermaid are all symbols for him of this impossible, fairy world. 'If thou beest born to strange sights' is no idle hypothesis, for the young Donne feels himself somehow *outside* life, alien, a sojourner in a strange land.

'Go and catch a falling star!'

he commands his listeners, but it is *he* who is the falling star, the meteor, child of the heaven's and earth's inexplicable, vaporous mating, that wild flaming tail of light which defies the analysis, since when people run to examine the body they are cheated by finding only a 'jelly'. The meteor which continues to fascinate him throughout life typifies the spirit of the young man which refuses to be caught and ignominiously labelled. In later life, writing to the Countess of Bedford, Donne even compares himself to one:

'. . . meteor-like, of stuff and form perplexed,
Whose what and where in disputation is . . .'

For the same reason he admires the watery elusiveness of the fish whose medium permits it complete discretion of movement. He advises his friend Sir Henry Wotton to imitate them, 'leaving no print where they pass,' (a simile which he uses with a sexual emphasis in another poem[1]) and to adhere so closely to his course that 'men dispute whether thou breathe or no'.

This last phrase shows his preoccupation with another theme, that of hibernation, or suspension of life. In *The Good Morrow* he uses the example of the seven sleepers of Ephesus who lay entombed in a dark, womb-like cavern for some 200 years, torpid, passive and unresponsive, neither attracted to nor repulsed by one another, whose sex therefore remained dormant and problematical. Over and over again in his prose writings he speaks of the child alive in its mother's

[1] *Heroical Epistle.*

womb who is yet imprisoned, asleep and unfulfilled, maintained in a balance of indecision and inaction. And at the close of his life the mature man chooses a sepulchral effigy which resembles either a caul or the silky cocoon spun by the larva, shrouding and shielding his body in such a way that, were it not for the disclosure of the face, one would be hard put to it to identify the sex.

Thus, in his early efforts to escape from reality, he attempted the elfin and alchemistic way out (which later developed into the spiritual), or the earthy and highly sensual. But no escape is possible and in his attempts to transcend life and achieve an otherness Donne slips mercurially out of one sex into the other, in one poem even interchanging the pronouns.[1]

This interplay, this merging and confusing of the sexes may be noted in *Break of Day*, a poem which appears to be addressed by a male lover to his feminine companion but which, upon close examination, proves to be the opposite. One may excuse this example by alleging it to be like so many of the Elizabethan lyrics in which the woman takes the lead, were it not for other examples. In the *Valediction: Forbidding Mourning*, quoted previously,[2] he uses the compass, a two-into-one symbol to express his preoccupation; allots the circle, a feminine symbol, to himself, and suggests that the feminine portion of the compass 'grows erect' when it senses the approach of the other. In his poems to Magdalen Herbert, in which he always attempts to remain most platonic, he plays with the idea of woman removed into another sphere, the sub or super human, in order that she may lose that part of her which torments him, her sex and her charm. This might prove an advantage but with the consequent disadvantage that, whether he reduce her below or magnify her above femininity, he loses that which also attracts him, and either substitution becomes monstrous and unthinkable.

[1] See *The Progress of the Soul*. [2] pp. 244-5.

In the *Dissolution* he thinks of his anatomy, now sunk into ashes, blended with those of the woman he has loved, become indistinguishable from hers and thereby defying the analyst to distinguish the sexes: and in the *Progress of the Soul* he goes through the wearisome business of finding new homes for the migratory soul, male and female alike.

But the wretched man, unable to escape into a different category, unable to invent another sphere of relationship, is caught in the web of his own weaving and one is never convinced in hearkening to him that he is able to distinguish fact from that which fact suggests, or reality from the image. Like the dog in his *Fifth Satire* he is cozened by his own shadow.

Just how much of this hermaphroditic interplay belongs to an original mind like Donne's with its amazing facility for 'mental osmosis',[1] and just how much is an offshoot of the tendencies of the period it is difficult to say. One of the chief allegations against prominent Elizabethans, like Hawkins, was that they suffered from the 'Norman vice', and a student of contemporary drama remarks that Inigo Jones' designs for the characters in his Masques portrayed a curious sexlessness, or mixture of the sexes. "Were it not for the external evidence we should be greatly at a loss in guessing the identity of many of the costume figures. The androgynous types admired at the Court of James the Ist and his son often make it difficult to determine even the sex of the personages."[2]

Shakespeare, and other dramatists, played upon the Rosalind theme of the girl who masquerades as a boy, (which cannot be entirely explained by stating the necessity of utilizing boy-actors in feminine parts): Donne, we have seen,

---

[1] Professor Mario Praz's phrase in his 'Donne and The Poetry of his Time' in *A Garland for Donne*, p. 62.

[2] *Designs for Masques and Plays at Court by Inigo Jones*. Introduction and notes by Percy Simpson and C. F. Bell. Vol. xii of the Walpole Society, Oxford University Press, 1924, p. 28.

used it in an Elegy in such a way that it appears as if he were dealing with an actual, not an imaginary suggestion, and examples of people putting the experiment to the test in real life were not isolated. All these tendencies and trends of thought, both national and individual, open paths for reflection and study in the light of modern psychological investigations.

5

Donne's was a dawning scientific mind clogged with mediaevalism and his pulpit oratory was a purge as well as a tonic. It was a salve to the sore which the religion itself influenced, a blessed relief to tormented heart and conscience, and through it Donne, though alternately chafed and chastened, freed the clot threatening his life and health and retained his very sanity. Had he and his contemporaries not voided some of the appalling wad of uncivilized emotion gathering from current theological teachings, a greater amount of national persecution, culminating in massacre, would probably have occurred.

The skein which tangled and muffled his mind in a kind of strangulation was the doctrine of Original Sin—the chief moral agent of the Middle Ages. Together with the belief in Hell Fire and Damnation, it paralyzed his reason, so ready for liberation, so eager to soar up into new thought and contentment, and chilled his impulses toward a Creator whom he needed, longed to love, and also to be cherished by.

It was this pernicious doctrine which caused Donne to write with all solemnity that man was less than the toad or spider:

'Miserable man! A toad is a bag of poison, and a spider is a blister of poison, and yet a toad and a spider cannot poison themselves: Man hath a dram of poison, original sin, in an invisible corner, we know not where, and he cannot choose but poison himself and his actions with that. . . .'[1]

[1] Sermon XIII. Preached at Whitehall, April 19, 1618.

and again:

'I have a sense of sin, a root that is not grubbed up, of sin that will cast me back again. Scarce any man considers the weight, the oppression of original sin . . . and though God deliver me from eternal death, due to mine actual and habitual sins, yet from the temporal death, due to original sin, he delivers not his dearest Saints.'[1]

It involves the notion of transmitted guilt and a revengeful creator, and Donne, like thousands of Christian men of his era, was taught to believe that this guilt, entirely unconnected with any recognized, personal act, tainted him at his conception and poisoned him for life: that the God who made him, while remaining the author of justice, mercy and loving-kindness, permitted and in no way hindered sin, until He became its author as well. Thus He is at once worshipped and vilified, loved and hated, supplicated and intensely feared. Why strive for salvation from a Being who decides irrevocably the fate of each palpitating human long before he is called into existence, who has predestined millions to hatred and eternal damnation?

'With this object He gave them being, with this object He withholds from them the assistance which alone can correct the perversity of the nature with which He created them. He will hate them during life, and after death will cast them into the excruciating torments of undying fire and will watch their agonies without compassion.'[2]

With such doctrines, incompatible with either an endearing creator or created, all sense of justice is perverted, reason is subjected and the lines of natural conscience, engraven upon every heart by a truly divine originator, are entirely obliterated, the lamp of conscience is extinguished and the inner voice is stifled as being that of a strumpet or a lying witness.

With the rise of rationalism and a dispassionate, scientific

[1] Sermon XII. Preached at Lincoln's Inn.   [2] Lecky, i, p. 389.

attitude, with the coming of Montaigne, Descartes, Hobbes and Locke, the nightmares of persecution, witchcraft and personal disapproval began to disperse, but the tragedy of Donne's is that his birth occurred before the ripening of their philosophy.

Such an attitude, imbedded like a hard and irritant pearl in the growing oyster, meant that Donne failed to be able to accept life, even the physical facts of life—birth, union and the act of dying. Its roots for him sprang from, and remained entwined in, unnatural filth. One has only to read the first half of *Death's Duell* to appreciate the appallingly unhealthy state of his mind, as darkness closed in and he reverted to the basic disease within him. Conceived in sin, born in sin, and wrapped in its consciousness throughout life, he waited for resurrection as the entrance to purity, half fearing that divine forgiveness and a paradisal respite might be denied him by a 'sportive', neglectful deity. And if so foully conceived, so foully born, so perpetually tainted, what hope of salvation might there be, except through constant, despairing, violent striving?

'Nor do all these, youth out of infancy, or age out of youth arise so, as a Phoenix out of the ashes of another Phoenix formerly dead, but as a wasp or a serpent out of carrion, or as a snake out of dung. Our youth is worse than our infancy, and our age worse than our youth. Our youth is hungry and thirsty after those sins which our infancy knew not; and our age is sorry and angry that it cannot pursue those sins which our youth did. . . .'[1]

The doctrine becomes entangled with the earlier unfortunate phantasy of birth which haunts him sleeping, waking and dying.

'. . . for in our mother's womb we are dead so, as that we do not know we live, not so much as we do in our sleep, neither is there any grave so close, or so putrid a prison, as the womb would be unto us, if we stayed in it beyond our time or died there before our time. . . . In the womb the dead child kills the mother that

[1] *Death's Duell*. A Sermon preached at Whitehall, Feb. 25, 1630.

conceived it, and is a murderer, nay a parricide, even after it is dead. . . . There in the womb we are fitted for works of darkness . . . and there in the womb we are taught cruelty by being fed with blood, and may be damned, though we be never born. . . . The womb which should be the house of life becomes death itself if God leave us there. . . . We have a winding sheet in our mother's womb which grows with us from our conception.'[1]

And much more in the same repulsive vein. The suppressed hatred of the creator-father, everlasting sin and damnation, the perpetual state of irredemption, the hopeless struggle lost at the outset, and the confirmation of his first and most terrifying suspicions, are all inarticulately expressed in this passage.

Even the bed which supports and restores him to rest is tainted with imagined filth:

'Therefore sanctify that place; wash it with thy tears, and with a repentant consideration; That in that bed thy children were conceived in sin, that in that bed thou hast turned marriage, which God afforded thee for remedy, and physic, to voluptuousness and licentiousness; that thou hast made that bed which God has given thee for rest and for reparation of thy weary body, to be as thy dwelling, and delight, and the bed of idleness, and stupidity.'

So much for his remorseful thoughts of Ann, and for the mediaeval attitude towards loving, conception and birth, which lingered on well into the nineteenth century, and which our own healthier generation regards with horror or indifference.

The current literature of the period is riddled with these gruesome thoughts: Chidiock Tichborne's Lament is only one of many examples:

> 'I sought my death and found it in my womb,
> I looked for life and saw it was a shade,
> I trod the earth and knew it was my tomb,
> And now I die, and now I am but made.'[2]

[1] *Death's Duell*. A Sermon preached at Whitehall, Feb. 25, 1630.

[2] *Sherborne Ballads*, p. 549. See also 'The Ballad on William Wrench', deserter, executed in 1600, p. 202.

Herrick follows apostrophizing his winding-sheet. But there is something peculiarly repulsive in Donne's method of brooding on corruption. Birth and death are irremediably locked together in his mind, not as natural processes, but as strange, unwholesome phenomena.

Yet his very avidity for life was the counterpart of his fear of death. At some time in childhood, or even in early manhood, perhaps at the loss of his brother, Donne had looked too closely into the face of death. She had breathed upon him like a stony Medusa, and having felt her breath striking so chill into the mind's interstices, he became one of life's most ardent champions. Death made him feel his inferiority, his vulnerability, above all, his frailty. He refused to accept its finality. But the pagan attitude to dying, whether that of the savages who look upon it passively as a necessary accident, or of the ancients who cherished the doctrine of immortality and contemplated death with stoic calm, was impossible for Donne. The heathen, contemplating death, 'neither seeth nor feeleth that it is God's wrath, but meaneth it is the end of nature and is natural; he dieth securely away,'[1] and Plato declared that 'The just man should take confidence in death'. But their serenity was alien to Donne. The 'insatiable whirlpools', 'the furnaces' of his 'spirit' suffocated him up to the last.

His attraction to the very thing which he feared was an offshoot of Christianity, for as Luther said: 'It is God's wrath which maketh death bitter to us.' A modern French writer puts it differently:

'In savage society, in which sensualism and licence abound, a man is careful not to represent death as anything hideous: the skeleton does not stand to him for the symbol of an unpitying god.

But when Christianity conquered the world, when a miserable eternity became the punishment meted out for errors committed

[1] Luther's *Table Talk*; translation by Bell.

on earth, death, which had been a matter of such indifference to the ancients, became something whose consequences for the believer were so terrible that he was forced to remind himself of it at every breath by startling the eyes with the very depiction of death.'[1]

It has been said that this preoccupation with death is a national characteristic of the English,—a 'Teuton wail' rising in the literature of every century in contrast with the more placid Latin acceptance. From the unknown Anglo-Saxon poet writing of the wretched beginning, the foul middle and the disgusting old age of man, ultimately food for worms, from Rolle of Hampole soliloquizing on the instability of life, Dunbar, writing, as Donne did, in a time of sickness, buttressing his poem with the constant refrain,

'Timor Mortis conturbat me'

which tolls like some great bell in Donne's *Devotions*, to Raleigh apostrophizing death so lovingly, and Hamlet lingering over Yorick's skull and addressing it rather than his human companion, the cry goes up unceasing.

In Donne's attitude to death there is none of that feeling of liberation and expansion which a nineteenth-century poet expresses:

'. . . it is the end, the high
Hope that is like a cordial that we buy
And till the even strengthens our weak knees;
Beyond the snow, the storms, the frosts that freeze,
The tremor of a light beneath the sky
Of visible darkness . . .
The door that opens on the unfathomed sky.'[2]

The melancholy messages of the scriptures fell on ground of peculiar fertility when the Church Fathers introduced them to Donne and his predecessors.

---

[1] Jubinal, *Sur les Danses des Morts*.
[2] Jourdain's translation of Baudelaire.

6

But the way is not entirely clouded by thoughts of death and the dark unsatisfying conflict. At his finest and most sincere the note of certainty and high contentment breaks out clear and untroubled. This joy of loving, which is part of his love of woman in the *Songs and Sonnets*, of life and the goodness of God in the Sermons, indicates the heights to which he might more often and more readily have attained.

'God shall never take from me ... my internal gladness and consolation, in his undeceivable and undeceiving spirit, that he is mine, and I am his: and this joy, this gladness, in my way, and in my end, shall establish me. ...

In the days of our youth, when the joys of this world take up all the room, there shall be room for this holy joy, that my recreations were harmless, and my conversation innocent. ... In the days of our age, when we become incapable, insensible of the joys of this world, yet this holy joy shall season us, not with a sinful delight, but with a rejuvenescence, a new and fresh youth, in being come so near to another, to an immortal life.

In the days of our mirth, and of laughter, this holy joy shall enter; and as the Sun may say to the stars at noon, How frivolous and impertinent a thing is your light now! so this joy shall say unto laughter, Thou art made, and unto mirth, what dost thou?

And in the midnight of sadness, and dejection of spirit, this joy shall shine out, and chide away that sadness, with David's holy charm, My soul, why art thou cast down, why art thou disquieted within me?'[1]

In his great Sermon of jubilation upon the Feast of the Conversion of St. Paul,[2] Donne speaks with an eagerness and conviction which testify to his own 'outer darkness' before he was reconciled and the abundant light which shone upon him afterwards. It might well be called the Sermon of Regeneration, or the New Man, as the husk of the seed splits and falls apart, the new growth thrusting towards immortal life.

'Saul was struck blind, but it was a blindness contracted from light: It was a light that struck him blind. ... This blindness

[1] Sermon LXXIX. St. Paul's 1620–22.   [2] January 30th, 1624/5.

which we speak of ... this holy simplicity of the soul, is not a darkness, a dimness, a stupidity in the understanding, contracted by living in a corner, it is not an idle retiring into a monastery, or into a village or into a country solitude, it is not a lazy affection of ignorance: not darkness, but a greater light, must make us blind. ...

Saul had such a blindness as that he fell with it. ... Men blinded with the lights of this world, soar still into higher places, or higher knowledges, or higher opinions; but the light of heaven humbles us, and lays flat the soul, which the leaven of this world had puffed and swelled up.'[1]

In this passage one hears the echo of the young man of twenty-four who wrote:

'And this blindness too much light breeds.'

And here is another magnificent passage from the great Christmas Sermon of pagan abundance:[2]

'If some King of the earth have so large an extent of Dominion, in North and South, as that he hath, winter and summer together in his dominions, so large an extent east and west, as that he hath day and night together in his dominions, much more hath God mercy and judgment together; He brought light out of darkness, not out of lesser light; He can bring thy summer out of winter, though thou have no spring; though in the ways of fortune or understanding, or conscience thou have been benighted till now, wintred and frozen, clouded and eclypsed, damped and benumbed, smothered and stupefied till now, now God comes to thee, not as in the dawning of the day, not as in the bud of the spring, but as the sun at noon to illustrate all shadows, as the sheaves in harvest, to fill all penuries, all occasions invite his mercies and all times are his seasons.'

And lastly here are two examples of Donne, the worshipper and believer in nature, both human and elemental:

'In that glistering circle in the firmament, which we call the Galaxie, the Milky Way, there is not one star of any of the six great magnitudes, which astronomers proceed upon, belonging to that circle: it is a glorious circle, and possesseth a great part of heaven, and yet is all of so little stars, as have no name, no know-

[1] January 30th, 1624/5.
[2] St. Paul's, Christmas Day in the Evening, 1624.

R

ledge taken of them; So certainly there are many Saints in heaven, that shine as stars, and yet are not of those great magnitudes, to have been Patriarchs, or Prophets, or Apostles, or Martyrs, or Doctors or Virgins; but good and blessed souls, that have religiously performed the duties of inferior callings, and no more.'[1]

. . . . . .

'There is nothing which God hath established in a constant course of Nature, and which therefore is done every day, but would seem a miracle, and exercise our admiration, if it were done but once; nay, the ordinary things in Nature, would be greater miracles, than the extraordinary, which we admire most, if they were done but once; the standing still of the sun for Joshua's use, was not, in itself, so wonderful a thing, as that so vast and immense a body as the Sun should run so many miles in a minute; the motion of the sun were a greater thing than the standing still, if all were to begin again: and only the daily doing takes off the admiration.

But then God having, as it were, concluded himself in a course of nature, and written down in the book of creatures, Thus and Thus all things shall be carried, though he glorify himself sometimes, in doing a miracle, yet there is in every miracle, a silent chiding of the world, and a tacit reprehension of them, who require, or who need miracles.'[2]

If we remember Donne for the dark side of his nature, yet we love and cherish the other, bright with an almost miraculous brightness, like the light, of which he was never tired of speaking, which blinded Saul, or that which shines from the wings of archangels. 'Miraculous Donne,' Ben Jonson called him, but it was the poet that he saluted, not the theological writer. If it is too much to ask of human nature to wish the Sermons more in number, we never tire of the *Songs and Sonnets*, the singing parts of the *Elegies*, those poems which their author labelled mere 'evaporations of wit' and for which, with characteristic irony, he made neither prophecy nor preparation.

The student may ponder Donne's sources, rhythms and

[1] *Six Sermons*, II, No. 29.
[2] Sermon, St. Paul's, Easter Day, March 25th, 1627.

craftsmanship, the scholar his metaphysics, mysticism, mediaevalism; the devout may learn the *Holy Sonnets* and the religious the *Devotions*; the historian may study the *Satyres* and *Letters*, 'through which the slow and massive movement of his mind turns and returns, before it draws towards a difficult conclusion.'[1] Yet Donne will remain the poet for lovers. His rebel spirit, his passionate intensity, no matter how complex the metrical form compressing it, nor how aggravating the wealth of scholastic divinity entangling it, will draw them as the sun draws rising sap, or a magnet flakes of trembling steel.

And so leave him, not dreaming in 'a winter-seeming summer's night', nor repenting with 'a kind of sorrowing dullness of the mind', but pleading with his mistress whose face, whose name, is unknown to us, in rough, abrupt, impetuous speech, or in lines of silken enticement. Her name, her features, do not matter. It is Donne's ardour and accents that live, and will live, as long as men and women love.

> ' 'Tis true, 'tis day; what though it be?
> O wilt thou therefore rise from me?
> Why should we rise, because 'tis light?
> Did we lie down, because 'twas night?
> Love, which in spite of darkness brought us hither,
> Should in despite of light keep us together.'[2]

---

[1] Hayward, p. 438.   [2] 'Break of Day.'

R 2

APPENDIX I

PEDIGREE OF JOHN DONNE'S MATERNAL ANCESTORS

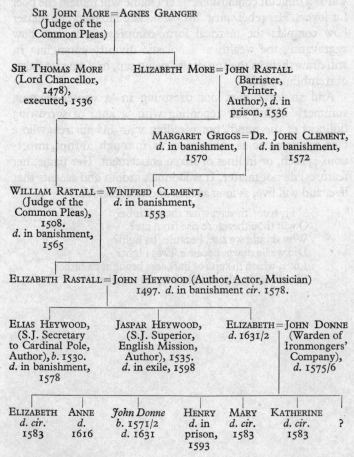

SIR JOHN MORE = AGNES GRANGER
(Judge of the
Common Pleas)

SIR THOMAS MORE   ELIZABETH MORE = JOHN RASTALL
(Lord Chancellor,   (Barrister,
1478),   Printer,
executed, 1536   Author), d. in
                                                     prison, 1536

MARGARET GRIGGS = DR. JOHN CLEMENT,
d. in banishment,   d. in banishment,
1570   1572

WILLIAM RASTALL = WINIFRED CLEMENT,
(Judge of the   d. in banishment,
Common Pleas),   1553
1508.
d. in banishment,
1565

ELIZABETH RASTALL = JOHN HEYWOOD (Author, Actor, Musician)
                                1497. d. in banishment cir. 1578.

ELIAS HEYWOOD,   JASPAR HEYWOOD,   ELIZABETH = JOHN DONNE
(S.J. Secretary   (S.J. Superior,   d. 1631/2   (Warden of
to Cardinal Pole,   English Mission,   Ironmongers'
Author), b. 1530.   Author), 1535.   Company),
d. in banishment,   d. in exile, 1598   d. 1575/6
1578

ELIZABETH   ANNE   *John Donne*   HENRY   MARY   KATHERINE
d. cir.   d.   b. 1571/2   d. in   d. cir.   d. cir.   ?
1583   1616   d. 1631   prison,   1583   1583
                                                 1593

See Jessop's *John Donne*, p. 223 and Wilson, *Notes on the Early Life of Donne*, p. 275.

260

APPENDIX II

EXTANT LIKENESSES OF DONNE

The Paintings

1. Miniature by Isaac Oliver, signed with Monogram and dated 1616, in the Royal Collection, Windsor, which is either identical with, or similar to, one formerly in the possession of Charles Sackville Bale in the 1860's. *c.* 2½ inches. Blue background.

2. Portrait in oil in the National Portrait Gallery. Head and shoulders, to left. Canvas: anon. after Isaac Oliver. 20¼ × 17, of the same type as the miniature with slight variations. (Engraved by Duncan when in the possession of the Rev. Jonathan Tyers Barrett, D.D. It remained in the possession of his descendants at Brandon House, Suffolk, until 1919, when it was purchased by the National Portrait Gallery.)

3 & 4. Two paintings in oil, similar to the engraving in line by P. Lombart. Both circular and of *c.* 25 inches in diameter. Head and shoulders, bare throat. One is in the Deanery of St. Paul's, the other in the Dyce Collection at the Victoria and Albert Museum.

5. Monumental Effigy by Nicholas Stone and his assistants in St. Paul's Cathedral. White marble, placed in grey marble niche with semi-circular head, above which is a white marble tablet and escutcheon with garlands. It stood on the south side of the choir of the old church, survived the Fire of London with little damage, and was re-erected in the south aisle of the choir of Wren's St. Paul's.

The Engravings

(From the published catalogue of Engraved British Portraits in the British Museum.)

	Painter	*Engraver*	*Copies of Books with portrait in B.M. Library*
1. Bust, to l., in gown and ruff; rect. Pl. to Walton's *Compleat Angler;* pub. J. Major, 1825. Line; $4\frac{1}{8} \times 3\frac{1}{8}$ in.		W. Bromley	
2. H.L., to r., in his shroud; oval. Front. to his *Death's Duell*, 1633. Line; $5\frac{1}{4} \times 4\frac{1}{8}$ in.		M. Droeshout	c. 53. k. 19
3. Bust, to l., in gown and ruff; rect. Pl. to *Effigies Poeticae*; pub. W. Walker, 1822. Line; $3\frac{7}{8} \times 3\frac{1}{8}$ in.		A. Duncan	
4. His monumental effigy, now in the crypt of St. Paul's cathedral. Pl. to Dugdale's *St. Paul's*, 1658. (Parthey 2277.) Etching.		W. Hollar	208. g. 13 (p.62)
5. Same figure, with emblems. Title to his *Devotions*, 1634. Line; $3\frac{3}{4} \times 2$ in.		W. Marshall	Copy of this edition not in B.M. Library
6. Bust, full face, with classical drapery; oval, with Latin inscription below. Front. to his *Poems*, 1633. Line; $5\frac{7}{8} \times 3\frac{7}{8}$ in.		P. Lombart	G. 11415
7. Copy from the last; oval at head of account of him. Pl. to *Biographical Mag.*, pub. Harrison & Co., 1798. Line; $1\frac{7}{8} \times 1\frac{3}{8}$ in.		P. Audinet	
8. Aged 18; H.L., to r., r. hand grasping hilt of sword; oval, with 8 lines by I. Walton below: 'This was for Youth, Strength, mirth and wit that Time,' etc. Front to his *Poems*, 1635, 1649 (1650). Line; $3\frac{1}{2} \times 3$ in.		W. Marshall	011641. de. 102

	Painter	Engraver	Copies of Books with portrait in B.M. Library
9. Aged 42; bust to r., in gown and ruff: Oval in rich architechural frame. Front. to his Sermons, 1640. Line.		M. Merian, jun.	480. f. 5
10. Mural Monument in St. Paul's Cathedral with W.L. effigy. Pl. to *The Walpole Society's* vol. 7, 1919. Process block.	N. Stone (sculptor)		

Mr. Geoffrey Keynes in his *Bibliography of Dr. John Donne*, 1914, pp. 157–8, and Mr. John Sparrow in *Donne's Devotions*, 1923, pp. xxix–xxx, have already dealt with the paintings and engravings extant of Donne but the details are here presented in a different manner.

The Mural Monument, (No. 10 above) was removed for safety from the Cathedral in 1940.

The Spanish motto, or 'word', on Donne's youthful portrait, (No. 8, p. 262) was incorrectly translated in the 1675 edition of Sir Isaac Walton's *Life of Dr. John Donne* as:

'How much shall I be changed
Before I am changed!'

Sir Edmund Gosse in his *Life and Letters*, v. 1, p. 24, repeats the error by interpreting it as 'Before I am dead, how shall I be changed.' But, as Senor Ugidos has pointed out to me, the correct meaning, 'Sooner dead than changed', is significant of the national trend of Spanish thought ever since the days of *El Cid*. It embraces the age-long Spanish conception of chivalry and betokens an obstinacy of mind general in Spanish thought and fable. Donne's adoption of this motto, about which I hope to make further discoveries, expressed his audacious stubbornness, and his admiration for Spanish romantic chivalry, but not his native piety.

AUTHOR'S NOTE.

APPENDIX III

DONNE'S HANDWRITING

Analysis

The writer is not a man who evades things; he faces them, and gives expression to what he means and feels. He opposes yielding, or the making of concessions, with the whole strength of his personality. He is satisfied only with the severest truth, fights for his opinions and tries to express them clearly. If he dislikes something he attacks it violently and is not content with half victories, but struggles to attain his ends. He asks for trouble—and gets it.

He is modest before God and confident of his own powers, but there is nothing of arrogance, or pretence, in his belief in himself. He has a strong will and a strong conviction that he acts rightly and that things are as he sees them.

This is not an intellectually striking personality, nor is the intellect even strongly developed. It is one in which feeling and impulse predominate dictating motive and action. His world of imagination is not primarily filled with spiritual or intellectual fantasies but with pictures of this world—of reality. Sexual images play a great, even a dominant part, and these are not concerned solely with feminine types but in some degree with juveniles of his own sex.

He is introspective, but never loses himself in introspection. His interests are external, directed towards the world with which he contends, and to which he wishes to dictate. His feelings are strong and genuine, not sentimental or vague. He is very sensual and his roots are in the earth. He is also an adventurer, never afraid to risk things.

He has encountered great difficulties in life. This is partly due to his inability to make concessions and to give in wisely where compromise would be advisable (as mentioned above); and partly due to his sensitiveness which causes him to take offence easily. He has therefore become nervous, highly-strung and irritable. He is good and bad in one; he can torture some people and can encourage others. His longing for truth often causes him to hurt the feelings of other people and sometimes to reveal matters which would

264

Prose	Publication
Sermon to the Earl of Dorset at Knole	July 27, 1617
Sermon to the Hon. The Virginia Company	Nov. 13, 1622
Sermon for Lady Danvers (Magdalen Herbert)	July 1, 1627
The *Devotions*, Winter 1623 - - - -	1624
Death's Duell preached before King Charles Ist Feb. 25, 1631 - - - - - -	1632
Six Sermons published during Donne's lifetime -	1622-1627
Eighty Sermons with Walton's Life, published -	1640
Fifty Sermons, published - - - -	1649
Twenty-six Sermons, published - - -	1660

(For occasional Pieces of Verse not included here see Geoffrey Keynes' *Bibliography of the Works of Dr. John Donne*, pp. 91-2.)

PRINTED IN GREAT BRITAIN BY ROBERT MACLEHOSE AND CO. LTD.
THE UNIVERSITY PRESS, GLASGOW

INDEX

[1] See Jessop, pp. 226-31 and Gosse, ii, pp. 359-63 for Donne's will and Gosse, ii, pp. 357-9 for the will of John Donne senior. (There are copyists' errors in the last.)